A Way of Music Education

A Way of Music Education
Classic Chinese Wisdoms
音樂教育之一道：經典智慧

C. Victor Fung

馮志強

Oxford University Press is a department of the University of Oxford. It furthers
the University's objective of excellence in research, scholarship, and education
by publishing worldwide. Oxford is a registered trade mark of Oxford University
Press in the UK and certain other countries.

Published in the United States of America by Oxford University Press
198 Madison Avenue, New York, NY 10016, United States of America.

© Oxford University Press 2018

All rights reserved. No part of this publication may be reproduced, stored in
a retrieval system, or transmitted, in any form or by any means, without the
prior permission in writing of Oxford University Press, or as expressly permitted
by law, by license, or under terms agreed with the appropriate reproduction
rights organization. Inquiries concerning reproduction outside the scope of the
above should be sent to the Rights Department, Oxford University Press, at the
address above.

You must not circulate this work in any other form
and you must impose this same condition on any acquirer.

Library of Congress Cataloging-in-Publication Data
Names: Fung, C. Victor, author.
Title: A way of music education : classic Chinese wisdoms / C. Victor Fung.
Description: New York, NY : Oxford University Press, [2018] |
Includes bibliographical references and index.
Identifiers: LCCN 2017034410 | ISBN 9780190234461 (cloth) | ISBN 9780190234478 (pbk.) |
ISBN 9780190234492 (oxford scholarly online)
Subjects: LCSH: Music—Instruction and study—Philosophy. |
Philosophy, Chinese.
Classification: LCC MT1 .F942 2018 | DDC 780.71/051—dc23
LC record available at https://lccn.loc.gov/2017034410

1 3 5 7 9 8 6 4 2
Paperback printed by Webcom, Inc., Canada
Hardback printed by Bridgeport National Bindery, Inc., United States of America

OXFORDSHIRE LIBRARY SERVICE	
3303413412	
Askews & Holts	29-Jun-2018
780.71	£18.99

CONTENTS

Preface   *vii*
Acknowledgments   *xi*

PART I: Classic Chinese Philosophies and Music Educational Interpretations
  1. Introduction   3
  2. Foundations of *Yijing*: An Organismic Worldview   21
  3. Foundations of Classic Confucianism: *Cheng* (Sincerity), *Shan* (Kindness), *Ren* (Benevolence), and *Junzi* (the Exemplary Person)   36
  4. Foundations of Classic Daoism: *Wuwei* (Non-egoistic Action), *Guan* (Observation), *Qiwu* (Equality), and *Rou* (Softness/Flexibility)   58

PART II: Complementarity and a Trilogy
  5. Complementary Bipolar Continua in Music Education   77
  6. Change   95
  7. Balance   117
  8. Liberation   135

PART III: A New Way of Thinking and Practical Implications
  9. A Way of Music Education as a Way of Life   153
  10. Toward Practical Implications   167

Epilogue   *173*
Glossary   *175*
Notes   *179*
Bibliography   *207*
Index   *215*

PREFACE

The idea of writing this book has been brewing in my mind for many years, but it did not materialize until I began a sabbatical in 2013. The most productive portion of the sabbatical was my six-month residency at the Graduate Institute of Musicology, National Taiwan University, Taipei, where I studied with phenomenal experts in early Chinese philosophies in the Philosophy Department. During that time, my thoughts developed substantially beyond my earliest published work in the area of music education philosophy based on Chinese thoughts: "Music and Culture: A Chinese Perspective," in *Philosophy of Music Education Review* (1994). While I was writing this book, my bicultural (Chinese and American) and bilingual (Chinese and English) background situated me perfectly, having lived half of my life in Asia and the other half in North America, to understand both Chinese and Western philosophical traditions and to commit myself to share my insights from a characteristically Chinese perspective. Furthermore, I have sufficient background in Chinese classic texts, from my schooling at a young age through undergraduate studies in Hong Kong, to cope with the demands of this project. My dual backgrounds have allowed me to develop unique perspectives, insights, and interpretations that can bridge an important gap between the two academic worlds.

This book presents a philosophy of music education rooted from the classic Chinese sources of *Yijing* (The Book of Changes), classic Confucianism, and classic Daoism. It puts humans at the center of an organismic world, in which all matters and events are connected. Musical experiences, including education, are key attributes to musical well-being throughout one's lifetime. In applying the concepts of *yin* and *yang*, "deep" harmony (*he*), and the teachings of the classic masters (Confucius, Mencius, Laozi, and Zhuangzi) in a classic Chinese philosophical way, I propose a trilogy of change, balance, and liberation as a way of practicing music education. The main threads of this philosophy are change, human-centric, and *dao*-centric.

This book fills a gap in the field of music education philosophy, which to date has been almost exclusively based on a Western lineage traced from the ancient Greek philosophers and thereafter. Profound Chinese philosophies found in *Yijing* (The Book of Changes), classic Confucianism, and classic Daoism have been obscured in the literature at best. These ideologies from early China form the basis of much of the Chinese philosophical milieu for more than two millennia but are neglected by most music educators in the West. This book brings these wisdoms to light for music educators, aiming to repossess these classic Chinese ideologies in a refreshing contemporary interpretation for music education practices.

The ideologies presented in this book are sustainable, valuable, and transcendental across time and space, much like the principles found in ancient religious texts that are championed by believers today. The human spirit is at the center. Music education is an essential and harmonizing part of life that promotes the well-being of the human spirit and fulfills the specific and changing needs of each individual across one's lifespan. The propositions presented in this book are suitable for anyone who comes into contact with music. They are active, adaptive, and liberating, leading to a fulfilling lifetime of experiences in music.

In this book I am reclaiming the long-held values of the classic Chinese philosophical schools from a music education perspective. The approach is holistic, rather than atomistic, in relation to the overall human spirit and the natural world. The philosophy presented in this book puts the human experience throughout the entire lifespan at the center. It is harmonizing rather than combative: there is no dramatic displacement of any other approaches. Music and music education are harmonizing endeavors to satisfy the spirit of the self, the relation with others, and the relation with *dao*—the underlying principles of the natural way and the path toward an exemplary person.

Throughout the book, I have decided to include names, terms, and classic texts in Chinese characters to safeguard against incomplete or improper translations. As any scholars dealing with classic Chinese text would agree, it is next to impossible to provide an accurate and complete translation. Furthermore, the references presented in Chinese are intended to facilitate reading by the growing number of Chinese readers. For Chinese names, I follow the common practice of putting the last name first in the name Romanization or pinyin, unless the Chinese author publishes in English and presents the first name first.

Since this book is not intended to be used as a textbook, the chapters are in uneven lengths due to the nature of the literature and of the themes presented in each chapter. The book is organized in three parts. Part I consists of four chapters that introduce the fundamentals of the classic Chinese philosophies and their music educational interpretations. Part II consists of another four chapters that synthesize the classic Chinese philosophies from a music educational standpoint and propose a new way of thinking in music education in the form of a trilogy: change, balance, and liberation. Part III, containing two chapters, works toward integrating the ideologies in life and seeking directions for practical implications in this new way of thinking.

ACKNOWLEDGMENTS

I could not have finished this book without the support of many. First and foremost I acknowledge the University of South Florida for granting my first sabbatical in 2013, which allowed me to maintain a high level of focus for an extended period to study Chinese philosophy and to develop my ideas. The most productive portion of the sabbatical was my residency at the National Taiwan University in Taipei. Without the kind hospitality of Wang Yuh-Wen, Director of the Graduate Institute of Musicology, I could not have gained so much during this residency. Her colleagues were most helpful, particularly the historical literary insights offered by Shen Tung. Thanks also to many friends and colleagues in Taiwan, such as Lin Sheau-Yuh and Lai Mei-Ling, who have helped in many ways. The most productive experience during this residency was my tremendous privilege to learn from Professor Fu Pei-Rong. Many thanks for the time he took to converse with me, as well as his permission for me to attend his classes and ask questions. Professor Fu has clarified for me how Chinese philosophy works and has reminded me that it is extremely important to respect the original source and interpret, examine, and evaluate it in its own way. I am also grateful for Wim De Reu, who allowed me to audit his classes. I have been privileged to be able to hold fruitful discussions with many Chinese philosophy scholars, including Chou Yu-Wen and Lin Hsiu-Chen of the National Taiwan Normal University, Dan Jau-Wei of the Taipei Municipal University of Education, Chen Chen-Chu of the Research Institute for the Humanities and Social Sciences, National Science Council (Taiwan), and Li Chun, who is retired in Tainan. Many individuals have facilitated discussions with these scholars, such as Sheu Tian-Ming and Fang Yong-Chuang of National Taiwan Normal University, and Hsieh Yuan-Mei of National University of Tainan. Furthermore, I appreciate the students and faculty who were at my lectures and seminars at National Taiwan University, National Taiwan Normal University, Taipei Municipal University of Education, and the University of South Florida, who raised stimulating questions that have helped me to consolidate my thoughts for this book. I am grateful for Leonard Tan of the National Institute of Education, Nanyang Technological University, Singapore, for his feedback on my earlier version of this manuscript. More personally, I am forever in debt to my family, who had to give up their precious time with me throughout the years so that I could study and work on this book.

Last but not least, I am so thankful for the anonymous reviewers and the editorial team at Oxford University Press. Their advice, guidance, and professionalism have brought this book to fruition.

A Way of Music Education

PART I

Classic Chinese Philosophies and Music Educational Interpretations

CHAPTER 1

Introduction

Thinking is a prerequisite for having a philosophy. A privilege of being human is that there is no limit to the number of ways we can think, which implies that there is no limit to the number of philosophies we could have for music education. Wayne D. Bowman and Ana Lucia Frega state that "philosophy's contribution to the music education profession involves asking tough questions about the full range of our beliefs, habits, and practices: seeking alternative possibilities, and interrogating habitual modes of thought and action with the intent of identifying better ones where needed—'better' in the sense of improving professional practice."[1] Since music education is a practicing profession, not a purely academic field, "philosophy improves practice not technically or directly... but incrementally and indirectly: by refining and improving habitual ways of thinking and acting."[2] Each way of thinking and its determinant actions have their own merits.

In this book, I offer a way of thinking about music education so it can be helpful to music educators interested in finding strategies that are based on a widely overlooked philosophical resource—wisdoms from early China—that is sustainable and transcendental across time and space. This different way of thinking contributes to the realm of music education philosophy in a unique way, making one more source available for professional consultation. It presents music education as a natural part of the human experience, which contributes to a holistic entity (*dao*) on an eternal path with ever-changing elements. The novel and mystical appearance of this approach warrants a close examination. The affirmation of early Chinese philosophy in a contemporary music education context is meant to repossess a firm and long-standing philosophical tradition and to bring it to a new level of understanding and interpretation in the field of music education. This philosophy is positioned to open a new horizon in the field of music education. This Chinese perspective presents music, its making, transmission, teaching, and learning as part of a larger scheme. This book is intended to explore a way of thinking that is distinctively Chinese but open for all humans to practice, much as ancient Greek philosophies are accessible for use by both Greeks and non-Greeks.

THE PREMISES

In this book, I explore a way of thinking in music education based on principles observed and articulated by some of the greatest thinkers during one of the earliest periods in the documented history of the humankind. Ideas presented in this book are based on two premises. These premises are necessary in an environment where multiple ways of thinking are valued. Whether these ways of thinking are long-standing or innovative, great thinking should be free from the constraints of time and space.

The first premise is that there are different valid ways of thinking in music education. Bowman and Frega observe that "music education philosophy is still very much in its nascent stages" and that "music education philosophy is . . . in many ways distinct from music philosophy, from educational philosophy, and from 'academic' philosophy in general. The confluence of music, education, and philosophy results in a distinctive practice with distinctive values, responsibilities, and concerns."[3] Philosophy of music education as a field certainly has much room to grow. It is an open field with great potentials for development in many directions. As Michael Mark and Patrice Madura put it:

> It is unlikely that music education will ever be guided by a single philosophical foundation. As soon as one position begins to gain ground, a new perspective on music education begins to overtake it. Continuing discussions and disagreements, often resulting in appropriate compromise, might well be the healthiest and most productive paradigm for the music education profession. As is true of any discipline, it is in the best interest of the music education profession for philosophers to debate long-held beliefs and to propose new doctrines.[4]

This book is positioned to contribute to the discussion with the intent to propose a set of new principles based on some long-held beliefs overlooked by many music educators, especially those who operate only in Indo-European languages.

The second premise of this book is in congruence with philosophers interested in metaphysics. The Chinese term for "metaphysics," *xing er shang* (形而上), comes from an accompanying essay to *Yijing* written during the Warring States period (475–221 BC). Above the physical matters (*xing er shang* 形而上) are *dao* (道) to include the ways, the ideologies, the rules, and the principles; below the physical matters (*xing er xia* 形而下) are materials, or *qi* (器), to embrace all things tangible and perceptible, including human behaviors.[5] If metaphysics is to be explained strictly from a Chinese perspective, it is *dao*. Although *dao* here is defined loosely compared to the specific meanings of *dao* in Confucianism and Daoism, the act of taking this concept from the accompanying essay to *Yijing* as a translation of metaphysics supports the belief that scholars are already interested in metaphysics—the principles and ideologies that have received consistent attention through the ages—in the Warring States period.

To take this idea of metaphysics and *dao* further, I borrow the framework of a highly regarded Chinese cultural historian and philosopher, Qian Mu (錢穆) (1895–1990), who describes in detail three layers of culture: material (*wuzhi* 物質), social (*shehui* 社會), and spiritual (*jingshen* 精神).[6] The first level—material—refers to the basic needs for human survival, such as food, clothing, shelter, and mobility, as well as any materials associated with human lives. Within this layer, humans are interacting with various objects, including those from nature. Materials (i.e., objects) in any given culture can change constantly. For example, means of transportation, means of communication, clothing, food, and tools and utensils in everyday living are materials that change rapidly. Even materials used in education change frequently, such as books and computer equipment. While they have cultural and philosophical significance, most of them remain at a level differing drastically across time and space. The second level—social—is characterized by interactions among humans, when relationships and organizations begin. Families, institutions and social organizations, legal systems, national regimes, and cultural practices are all realizations of this cultural layer. Systems can be modified as the consensus of the society changes. This systemic change is evident in various policy, legal, or social changes in nations, regions, and organizations. For example, the suggestion of education for political ends in Confucius' teaching is situated in the social system of his time. It would be a hard-pressed proposition to apply his concept of *yue jiao* (樂教 education of *yue*) or *liyue jiaohua* (禮樂教化 *li* and *yue* in education and acculturation) in a contemporary social system.[7] The value of studying Confucius, and other Chinese classics, in contemporary societies is shown on the third layer—spiritual, consisting of all types of ideologies,[8] including philosophy, morality, and humanities. By and large, they transcend time and space. Similar to metaphysics, this is the layer that far more philosophers are interested in interrogating. Long-standing ideologies tend to capture the essence of being human, regardless of changes in social systems and materials. For example, certain expectations between parent and child, between superior and inferior (e.g., employer and employee, or leaders and lay persons), among siblings, and among friends seem to remain stable regardless of changes in the system or materials across time and space. The relationship between human and nature also remains rather stable (e.g., humans relying on natural resources to fulfill basic needs). Ideologies, rather than social systems and materials, are much closer to these ever-existing relationships and expectations. The longevity of an ideology depends much on its ability to transcend systems and materials. The main concern of this book is an examination of a set of ideologies that has gone through the test of time, in how early Chinese wisdoms could be applied to music education and the broader human spirit. Too much attachment of the material and social system to the ideologies under discussion would make them look outdated and, at the same time, further removed from the very nature and essence of being humans, and most important, lose the power to transcend across time and space. Therefore, it is important to focus on the lasting spiritual ideologies. Fu Pei-Rong (傅佩榮) (b. 1950), a phenomenal scholar of Chinese philosophy,[9] elaborates when describing the greatness of Confucius' ideologies in that Confucian ideals "transcend across time and space, break boundaries set by language, ethnicity, and religion, and at the same time venerated by those who know them."[10] Great ideologies should transcend time and space. Seemingly archaic ideologies can contain some of the most important essence of being human. It is similar to how believers of many religions today find ancient texts of their own religion applicable in contemporary lives. Desirable behaviors and expectations persist while the social context and material culture are drastically different. This philosophical transcendence seems to have thrived within Chinese communities. While music is a human activity and product attached to its root culture, it is worthy to explore if this transcendental way of thinking is to be developed beyond Chinese communities and applied to the field of music education.

WHY EARLY CHINESE PHILOSOPHIES?

Most contemporary philosophies of music education found in the literature are rooted in a Western lineage. They can be traced back to the ancient Greek philosophers, whose philosophies, in part or in whole, have been explored, modified, restructured, refuted, and clarified by many philosophers, musicians, and educators across the world. By contrast, philosophical traditions not rooted in ancient Greece have been given little consideration.[11] Even in the East Asian region, Western philosophies of music education play an important role in contemporary practices. Major philosophical works in the West are being translated into various Asian languages, including Chinese, and being studied by music education students and leaders in the field throughout Asia. Coupled with waves of economic, sociological, and political influences from the West via trade, religious activities, military presence, political alliance, and so forth, many ideologies and values indigenous to Asia have gone under the shadow of these influences. Only recently, articles by Leonard Tan have drawn upon ancient Chinese thoughts in explaining contemporary Western music education.[12] Other and earlier writings on this topic in the West have been sporadic at best.

Although Chinese philosophies were documented in abundance at about the same time as those of the ancient Greeks (i.e., around the fifth century BC), they have not been utilized by Western-trained music educators and are still foreign to most music educators in the West. Perhaps there is a need to clarify issues and concepts, address key questions, expose their assumptions and arguments, organize them in a sensible way, and draw implications for practitioners in the field of music education based on these earliest Chinese philosophies.

The focus on early Chinese classics is a tribute to the idea of "root seeking" (*xungen* 尋根), similar to the spirit of genealogy in the West, though this is a genealogy of philosophical schools in China.[13] The roots of the lineage in Chinese philosophy may shed light on new space for development and direction in music education. Eventually, a new way of thinking in music education could be developed.

Any attempt to draw from thousands of years of philosophical ideologies, Western or Chinese, to contemporary practice in music education is a daunting task. I have selected a critical historical period in China, from the mid-sixth to the mid-third century BC, when the classic, mature, and genuinely Chinese philosophical sources were coming together in one manageable philosophical, cultural, and geographical space before they evolve into multiple schools, amid external influences and mixtures of different sorts. This three-century period is a significant period in the history of the development of Chinese philosophies in that it forms a firm philosophical core that permeates much of the Chinese culture and philosophy for the following two and a half millennia. I use the term "classic" to denote the original, high-quality, definitive ideologies found in this period and to distinguish it from those that diverged and evolved after this period, some of which have been described with the prefix "neo-" and even as "religious," "new," or "contemporary."[14]

Ancient wisdoms should not be relegated simply because they are ancient. To the contrary, we should cherish them because these wisdoms represent the earliest pinnacles of human thought pioneered by some of the most intelligent and broad-minded observers of phenomena and relationships, without the distraction of the hustle-bustle and politics of the contemporary world. They help us to reconnect to the nature of being human and the natural environment in which we live. They are perspicacious and timeless. Furthermore, these chosen classic Chinese wisdoms have been subjected to political, religious, and folkloric twists and turns, and have thus potentially been removed from their original and genuine human-centered focus after their maturity in the third century BC. A desire to repossess these classic wisdoms has been noticeably expressed since the early portion of the Qing Dynasty (1644–1911).[15]

Let me use salad as an analogy. Looking at ancient wisdoms is like looking at a salad with no dressing. A mixture of raw vegetables, and sometimes other raw or cooked food, forms the basis of what a salad is. This mixture of ingredients presents the salad's original flavor, color, and nutrients. The consumer may choose which and how much salad dressing to use, or not to use any dressing at all. The same salad could look, taste, and function differently when it falls into the hands of a different consumer, who may use a different amount of dressing of a different kind. Once the dressing is used habitually on the salad, a consumer may come to believe that the dressing is an essential part of the salad and not to think much about the flavor, color, and nutrients of the original ingredients. For some consumers, the flavor, color, and nutrients of the dressing might have taken over. Similarly, this book presents ideologies about human nature (i.e., the original ingredients of the salad) before the human mind is tainted by too many preconceived notions and before the ideologies turn into something that look and function differently (i.e., the salad with the dressing used by different consumers). A wide latitude of development is to be expected once the original is settled, just like the multitude of possibilities that exist for a consumer in choosing which and how much salad dressing to be used.

After reading this book, readers are free to apply these ideologies in their own way, just like adding their favorite type and amount of dressing on a salad. A triad of early Chinese philosophical sources—*Yijing* 《易經》, classic Confucianism (傳統的儒家), and classic Daoism (or Taoism) (傳統的道家)—are chosen to represent the origin of many possibilities that are genuinely Chinese, before mixing in with anything from the outside or any altered interpretations from the inside.

Yijing, classic Confucianism, and classic Daoism were intricately connected. Although *Yijing* was written long before it became a must-read for Chinese scholars in the pre-Qin period (pre-221 BC), foundations of all three sources as key scholastic and philosophical studies were formed in the same period, around the mid-sixth to the mid-third century BC, covering part of the Spring and Autumn period (770–476 BC) and the Warring States period (475–221 BC). As the name of the latter period suggests, these three centuries were a time of political turbulence. Forms of nihilism were pervasive throughout various strata of society. The common people, the thinkers, and the rulers alike were experiencing a great deal of social instability. Everyone was searching for a way to settle for a better life. It was congenital for scholars, philosophers, and rulers to look to supernatural powers and a variety of ways in search of a better life for everyone. The birth of a new, strong, and deep philosophical milieu during this period is profound.

Views from both Western and Chinese scholars agree that there is a dramatic contrast in the philosophy and development between the two civilizations. From a Western perspective, David L. Hall and Roger T. Ames recognize the intense difference in the two modes of philosophical thinking. They describe that European philosophers have a tendency "to seek out the being of things, the essential reality lying behind appearances," while Chinese thinkers' "principal interests lie in the establishment and cultivation of harmonious relationships within their social ambiance. . . . [T]he thinking of the Chinese is far more concrete, this-worldly and, above all, practical."[16] Hall and Ames go on to state that there are distinctive origins and histories of Chinese and Western civilizations. Logical reasoning has been a priority in the West, whereas harmonious interaction has been more important to the Chinese.

Chinese scholars also see the distinctiveness of the Chinese philosophical tradition. The sharp contrast between the Chinese and Western philosophical traditions is manifested in two notable ways. First and foremost, the Chinese presents an organismic worldview at least five thousand years ago. In this organismic worldview, each element of the world must be viewed in relation to all other elements. If the world is analogous to the human body, pulling one hair from the head can be felt by the entire body, not just the scalp where the hair is pulled.[17] All elements within the organism are connected via an exceedingly sophisticated network.[18] All matters are synchronized[19] based on rules of nature or events that occur with or without any noticeable intention or meaning. This differs dramatically from the earliest Western thought, in which elements of the world were considered separate components that work together. The Western way of thinking is much more atomistic, mechanistic, and compartmentalized.[20] Psychologist Carl Gustav Jung hits at the center of the Chinese organismic worldview and describes methods of explaining various phenomena presented in *Yijing* as an "intuitive technique for *grasping the total situation* [emphasis original] which is so characteristic of China. . . . Unlike the Greek-trained Western mind, the Chinese mind does not aim at grasping details for their own sake, but at a view which sees the detail as part of a whole."[21] He even called the *Yijing* as an "experimental foundation of classical Chinese philosophy" and "one of the oldest known methods for grasping a situation as a whole and thus placing the details against a cosmic background—the interplay of Yin and Yang."[22] He also referred classic Daoist view as "a thinking in terms of the whole."[23]

The second characteristically Chinese quality in the philosophical quest is that it propagates a harmonious phenomenon. This is, again, in sharp contrast with early Western thought. As the highly respected Chinese philosophy scholar Thomé H. Fang (方東美) puts it:

> Western thought is often permeated with vicious bifurcation which sets a number of things in implacable hostility. The universe seems to be a theatre of war wherein all sorts of entities or phenomena are arrayed one against another. As the Evil One vies with God, . . . As Nature is set in opposition to the Supernatural, . . . And as Nature is made incongruous with Man, . . . The instances of antithesis of this kind might be infinitely multiplied. . . ., the extreme importance of harmony is either simply ignored or hopelessly misconstrued.[24]

He then continues to describe a different philosophical temper that is characteristically Chinese: "For several thousands of years, we Chinese have been thinking of these vital problems in terms of *comprehensive harmony* [emphasis added] which permeates anything and everything."[25] The "anything and everything" here I take it to include music education. This suggests that the huge network of elements in the world works as a whole in harmony and that music education, as one of the elements, should work within and outside of the field in harmony. The Chinese emphasis on harmony warrants a deep reflection for music educators and their broader lives. Among extant philosophies of music education, the Chinese notion of harmony could contribute to a more harmonious and complementary ambience among schools of contemporary diverse, and sometimes divisive, propositions.[26]

Another distinctive feature of the harmony postulated in early Chinese philosophies, especially in Confucianism, is that it is of a horizontal type, going across different human relationships, beginning with a private life, to filiality and other virtues in family life, to accordant social and political affairs, congenial order to the state, and peace to the world. This is often characterized as "social harmony." Due to the built-in tension and the absence of a pre-set order in interacting between humans, the sense of harmony exists from deep inside an individual. For Confucians, "tension is transformed and conflict is reconciled into favorable conditions for each party to flourish."[27] Harmony is renewed continuously deep inside the individuals. Therefore, it is also described as "deep harmony."[28] The Daoists also found a similar sense of harmony between heaven and humans. Harmony has been a focus of attention since the earliest identifiable Chinese thoughts. The broad and deep coverage of harmony found in early Chinese philosophies is unique in many ways. Once again, this is in sharp contrast with the type of harmony posited by many Western philosophers. For example, Plato accentuated a harmony among such domains as poetry, gymnastics, mathematics, geometry, astronomy, and dialectic. For him, truth cuts across all disciplines, thereby maintaining harmony in a vertical sense. Some may call this "intellectual harmony,"[29] which is focused more on the type of harmony found *within* an individual. Since this type of harmony conforms to a static, pre-set, rational order imposed onto the world, it is described as "harmony of conformity."[30]

When describing the special qualities of Chinese philosophy, Mou Zongsan (牟宗三) juxtaposes them alongside with the special qualities of Western philosophy. He bases his observations on the three main streams of Chinese philosophy—Confucianism, Daoism, and Buddhism,[31]—and on the assumption of Confucianism being the "mainstream of the mainstreams."[32] He posits that since the early stages in the development of Chinese philosophy, the emphases have been placed on subjectivity and inner morality. In contrast, since the early stages of Western philosophy, the emphases have been placed on objectivity and knowledge. The subjectivity and inner morality found in the Chinese go along with the ideas of horizontal harmony or deep harmony, where it begins deep inside the inner self and expands in concentric circles, from self, expanding outward to include the family, the society, and eventually, the world.

Cultural historical analysis provides insights into the Chinese horizontal harmony that demonstrate this fundamental philosophical difference between the Chinese and the West. The renowned Chinese historian, philosopher, and educator Qian Mu sees a distinctive difference in the evolutions between the Chinese and the Western civilizations. He characterizes the advancements in Chinese civilization as cultivational change (*zhuanhua* 轉化) and extension (*mianyan* 緜延) through the ages based on a singular root. This is in stark contrast with the West, for which he characterizes as revolutionary change (*biandong* 變動) and progression (*jinbu* 進步). For this reason, Western civilization is more prone to tensions between the conqueror and the conquered, while the Chinese cares more about harmony from within, and to be extended to the world.[33] These distinctions between the Chinese and Western civilizations and philosophical developments call for a need to better understand the Chinese way of thinking in music education. Because of the values that the Chinese place on changes from a singular root, it adds weight to the importance of looking deeply into this root as presented in the next three chapters: *Yijing*, classic Confucianism, and classic Daoism.

Since there are many music educators throughout the world with a Chinese background and the ways of thinking presented in this book are characteristically Chinese, perhaps some elements of the ideologies presented in this book have already been incorporated in their music education practices, either by conscious efforts or by subconscious assimilation. Nevertheless, genuinely Chinese philosophies as applied to music education in China often appear in passing under the shadow of Western philosophies.[34] Only on rare occasions do Chinese music educators dedicate space to discuss the topic.[35] Amazingly, most of these brief remarks and dedicated short papers refer to more or less the same few popular quotes from the classic texts. There is little, if any, synthesis, systematic reflection, or scholastic deep insight presented in a schematic way. This book, however, is designed to bring such a Chinese way of thinking to the field of music education in a structured, systematized, and philosophical way, so it can be shared, discussed, developed, and used by all music educators.

In this book, early Chinese philosophies refer to the ideologies presented in one of the oldest Chinese books, the *Yijing*, and the two earliest and most prominent Chinese philosophical schools, the classic Confucianism and the classic Daoism. *Yijing* has been an inspiration for both Confucianism and Daoism. Although their philosophical foundations vary, their different emphases have made them compatible in the practical lives of many Chinese, just as one takes in different types of food for different meals throughout the day. Variety and flexibility are expected to maintain the well-being in changing conditions. The differences among these three Chinese philosophical sources serve different human needs in different situations. Separate chapters in this text are dedicated to each of these philosophical sources. Of the three sources, the classic Confucians have the most extensive and direct commentaries on music and music education. The majority of what I draw on, however, is not specifically musical but rather ideologies and principles that govern multiple entities and phenomena. Music and music education are part of the larger entities and phenomena, be they the society, the nation, or the universe, that cut across time and space despite changes in materials and social systems.

Like most ideologies, Confucianism and Daoism have evolved through time and space with new interpretations, modifications, and branches.[36] I have chosen to focus on the original classic ideologies, which could be argued as the philosophical roots of the Chinese civilization. Except for the imports from outside China, other Chinese philosophical schools and many elements of the Chinese civilization are deeply rooted in these sources. My background in academic scholarship has guided me to focus on these earliest Chinese philosophical sources. Their primary sources would receive the ultimate attention and respect. In other words, interpretations of these philosophies after their formative years should be based on the original texts. Rather than considering a multitude of these interpretations, modifications, and branches throughout the 2,500 years, I revert back to the earliest available Chinese philosophical source—the *Yijing* (collectively dated from the twenty-ninth to the sixth century BC), the ideologies of Confucius (551–479 BC) and Mencius (372–289 BC) on classic Confucianism, and the ideologies of Laozi (b. ca. 570 BC) and Zhuangzi (369–286 BC) on classic Daoism.[37] Evidence suggests that *Yijing*, being one of the oldest and most comprehensive books based on thousands of years of observations of how the world works, has been an inspiration in the formation of Confucianism and Daoism.[38] A timeline of these classic Chinese wisdoms is presented in Figure 1.1. From the formation of the surviving version of *Yijing* to the times of Mencius and Zhuangzi, it covers about three centuries from the mid-sixth to the mid-third century BC.

At times, I draw upon literary and historical texts written during, and within a few hundred years of, their times, notably *Shijing* 《詩經》, *Shangshu* 《尚書》, *Shiji* 《史記》, *Chunqiu Zuozhuan* 《春秋佐傳》, *Lushichunqiu* 《呂氏春秋》, *Guoyu* 《國語》, *Liji* 《禮記》, *Liezi* 《列子》, *Xunzi* 《荀子》, and *Guanzi* 《管子》. Although the dates of some these texts are hard to verify and there could be edits and modifications throughout the last two millennia, relevance of these texts to the classic Confucian and classic Daoist ideologies are undeniable. Due to the inclusion

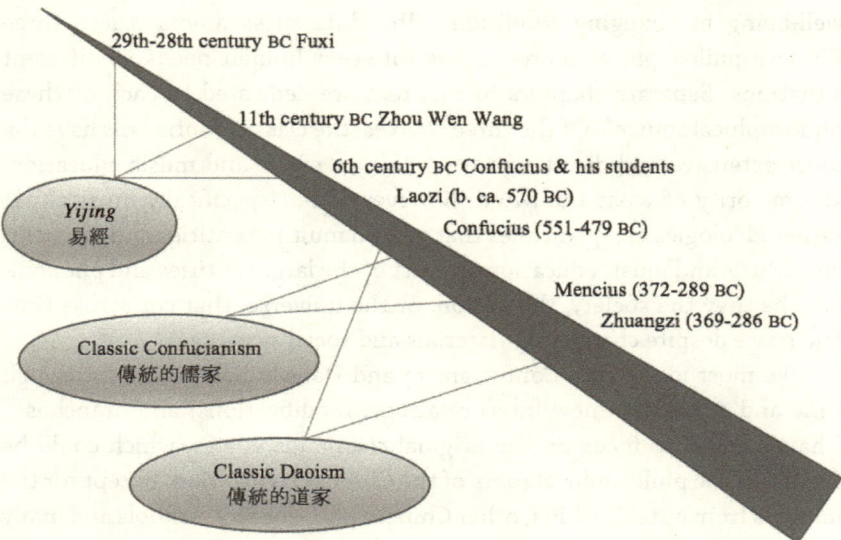

Figure 1.1: Timeline of the classic Chinese wisdoms.

of some non-classic ideologies in some of these texts, only the portions that corroborate the classic ideologies are cited, not to diminish any of the non-classic ideologies but to maintain a focus in the current inquiry. The purpose of looking into these historical sources is to interrogate the original ideologies before their interpretations and meanings were modified.[39] To get to the ideas and principles that truly represent the essence of being human with the respect for the original ideologies, writings, and observations of the founding philosophers without the alterations of their successors, it would make sense to focus on these earliest wisdoms within the confines of this book.[40]

The importance of early Chinese wisdoms in the contemporary world was explicitly stated by Hannes Alfvén, a Nobel Prize winner in physics (1970), approved by seventy-three other Nobel laureates in a meeting in Paris in 1988 and acclaimed by Maotian Fang, the Secretary-General of the China National Commission for UNESCO, and participants of the First Nishan Forum on World Civilizations involving an international community of Confucian scholars. Alfvén's statement has been quoted widely: "Humanity must return to 2,500 years ago and draw wisdoms from Confucius if it is to live on in the 21st century."[41] The importance of Confucian ideologies in contemporary lives is supported by many others, including Weiming Tu, a professor and advocate of Chinese philosophy in the United States.[42] Although Confucian and other classic ideologies included in this text come from about two and a half millennia ago, its importance must not be overlooked.

SCHOLARSHIP IN EARLY CHINESE PHILOSOPHIES

Those who study early Chinese philosophies understand the complexity and the multiplicity of the dimensions in the field. Ancient texts are the main evidence for these philosophies. Embedded in them are some of the most sophisticated literary and semantic nuances. On the literary front, some ancient Chinese classic texts could appear as a set of nonsense Chinese characters if one does not know the ancient usage of the language. Such usage takes years to learn. Learning such usage was considered an important component of the cultivation process for the nobles. Even today, skills in Chinese classic text, alongside with foreign languages, are important parts of the education system in many Chinese communities. Students in various Chinese communities start on it somewhere between their preschool years, on simple and short classic phrases, and their secondary school grades, on entire essays appropriate to their level. It would be safe to state that all Chinese people who have gone through schooling in China and its traditions would know some Chinese classic texts, but that their degree of skillfulness and fluency depends on how much they have studied during those years, from minuscule to profound. Just like any linguistic skills, it takes time to improve and the learning process never ends.

On the semantic front, it is tremendously difficult to translate Chinese classic texts. A word-for-word literal translation is almost a guarantee for inaccuracies or incompleteness. Many Chinese characters, especially those found in classic texts, are not fully translatable. Various forms of figures of speech, metaphors, and poetic insights are common. One Chinese character often has multiple meanings, each depending on its context. Some ancient use of Chinese characters may take a similar-sounding word to refer to the meaning of another word. Meaning of the text is often fluid and associated with its historical, social, and functional contexts. These semantic variations are prone to influence word order and other issues in grammar. In other words, demand for insights across history, philosophy, cultural studies, and language is common in classic text interpretations. After an extensive explanation on such linguistic concerns, Hsü Fu-kuan (徐復觀) is convinced that interpreting historical Chinese thoughts merely through a linguistic view is inadequate.[43] Chinese scholars often refer to the need to understand classic texts through the flow of the "pause and blood vessels" (*mailuo*, 脈絡, also interpreted as context). Taking the *Yijing* as an example, a Danish scholar Bent Nielsen commented on its early translations to Latin, French, and English and stated that they "were based on commentaries and interpretations of a handful of influential scholars of the Song dynasty (960–1279), most notably Cheng Yi (1033–1107) and Zhu Xi (1130–1200)."[44]

> When translators encountered difficult passages in the text, they sometimes—as in the case of James Legge, the great 19th century translator of the Chinese classics—translated the paraphrases of the commentaries instead. The original meaning of [Yijing] lay buried beneath layers of mainly Confucian interpretation, and the sinologist of the 19th century simply was not equipped to penetrate these layers.[45]

However, archeological evidence found in 1899 has guided scholars to "interpretations based on knowledge of grammar, syntax, and vocabulary obtained from studies of the oracle-bone and bronze inscriptions." Nevertheless, "[t]he contextual studies of [Yijing] were very slow to catch on in the West. Although Arthur Waley (1889–1996) first communicated these studies to the West in 1933, they had virtually no effect on Western scholarship on [Yijing] until the beginning of the 1980s."[46] This example of Yijing scholarship points to some difficulties of relying exclusively on Western scholarship, namely translations of commentaries and interpretations, rather than on the original.[47] There has been a gap both linguistically and contextually. The ability to comprehend the connections across various writers' intentions, meanings, interpretations, contexts, and relationships is critical. Only through rigorous scholarship can meanings and interpretations be flowed seamlessly from these classic texts. Without this rigor, meanings and interpretations can easily become an "I think" or "I believe," which may either be presentations of insightful personal opinions or symptoms of weak scholarship. The former could be desirable in some cases, but the latter is not.

Relying on English sources in studying Chinese philosophy can be problematic. It may create more confusion than help understanding the subject. As recent as 2015 in the introduction of UNESCO's report on *Rethinking Education: Towards a Global Common Good*, a quote from Confucius is featured prominently.[48] However, the Chinese translator could not find a match in any of the Confucius' original literature, even after consulting with experts. The translator had to choose a "closest" quote from the *Analects* for the "original" English quote from Confucius.[49] The difference between the English quote and the reverse translation in Chinese is astonishing, to say the least. Even this day and age, there are still obvious gaps in the transmission of meaning of classic Chinese texts between Chinese and English sources. For this reason, I rely more heavily on sources available in the Chinese language in its traditional form rather than the simplified form to ensure accuracy in extracting original meanings.

To these ends, I have learned to depend on reliable sources, some of which are the results of examining hundreds of interpretations and explanations since the appearance of the original, with explainable "pause and blood vessels." The same principle should be consistent in running through all of the arguments.[50] I refer to the writings of many master leaders in the field, such as Qian Mu (錢穆, 1895–1990), Feng Yu-lan (馮友蘭, 1895–1990), Thomé H. Fang (方東美, 1899–1977), Hsü Fu-kuan (徐復觀, 1903–1982), Tang Junyi (唐君毅, 1909–1978), Mou Zongsan (牟宗三, 1909–1995), Jao Tsung-I (饒宗頤, b. 1917), Nan Huaijin (南懷瑾, 1918–2012), Lao Siguang (勞思光, 1927–2012), Feng Dawen (馮達文, b. 1941), Fu Pei-Rong (傅佩榮, b. 1950), and Li Zonggui (李宗桂, b. 1952), in laying a foundation for this text. I nevertheless take up the challenge of translating key Chinese texts, unless specified otherwise. Ultimate respect for the original texts and interpretations is a key to success in delving deep into this subject matter. A former president of the Social Science Research Council in New York, Kenneth Prewitt, reminds us that many social scientists and humanities scholars in East Asia "work only in local languages" and that "the foreign-educated scholars, with whom we comfortably interact, are a distinct minority when viewed from within Korea, Japan or China."[51] My Chinese background, fortunately, has availed me of many comfortable interactions with experts who are almost unnoticed in the English world but phenomenal in the Chinese world.

Scholastic debates are commonly found concerning the time and authorship of some of the classic texts. These debates rely heavily on archaeological discoveries and the interpreters' ability to make the meaning flow seamlessly through various classic texts. Rather than dwelling on such debates, I have chosen to accept agreeable interpretations until further discoveries are ungrounded or new and insightful meanings are unfolded. Classic texts used in this writing are based on, or cross-checked with, the most authoritative sources in early Chinese philosophies, namely the *Thirteen Classics* 《十三經》[52] and *Twenty-Two Masters* 《二十二子》,[53] unless there is overwhelming support to use otherwise.[54]

Finally, the original ideology must be the foundation of all of its interrogations and should receive ultimate respect. While scholars have all the rights to develop their own ideologies based on those who went before them, remote interpretations and modifications of the original ideology should not be the basis of an interrogation of the original ideology.

In the realm of early Chinese philosophies, there is little doubt that both Confucianism and Daoism were inspired by ideas found in *Yijing*, and that classic Confucianism and classic Daoism had begun to derail from their original philosophical system after Mencius and Zhuangzi respectively.[55] For these reasons, I focus my inquiry on the ideologies found in *Yijing* and those suggested by, and in congruence with, Confucius, Mencius, Laozi, and Zhuangzi. I may also refer to others' works consisting of these classic elements. At the same time, I have limited the use of translated texts, or interpretations of those that do not seem to stay on the grounds of the original classic philosophies, as well as those that are considered to be speculative rather than scholarly.

A CAUTIONARY NOTE ON CHINESE PHILOSOPHY, CONFUCIANISM, AND DAOISM

I would like to conclude this chapter with a cautionary note, especially for those who are new to the area of Chinese philosophy. While the bases of this book (*Yijing*, Confucius, Mencius, Laozi, and Zhuangzi) are foundations of many schools of Chinese philosophies, they do not constitute "Chinese philosophy" as a whole. They simply represent the root of the Chinese philosophical milieu that followed. Furthermore, no consideration has been given to a significant ideological import in the second century AD, Buddhism, as the aim of this text is to search for a philosophical direction based on the earliest and the most genuinely Chinese ways of thinking. The focus of this text is on early Chinese philosophical ideologies, not religious ideologies.

Confucianism has been described as the "mainstream of the mainstreams"[56] in Chinese philosophy. Ideologically, many philosophers after Mencius have reshaped, refocused, and reinterpreted elements of Confucianism, so that the basic framework has been shifted. Xunzi (313–238 BC) reportedly began such a shift.[57] New schools and branches of Confucianism sprawled substantially in the eleventh century. Scholars have used the term "Neo-Confucianism" to distinguish it from the classic Confucianism. Much of the contemporary Confucian influences in various Asian communities come from Neo-Confucianism, because of its spreading power of the time. As Peter K. Bol explains:

> Neo-Confucianism was spreading at precisely the moment when commercial printing was becoming common, and many counties [in China] had a printer or two, thus ensuring that more texts were put into circulation and more survived;

communities were investing in local schools and academies, providing intellectuals with careers and students with places to gather; local historical records were being compiled, giving local people a way to record their accomplishments and providing us with details unavailable for earlier periods; and private wealth was increasing, making it possible for Neo-Confucians to raise the money necessary to print their books, build their shrines and academies, organize charitable activities, and gain fame locally when they could not nationally. In other words, we can know more about the Neo-Confucians themselves and the world in which they lived than we can about intellectuals of any earlier period.[58]

The influences of Neo-Confucianism were powerful across Asia since the burst of Neo-Confucianism and its branches in the eleventh century. While a description, let alone an interrogation, of Neo-Confucianism is rather complex and beyond the scope of this text, the easiest way for readers to distinguish between classic Confucianism and Neo-Confucianism is to pay attention to the timing and authorship of the Confucian sources. This is not to say that classic Confucianism did not persist. In fact, it has persisted and is still current as one of many subdivisions of contemporary Confucianism. On the one hand, Confucian ideologies since Xunzi have already shown signs of departure from classic Confucians. On the other hand, some fundamental elements of classic Confucianism persist in Neo-Confucians ideologies, such as the focus on humans and the society and the importance of education. To push "Confucianism" further, the Chinese government sanctioned the New Confucianism movement in 1986, emphasizing more the political and cultural interpretations of the ideology. In other words, the substance in various forms of "Confucianism" might be different and worthy of readers' attention.

Daoism, like Confucianism, has gone through a lot of modifications and development throughout the last two millennia since the time of Zhuangzi. Using the *Yijing* as a classic text, Daoism, as a philosophy, quickly branched out to a religion in the Han Dynasty (206 BC–220 AD). The change was based on folklore of the time in combination with the classic Daoist ideologies. Some schools of Daoism focus on the divinatory aspect, and others are eager to turn the ideology into a religion. Daoism as a philosophy has been dissolved into many aspects of Chinese life. Many of the later developments consist of a mixture of other ideologies and folklore. Again, as in the case for Confucianism, readers should be cautious when reading about Daoist ideologies, the substance of which can be quite far apart at different times and in different branches.

While I refer to the classic texts as well as other relevant literary and historical texts, some of the relevant literary and historical texts comprise a mixture of ideologies of the time of writing to include the classic ideologies, as well as some expansions, modifications, or additions. One of such notable example is the *Yueji*, which is part of *Liji* that recorded musical and ritualistic ideologies from the classic Confucianism as well as expansions with no hint of congruence with any other classic Confucian texts. Such sources with mixed ideologies are treated with great caution. These sources include ideologies that parallel those of the classic Confucians and those that were new at the time of writing, after the classic ideology was formed. At the same time, these sources provide important contexts, and sometimes explanations, for the classics.

The following three chapters are dedicated to discussing the foundations of *Yijing*, classic Confucianism, and classic Daoism, and their relevance to music and music education. Chapter 5 is a pivotal chapter that focuses on the development of a set of complementary bipolar continua in music education based on those foundations. Chapters 6 through 8 present a trilogy in a way of thinking in music education: change, balance, and liberation. The book then concludes with suggestions on how this way of thinking in music education should be seen as a part of a way of living (Chapter 9) and a way of practicing music education (Chapter 10).

CHAPTER 2

⚬⌄⌃

Foundations of *Yijing*

An Organismic Worldview

In the late Spring and Autumn period (770–476 BC) and the Warring States period (475–221 BC), when rulers and laypersons alike were searching for better lives, *Yijing* 《易經》 was already an important source of reference to relate humans with natural and supernatural powers. Laying a foundation of an organismic worldview, it was mainly used as a tool for divination practices. *Yizhuan* 《易傳》, consisting of ten accompanying essays (or the Ten Wings) to explain *Yijing*, was written during the Warring States period[1] and has been incorporated in *Yijing* in contemporary publications.[2] *Yijing*, along with *Yizhuan*, has been a critical philosophical source for studies in China throughout the last two and a half millennia.[3]

Although *Yijing* and *Yizhuan* in combination do not present a complete philosophical system, their principles are key building blocks in the formation of classic Daoism. From its organismic view of the universe to the entangled *yin* and *yang*, they align with the classic Daoist philosophy. Considering *Yizhuan* as an illuminating collection of explanatory essays for *Yijing*, there is general consensus that *Yijing* contributed substantially to the foundation for classic Confucianism as well, although a few would disagree and claim that it belongs only to the Daoist tradition.[4] In this text, I have taken the position that *Yijing* is an inspiration for both classic Confucianism and classic Daoism and that *Yizhuan*, the accompanying essays, was written by Confucius and his students.[5] Furthermore, I join the consensus that *Yizhuan*'s moralistic views are aligned with Confucianism and that its heavenly ways belong to Daoism.⁶ Confucians focus on the cultivation of self and human relationships in forming an ideal society, while Daoists promote a harmonious way of life with nature. The richness of *Yijing*, along with *Yizhuan*, has allowed much room for philosophical meanings and interpretations. Both Confucians and Daoists have mined this profound richness of *Yijing* and developed two different yet by-and-large compatible schools of philosophy.

This chapter and the two that follow offer an overview of the main aspects of these philosophical sources as they are helpful in promoting the development of a way of thinking in music education. Each of these three chapters ends on some notes on music and music education. For more comprehensive overviews of these philosophical sources, readers should read further on each of these richly compelling philosophical ideologies. Many experts devote their entire career in studying them as philosophies, as historical phenomena, and as Chinese culture and civilization. The brief account of the philosophical sources in these chapters is designed only to align the flow of this book and to maintain a focus in working toward a way of thinking in music education.

YIJING

Yijing 《易經》 is one of the earliest, and most profound, philosophical sources found in the Chinese civilization. Scholars have generally agreed that Fuxi (伏羲) (c. 29th–28th century BC) was the original creator of *bagua* (八卦, the eight trigrams) and the sixty-four *gua* (卦, hexagrams). The *bagua* and *gua* are simple symbols to represent how elements are changed and connected as the world moves on. Zhou Wen Wang (周文王, 1152–1056 BC) was the main commentator on the *bagua* and *gua*. By the time of Confucius and Laozi in the sixth century BC, *Yijing* had already been a culmination of Chinese wisdom for more than two thousand years. After Confucius and his students contributed the *Yizhuan*, the contemporary version of *Yijing* is based on the version transmitted via generations of students of Confucius to key scholars and editors, Wang Bi (王弼, AD 226–249) and Han Kangbo (韓康伯, AD 332–380). A highly respected scholar, Kong Yingda (孔穎達, AD 574–648) studied the lineage of *Yijing* and clarified many of the issues regarding the transmission of *Yijing* for generations.⁷ Contemporary studies of *Yijing* have to depend on trustworthy scholarship and consensus formed throughout the millennia.

Yijing is usually translated as *The Book of Changes*, which reflects only a portion of its meanings. The *"jing"* (經) portion of *Yijing* simply means "book," with the connotation that it is classic and authoritative. The "*yi*" (易) portion of *Yijing*, however, contains three meanings.[8] First, *bian yi* (變易), refers to all types of changes in nature, including human experiences. A state of being safe and prosperous may not last forever. Danger and deprivation could be coming. The reverse is true as well. *Bian yi* reminds us that we should be vigilant for the changes ahead so we can live a satisfying life. Second, *bu yi* (不易), refers to the unchanging principles while phenomena change. These revelatory principles contribute substantially to the book's significance and sustainability for millennia in China. Third, *yi jian* (易簡), should be broken down into *yi* and *jian*.[9] The former represents the *easiness* of the way of *qian* (乾), signifying heaven or sky, which operates as the energy source of all beginnings. The latter represents the *simplicity* of the way of *kun* (坤), signifying the earth, which works in creating all matters as energy is received. The ease with which *qian* works helps the common people to understand, makes it approachable and long-lasting, and promotes ethical behaviors. The simplicity of how *kun* operates allow the common people to follow, be successful, grow, and be righteous. Relying on these simple and easy principles, everyone would be able to understand the universe and its principles and to be able to take proper actions. Another interpretation of *yi jian* is to represent changes across time (as implied in *yi*) and space (as implied in *jian*). As circumstances change through time and space, principles included in the book should be interpreted with a good deal of flexibility. In brief, the semantic meaning of *Yijing* is the classic authority of changes, unchanging principles, and easy and simple operations across time and space.

The profundity and longevity of *Yijing* lays in its universality. Based on the observations of all things, the ancient Chinese have accumulated and recorded their wisdoms in *Yijing*, which is one of the most complete and reliable sources with principles that are omnipresent, all-purpose, and ubiquitous. *Yijing* entails explanations of all things in three ways: *xiang* (象), *li* (理), and *shu* (數). *Xiang* refers to phenomenon. All things are phenomena. Each phenomenon has an explanation behind it, that is the *li*, which may be referred to as philosophy, principle, or theory. In other words, all *xiang* has *li*, and all *li* has *xiang*. Furthermore, each phenomenon has numbers attached to it. For example, music is a phenomenon (*xiang*) that can be explained by various philosophical principles or theories, be they cultural, acoustical, perceptual, or otherwise (*li*). The phenomenon of music has numbers attached too, such as the length of a string or a vibrating air column, the frequency of vibration, the duration of each sound, the number of instruments, and so forth (*shu*). Similarly, music education is a phenomenon (*xiang*) in which music is learned and is supported by philosophical principles on why music should be taught (*li*). At the same time, numbers can be extracted from this phenomenon (*shu*) so the learning can be described and assessed. Although much of the meanings of *xiang, li, shu*, and their intersections of all matters are understood by only a few who dedicate their lives to studying and practicing *Yijing*, most others may glean from its broad principles a frame of reference for further exploration. In fact, Nan Huaijin (南懷瑾, 1918–2012), a renowned sinologist, suggested that one should not completely understand *Yijing* so that life could remain partially mystical to be interesting.[10]

The original *Yijing* itself contains only 64 *gua*[11] sentences (卦辭) and 384 *yao* sentences (爻辭). Each of these sentences explains the meaning of the *gua* or the *yao* by describing (a) changes in nature that correspond with human phenomena, (b) gain or loss as a result of human behavior, or (c) evaluations of phenomena that are good or bad.[12] It is a record of observations on how various matters work and interact, with frequent references to natural phenomena. The *gua* sentences are based on the 64 hexagrams (*gua*), which are constructed from *bagua* (eight trigrams) using all its possible trigram pairs (i.e., 8 × 8 = 64), one laying on top of another. Each hexagram comes with a line of text. Since each trigram in the *bagua* contains three *yao*, the 64 hexagrams make 384 *yao* (i.e., 3 × 2 × 64 = 384). The original book is not very long in contemporary printing. However, *Yizhuan* is included in contemporary publications of *Yijing*, making the book longer. Adding the editor's commentaries on both *Yijing* and *Yizhuan* makes the book look fairly thick.

Since the use of symbols is a universal human characteristic, *Yijing* involves the use of simple symbols to represent an immensely complex network of matters and their operations. These symbols can be viewed as codes that represent all observable phenomena, which operate under everlasting principles as time and space change. These codes are deciphered only by those who study them. They represent how every element is changing and connected as the world moves on. They are intended to offer insights into a phenomenon at a given time and situation, so those who understand them might use them as a source for consultation or encouragement. Those who consult it can improve their morale, increase their abilities, and accumulate their wisdom, and life can be better as a whole.

The earliest element of *Yijing* (i.e., *gua*) was already an ancient record, over two thousand years old, by the time of Confucius (551–479 BC) and Laozi (b. ca. 570 BC). Both of them studied it, but they each takes on a different perspective. Confucius and his students had many discussions on it, and *Yizhuan* includes some of their conversations, in which explanations of *Yijing* and its philosophical elements are found.[13] The ten essays in *Yizhuan*, in varying lengths, collectively explain (a) the formation, operation, and meaning of *yin, yang, yao*, and *gua*; (b) the meaning embedded in the positioning of *yao* in *gua*; and (c) the way of a sage in the context of the organismic worldview presented in *Yijing*. Beyond explaining some of the meanings and technicalities of *Yijing*, *Yizhuan* can be seen as work that reveals much of the philosophical principles in *Yijing*.

Essays in *Yizhuan* have not only clarified some of the meanings of *Yijing*, but they also confirm the foundations for both Confucianism and Daoism. The emphasis on the importance of virtue and sincerity and the avoidance of evil[14] are in accord with the classic Confucians. The juxtapositions of *yin* and *yang* being a main thread of the *dao*[15] and the concept of opposing poles working together in creating change in everyday lives[16] are clearly precursors of classic Daoism.

Yijing and *Yizhuan* contain two important aspects for studies. The first aspect is its philosophical connotations. Principles of changes in nature and connectedness of all elements in the world become explanations of natural phenomena and proper guides for human behaviors. Whether they are observable or non-observable, intended or unintended, all events are synchronized in a way that is in accord with the natural occurrences of events at any given moment. Everything is changing constantly and dynamically. The universe is operating under a complex web of constantly changing parts. Any one part affects the rest of the whole while its *principles* of change remain stable. All changes are due to a constant flow of energies, from one side to the other and from one part to another, back and forth. All elements should be in sync with each other so there are healthy motions to move forward.

The second aspect for study is numerology, which uses the eight trigrams (*bagua*), the 64 hexagrams (*gua*), and numbers to explain and predict certain phenomena. This is known to the common people as divination (*zhan gua* 占卦). However, Fu Pei-Rong reminds us that "it is easy to *zhan gua* but difficult to interpret the meaning of the *gua* sentences and the *yao* sentences."[17] Proper interpretation of these sentences is key to finding the proper meaning of the phenomenon. Nevertheless, in this text I focus on the philosophical connotations only. The divination portion of *Yijing* is beyond the scope of this text.

YIN AND YANG

From the perspective of *Yijing*, nothing occurs without a reason. There needs to be some type of energy to make things happen, and thereby create all matters. The source of all matters as described in *Yijing* is initiated by motions of energy flow between the dyadic *yin* (陰) and *yang* (陽). *Yang*

Figure 2.1: Contemporary *Taiji* diagram representing qualities of, and interactions between, *yin* and *yang*.

is on the active and energetic side, and *yin* is on the passive side receiving the energy. This idea was first recognized no later than the time of Fuxi (c. 29th–28th century BC).[18] Since the time of Chen Tuan (陳摶, AD 871–989), scholars have been using a *taiji* (太極), or the Great Extreme, diagram to represent the qualities of *yin* and *yang* as described in *Yijing*. Figure 2.1 is a contemporary rendition of a typical *taiji* diagram, in which the bright side is *yang* and the dark side is *yin*. The diagram could have been inspired by a variety of sources, but it is first associated with Chen.[19] Through centuries of modifications, the idea of "*yin-yang* fish *taiji* diagram" (陰陽魚太極圖) appeared in early Ming Dynasty (1368–1644).[20] It is important to note that, first, the diagram represents two fish, *yin* and *yang*, showing a curvy division rather than a straight line. Second, the two fish are in a circle, depicting perfection and completeness. *Yin* or *yang* alone is incomplete. Third, the two fish are swimming in a circle, pushing each other, representing the dynamic motions between *yin* and *yang* and providing the momentum for change and to move forward. They have to coexist and help each other, so that change can occur. A giver (*yang*) gives and a receiver (*yin*) receives, though in a different situation, the giver may become the receiver and the receiver may become the giver. Through this interaction, things change and the world moves forward. Fourth, the eyes of the fish are marked in opposing colors, showing a dot of *yin* inside *yang*, and a dot of *yang* inside *yin*. These dots are symbolic of their complementary nature and to the non-mutually exclusiveness of *yin* and *yang*. There is no pure *yin* and no pure *yang* if the world is to move forward.

In *Yijing*, *yin* and *yang* appear in the form of *yao* (爻). The *yang yao* is represented by a horizontal solid line. The *yin yao* is represented by a horizontal broken line (see Figure 2.2). Each *yao* could form the basis for another

Figure 2.2: *Yin yao* (below, the broken line) and *yang yao* (above, the continuous line).

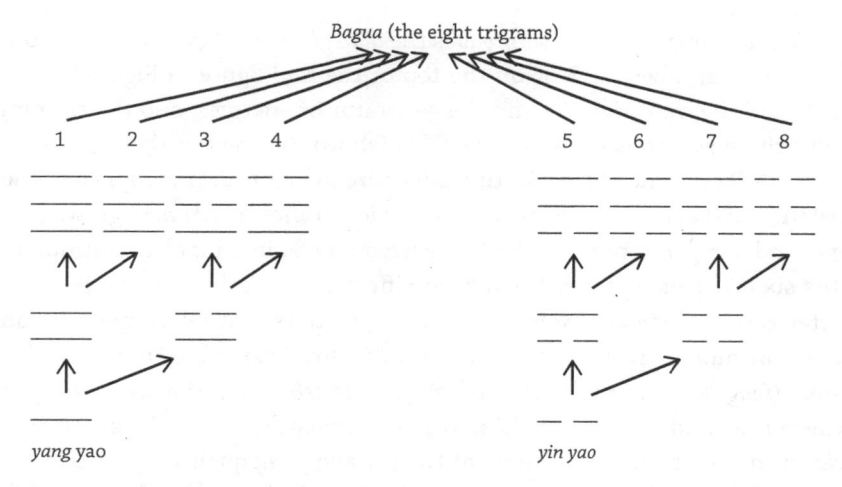

Figure 2.3: Formation of the *Bagua* (the eight trigrams) based on the *yin yao* (right side) and *yang yao* (left side), from bottom to top.

yin yao or *yang yao*. With all possible formations of the *yang yao* and *yin yao* in trigrams, the eight trigrams (*bagua*) are formed (see Figure 2.3). Contemporary representation of the *bagua* is often arranged around a *taiji*. Figure 2.4 shows a common contemporary way of arranging the *bagua*.[21] The eight trigrams represent various gradations of *yin* and *yang* as changes are made to represent various matters found in nature. Each trigram is constructed from bottom to top, and from inside to outside the *taiji* circle.[22]

Figure 2.4: A contemporary *Bagua* figure.

The trigram with three *yang yao* is the *qian gua* (乾卦) (shown on the top left corner in Figure 2.3 or on the top of the *taiji* figure in Figure 2.4) to represent heaven (*tian* 天) and the generator of energies, and the trigram with three *yin yao* is the *kun gua* (坤卦) (shown on the top right corner in Figure 2.3 or at the bottom of the *taiji* figure in Figure 2.4) to represent the earth (*di* 地) and the receiver of the energies to allow matters to grow. *Qian gua* and *kun gua* represent the two extreme ends in a bipolar continuum. The six trigrams between them have different strengths or levels of characterization of *yin* and *yang*, representing matters that fall somewhere on the continuum. They represent lake (*ze* 澤), fire (*huo* 火), thunder (*lei* 雷), wind (*feng* 風), water (*shui* 水), and mountain (*shan* 山). The positioning of the *yin yao* and *yang yao* in these trigram formations is significant in representing the relative positions of the *yin* and *yang* qualities. The trigram representing a lake consists of two *yang yao* at the bottom, indicating solid matters at the bottom, and one *yin yao* on the top, indicating floating water on top, which is non-solid and relatively lighter. The trigram representing fire is made up of one *yin yao* in between two *yang yao*, which indicates that air is needed in the middle of the fire. The trigram representing thunder has one *yang yao* at the bottom with two *yin yao* on top, which represent that the energy of the thunder is transmitted through the ground. The wind trigram has one *yin yao* at the bottom with two *yang yao* on top. This represents that the energy of the wind comes from above the ground. The water trigram is just the opposite of the fire *gua*, with a *yang yao* in the middle of two *yin yao*. This represents water flowing alongside with a solid line as support. Incidentally, this trigram looks similar to the earliest Chinese character for water (水) (see Figure 2.5). The mountain trigram has two *yin yao* at the bottom and a *yang yao* on top. This arrangement of the *yao* is symbolic of strong energy laying on top of the weak, which parallels the meaning of mountain wherein the path to move forward is barred.

Heaven and earth, lake and mountain, fire and water, and thunder and wind thus become four opposing pairs of trigrams in the *bagua*, with the first pair containing the most extreme ends of *yin* and *yang*. The other three pairs are somewhat opposites, but they are derived from varying gradations

Figure 2.5: The earliest form of the Chinese character water (水) found in oracle bone inscriptions.

of *yin* and *yang*. They are placed on the opposite sides of each other in this *bagua* arrangement. There are many representations of the *bagua*, and all of them are based on the same principle. The *bagua* can represent parts of the human body (*qian gua* and *kun gua* represent head and abdomen, respectively), while the other six *gua* represent mouth, eyes, feet, bottom, ears, and arms. The *bagua* can also represent parts of a family, various animals, various situations, time of year, time of the day, cardinal and intermediate directions, and so forth. Regardless of what it represents, it is clear that the trigrams with all *yang yao* and all *yin yao* represent the most active and passive ends. The characterization of the other six trigrams depends on the variations of energy flow between the two extreme ends. While the six trigrams show varying strengths of *yin* and *yang* from heaven and earth, each of the six trigrams can represent an extreme of its own. For example, the *gua* for mountain can represent series of steep mountains that cover an entire region, not only a typical mountain that one might imagine. This same idea applies to the *gua* for lake, fire, water, thunder, and wind. An extreme end of its own should be included as well as the typical. While the extreme ends rely on each other, representations in the eight trigrams are all connected. The system is incomplete without any of the trigrams.

Further variations of the eight trigrams are generated as extensions are made in trigram pairs, one trigram laying on top of another. All possible combinations of the eight trigrams create the 64 hexagrams, which becomes the main body of *Yijing*. These hexagrams are elaborations of the trigram representations. Their formation represents changes and interactions of various matters with well-connected elements. The 64 hexagrams have added a lot more complicated layers in describing and explaining various changes. When drawing meaning from and explaining the hexagrams, one can look at (a) the corresponding *yao* between the lower trigram and the upper trigram; (b) the pairs of *yao* with the two lowest *yao*, the two middle *yao*, and the two top *yao*; (c) the position of the concerned *yao* in the hexagram in relation to earth, human, and heaven; (d) the complementary hexagram, that is, changing the *yin yao* to *yang yao* and vice versa; (e) the component trigrams in each hexagram; (f) the overturned hexagrams, in which the upper trigram and the lower trigram is a reflection image of each other; (g) the entire hexagram turning upside down; and (h) the exchanged hexagram, in which the upper trigram and the lower trigram are exchanged in position.[23] All these variations are represented by the simple symbols of *yin* and *yang*, yet producing an astronomical set of possibilities, interpretations, and connections. While these variations have tremendous implications for divination, philosophically they present complex webs of explanations regarding how matters, elements, and actions are connected and how variations of *yin* and *yang* form the bases for change and forward motion.

THE SIGNIFICANCE OF AN ORGANISMIC WORLDVIEW

There is no mystery in *Yijing*, in that its ideologies are based on a set of simple symbols, *yin* and *yang*. They explain how complex matters and phenomena are not only connected but also dependent on each other. They show how the universe is changed due to the interactivities of the elements. Principles of the world's operation are modeled after those of *tian* (天 heaven, represented by *yang*) and *di* (地 earth, represented by *yin*), where all matters and phenomena occur. As all matters and events are dependent on each other, motion in one part affects the rest. Everything that exists has a role in it. Everything that exists has a reason.[24]

In *Yizhuan*, we are reminded of the importance of observing this organismic world regardless of our state of motion. In the state of stillness, one is to observe the phenomena; in the state of motion, one is to observe the changes.[25] This is how one can understand the operations of the world. Comprehending the changes and their connections in relation to their state and position can bring stability in accord with the rules of nature. Comprehending the rules of nature can contribute to a satisfying life. Recognizing one's position in the organismic world can free one from worries.[26] For example, one would know how to avoid dangers from weather elements or wildlife and to survive by understanding seasonal patterns for agricultural purposes. Positioning oneself is highly desirable to promote good outcomes.[27] The connections presented in the *yin* and *yang*, the trigrams, and the hexagrams clearly show an organismic worldview for thousands of years already by the time of Confucius and Laozi.

Yijing is a very important book for scholars throughout much of the history of China. Its content is based exclusively on the *gua* sentences and *yao* sentences, both using *yin* and *yang* as the basic elements and their interactivities as the principles of completeness, stability, and change. It explains the principles of how matters and phenomena work, which can be used to predict future events and guide human actions. It is a foundation for a Chinese way of thinking. Key figures in Chinese philosophy through the ages seem to have studied it and have gained philosophical insights from it. Since the sixth century BC, the stature of *Yijing* is reaffirmed and moved from a book of describing and predicting various phenomena to a book that is filled with philosophical implications. Chinese philosophers have built from this organismic foundation as they develop various ways of thinking for the following two and a half millennia. As principles found in *Yijing* are meant to be applicable to all aspects of life, music and music education are subsumed under these principles.

MUSICAL NOTES: CHANGE IN AN ORGANISMIC WORLDVIEW

The musical perspectives presented in this section are based on the philosophical threads suggested in *Yijing*, mainly referencing to the concepts of change, unchanging principles, easy and simple operations, *yin* and *yang*, and an organismic worldview. Based on these philosophical foundations, neither music nor music education should be conceived with static definitions. They change constantly but their *principles* of change remain constant. Some changes can be slow and gradual, others fast and dramatic. Changes are not unidirectional either. They are results of complex interactions of all connected elements. They follow the flow of changes in all matters. They change to meet the needs of the moment. Grasping these moments and resolving to simple and easy actions would be conducive to dissemination and growth. Musicians and music educators alike can seize these opportunities and spread the power of music through friendly and accessible engagements. To apply these ideas in the context of contemporary musical experiences, it is clear that music making and consumption are evolving along with trends that are available in many societies, such as microcomputer technology and the Internet. With strong traditions of musical experiences through acoustic musical instruments, musicians and educators cannot ignore the phenomenon and the need for high-quality musical experiences via electronic media. When one medium of music making, consumption, or instruction is effective for a given group, it does not mean that it will be effective for another group, however. Acoustic, electronic, or mixed, any medium might offer good or bad experiences, depending on the situation. When one studies the *Yijing*, one cannot miss the hint of the need to be flexible.

One simple idea about how flexibility works is found in the principles of *yin* and *yang*, which represent two extreme but complementary poles where energy flows from *yang* to *yin*. *Yin* represents the passive, soft, cold, and slow side of matters, while *yang* represents the active, hard, hot, and fast side. In addition, *yin* is associated with water, earth, the moon, and nighttime, and *yang* is associated with fire, sky, the sun,[28] and daytime. Musically, these could be interpreted in many ways. I suggest only a few here. Fundamentally, the interactions between *yin* and *yang* are driven by the flow of energy. It is obvious that energy is required to make music and to receive music. In normal circumstances, making and receiving music occur at the same time, and most likely in the same person, just as how *yin* and *yang* work. While actively making music, the musician would be receiving it simultaneously; while an audience receives the music, music is being recreated in the listeners' minds. In some cases, the musician and the listener are two in one, almost equally, as in improvisation. It also implies that when one is listening to music, the listener is not totally passive. Listeners could be actively making music in their minds. Music making and listening are complementary to each other as in *yin* and *yang*. There is always a *yin* inside *yang* and vice versa to propagate motion and change. By way of the interactions between music makers and music listeners, who can be the same person, the music becomes alive and moves forward. Musical style, medium, and meaning are changed to meet the needs of the audience of the time.

Within a piece of music, there can be moments of musical actions, such as extremely loud dynamics, rapid rhythms, aggressive chord progressions, active melodic movements, or fast-changing timbre. These are reflective of a *yang* quality. In contrast, there could be moments of musical inactivity, such as extremely soft dynamics, stagnant rhythm, unchanging or nonexistence of harmony, little or no melodic movements, or unchanging timbre. These are reflective of a *yin* quality. In reality, musical pieces would contain variations of these qualities and in different gradations, as in the 64 hexagrams, except the *qian* and *kun* hexagrams, in which one is made up of purely *yang yao* and *yin yao* respectively. Various musical elements change in different gradations at different moments, creating multiple possible combinations. Musicians make use of these various qualities and gradations as the piece moves forward and ideally maintain a complete entity and a balance for the piece as a whole. This is exactly how *yin* and *yang* work. The extremes rarely appear, but the gradations in between are common. Qualities of *yin* and *yang* are simultaneous and complementary to each other, as shown in musical pieces.

The 64 hexagrams, each containing six *yao*, allow for variations capable of describing potentially all types of changes. The key is to consider the possible combinations of the *yao* (*yin* or *yang*) in 64 hexagrams. Since there is no documentation to reveal the exact matches between specific musical phenomena and each of the 64 hexagrams, including the 384 *yao* within them, it is no more than a speculation in any attempt to do so. However, there is sufficient confidence to state that the possible combinations of various musical elements in different gradations at different times are in line with the principle that energy flows from one pole to the other, and various gradations of the extreme poles are used to create music while the extreme ends appear only in rare circumstances, if at all. In most musical situations, qualities of *yin* and *yang* in various musical parameters appear in meaningful synchronicity as generated by the music maker.

To consider the musical pieces as a whole, musicians and audience are likely to deal with musical experiences with which they are extremely familiar and those with which they are totally unfamiliar. Familiar musical experiences could be those that have been exposed for an extended period, in the family, in the local culture, through peers, through an education experience, or through traveling experiences. Unfamiliar music experiences could be those to which the musician or the audience have no prior exposure; perhaps they are based on a musical tradition that comes from afar or based on a new invention, such as the initial appearance of music in integrated multimedia or the music made by a new musical instrument. While these are descriptions of the extreme poles, most musical experiences lie somewhere in between the familiar and the unfamiliar. It could be a familiar style but an unfamiliar piece, a familiar instrument but an unfamiliar style, a familiar rhythm but an unfamiliar harmony, a familiar melody but an unfamiliar timbre, a familiar emotion but an unfamiliar structure, and so forth. Musicians and listeners create, recreate, and seek meanings in between the familiar and the unfamiliar. These permutations of *yin* and *yang* qualities in music and musical experiences are not unlike the complex web of connections described in *Yijing*, yet they all germinate from the simple concept of two extreme ends and their gradations in between.

NOTES ON MUSIC EDUCATION: AWARENESS OF SYNCHRONICITY AND ASSOCIATION WITH *YIN* AND *YANG*

In music education, the same principles of energy flow, connected elements, changing phenomena, consistencies, and complementary qualities of *yin* and *yang* can be applied. Worth mentioning is the idea of elements being in sync, regardless of whether the music teacher or the learner is aware of it. For example, if one stands on a sidewalk at a main intersection in a major metropolitan area, one can observe various people walking by, cyclists passing by, and cars driving by. The constant flow of pedestrians, cyclists, and automobiles creates ever-changing pictures that can never look the same. In any single picture, everything is in sync based on the natural occurrences of events, which include the stories of the individuals, the weather, and other natural events, all occurring in a synchronized way regardless of them being noticed. Now observe the same in a corner of a music classroom. Every student who comes through this classroom has a story and other natural events that occur in sync to make the specific combination of students and behaviors at that moment. If teachers are aware of this synchronicity, they would be more aware of the stories behind each student and natural events that have occurred to them to bring them to this classroom with their attitudes, behaviors, and abilities. In other words, there is a reason for everything to occur in that specific way and moment. Everyone has a role to play. Awareness of this synchronicity would allow teachers to understand the moments they have with their students. Since most of the synchronized elements are not easily noticeable (e.g., an uncle played the guitar for her on Skype the day before, or she saw a cartoon figure beating on a drum on television the night before), teachers may need to attend to the stories behind each student to help their teaching to be more effective.

Music education practices obviously involve the teacher, the learner, the music, and a process. The first two, the teacher and the learner, clearly show opposing qualities, as in *yin* and *yang*. The music teacher is often the manager, the leader, the instructor, the facilitator, the counselor, and the producer for music learners, whereas the music learner is at the receiving end while activities are initiated by the music teacher. The teacher-learner relationship reveals all qualities of *yin* and *yang* in that (a) they hold opposing roles with one mostly "giving" and the other mostly "receiving"; (b) they depend on each other for music education to take place; (c) they are not mutually exclusive of each other; (d) one is a component of the other, that is, teaching is part of the learning and learning is part of the teaching; (e) there are various gradations of teaching and learning for both the teacher and the learner; (f) the teacher can become the learner, and vice versa, as time, place, and context change; (g) intrinsically, not one of them is better than the other; and (h) both of them work together to create change and move music education forward.

To consider the *process* of music teaching and learning, one may derive from the same principles and draw parallels from the roles that the teacher and the learner have. Activities in music teaching and learning can be driven by the teacher or by the learner. Similar to the teacher-learner relationship, this process engaged in teacher- and learner-directed activities shows all qualities of *yin* and *yang*. If there is no interaction between teacher-directed activities (e.g., lecturing, conducting an ensemble, or close-ended exercises) and learner-directed activities (e.g., homework, practice on an instrument, or open-ended exercises), the process of music teaching and learning is not complete, and music education is not going much further. Moreover, whoever directs the activity, there is interaction between high-energy activities and low-energy activities, which is explored later in Chapter 5.

As seen in these derivatives of *yin* and *yang*, they can explain various phenomena in music and music education. The *qian* and *kun* trigrams and hexagrams represent only the extreme ends. Almost all phenomena in music and music education appear to be somewhere in between them, with various gradations of *yin* and *yang* qualities in various elements of the music and of the music education practice. While a one-on-one relationship between a trigram or a hexagram and a specific musical phenomenon cannot be drawn, it should be safe to assume the underlying principles of change, connectedness, consistency, dependency, and complementarity. These are the same principles that have become important foundations of much of the characteristically Chinese philosophical milieu, most directly in the formation of the classic Confucianism and the classic Daoism, which are addressed in the following two chapters.

CHAPTER 3

ojo

Foundations of Classic Confucianism

Cheng *(Sincerity)*, Shan *(Kindness)*, Ren *(Benevolence)*, and Junzi *(the Exemplary Person)*

BACKGROUND OF CONFUCIANISM

Confucianism is a philosophical mainstream in Chinese communities[1] named after the philosopher and educator Confucius (551–479 BC). The connection between "Confucius" and "Confucianism" in English is different from that in Chinese, however. In English, Confucianism and Confucius share the same stem, with the connotation that the former comes from the latter. While this is true to a great extent, in Chinese linguistic terms Confucianism (*rujia* 儒家) and Confucius (*Kongzi* 孔子) do not share any common Chinese character. The labeling of the two names are completely different. This illustrates that Confucius did not intend to establish his own school. Rather, others have labeled Confucian ideologies after him in English and in other languages of the Western world.

In fact, the basis of Confucian ideologies appeared before Confucius. The Chinese term for Confucianism, *rujia*, is to describe the mainstream spirit of the Huaxia (華夏) culture, which originated about 5,000 years ago along the banks of Yellow River (黃河) and Changjiang River (長江). The Chinese character *ru* (儒), as in the Chinese language for Confucianism, referred to technicians in charge of rituals (*li* 禮). They continued to serve to maintain order in the Zhou dynasty (1066–256 BC) and became a community of scholars knowledgeable in rituals of all sorts.[2] Cultural historians suggested that the idea of rituals existed prior to Confucius' propositions and teaching.[3] There is no doubt that he was the person who had developed it as a philosophical system, adding to it, clarifying it, practicing it, and teaching it throughout his lifetime. The word *ru* was ascribed to a spiritual meaning beyond the technical aspects of *li* after Confucius.

The classic Confucian philosophy described here is a continuation of the development of Chinese civilization based on the knowledge, the thoughts, the culture, and lives that preceded Confucius. It is obvious that he and his students were familiar with *Yijing*. There is plenty of evidence to support the belief that he and his students were authors of the ten accompanying essays, the *Yizhuan*,[4] which contains key technical explanations and philosophical interpretations of *Yijing*. Many philosophical ideas found in *Yijing* were thereby better understood. The interactions between *yin* and *yang* are the ways of nature in all things. They are the ways that lead to prosperity and that humans are in good terms with the heavenly ways and the earthly ways.[5] The idea that *yin* and *yang* are relative to the circumstances is made explicit. An entity could be in a position of *yin* or *yang* depending on a relational context. For example, a wife is *yin* in relation to her husband but *yang* in relation to her children, which is a reflection of an essential principle of change and in line with the logic that there is *yin* within *yang* and vice versa. Rather than seeing *yin* and *yang* as competing opposites, they are complementary pairs that depend on each other and work together in harmony and peace. Confucius was able to relate the organismic worldview and the concept of *yin* and *yang* to a way of understanding, reasoning, and living. The ideas of change, connectedness, dependency, and complementarity are clearly documented. Confucius inherited a great Chinese tradition and took it to new heights in a way he himself could not have imagined.

THE GREATNESS OF CONFUCIUS AND MENCIUS

The greatness of Confucius is attributable to the fact that he began his life as a layperson, just like typical citizens of the time, a time of internal political conflicts known as the Spring and Autumn period (771–476 BC). He lost his father at age three and his mother at age seventeen. He was raised as a peasant but decided to pursue knowledge as a teenager and ended up being a master of knowledge. He had managed a warehouse and a farm and had assisted in a funeral home when he was a young man. He began to have followers at around age thirty. He held government office in his fifties with splendid accomplishments despite the mediocrity of his ranks.[6] He spent most of his life teaching his philosophical ideologies. He was not a rich person by any standard. Rather, he lived humbly as an educated layperson most of his life. His ideologies were so integrated into his life that he was a living example, showing to the world that anyone can be great. One does not need to come from a noble family or be backed by special connections with those in power. Everyone can work hard to achieve the ideals as proposed. Normalcy and ordinarity are great virtues to live by. If he were still living today, he would be shocked to see how others have used his teaching and his name for more than two millennia in ways that he could not have imagined, becoming a major philosophical school throughout the world, modifying his ideologies or mixing his ideologies with others as propaganda, building a religion after him, establishing institutes after his name to promote Chinese language and culture across the globe, and much more.

Mencius (*Mengzi* 孟子) (372–289 BC) was a fifth-generation scholar after Confucius, following his legacy to further elaborate and clarify the ideologies within the same philosophical system, which is termed classic Confucianism throughout this text. Mencius lived during a time of wars, in the middle of the Warring States period (476–221 BC), in which there were about twenty Chinese states. Due to his reputation of being wise and knowledgeable, he was consulted by many feudal lords. Although there is relatively little documentation available about his life, one could deduce that his ideologies were impractical during such a turbulent time. He held the conviction of *ren zhe wu di* (those with benevolence will not have enemies 仁者無敵) even during his time of wars.[7] Since none of the state lords could achieve *ren* (benevolence 仁), no one could tell at the time if the principle of *ren zhe wu di* could work.[8] Nevertheless, he held firmly to his beliefs such that those after him could see the value of the philosophy, which had become a model for classic Confucians.

Mencius' complete loyalty and consistency with the ideologies of Confucius have been supported by many historians and philosophers, past and present.[9] Some even state that Mencius completed what Confucius began.[10] Their ideologies, collectively called classic Confucianism throughout this text, are documented in their own writings and those of their students, who documented their teacher's words and life stories. After rounds of editing and reorganization, these writings are collected in the *Analects* 《論語》 (*Lunyu*), *Mencius* 《孟子》 (*Mengzi*), and parts of *Liji* 《禮記》 (*Book of Rituals*), particularly *Great Learning* 《大學》 (*Daxue*) and *Zhongyong* 《中庸》. Many musical and educational ideologies are found in other parts of *Liji*: notably *Yueji* 《樂記》 (*Record of Music*) and *Xueji* 《學記》 (*Record of Learning*), respectively. However, due to the lack of evidence to support a consistent philosophical thread with Confucius and Mencius, many claims in *Yueji*[11] and *Xueji* are debatable in light of classic Confucianism up through Mencius. They are highly suspicious of works of a much later time, the Han Dynasty (206 BC–AD 220). There could be sporadic references to their ideologies in other sources as well, some of which could be questionable in terms of authorship, ideological consistency, or both. Nevertheless, sources used here have strong evidence to authenticate their authorship or are in line with the philosophical system of classic Confucianism as defined by Confucius and Mencius.

HUMAN-CENTRIC IDEOLOGY

The fundamental premise of classic Confucianism is to place humans at the center. It begins with sincerity within the individual. Humans have the ultimate value and can make changes in the self, others, the nation, and the world.[12] The value of humans is reflected in the *Analects* when describing the incident after Confucius returned home and learned about the accidental fire of his stable. "He asked, 'Did anyone get hurt?' And he did not ask about his horse" (*Analects* 10.17; 廄焚，子退朝，曰：「傷人乎？」不問馬。). Logically, one should be most concerned with the horses when a stable catches fire. The horse is the reason to have the stable. Confucius went against this logic and cared about the people who worked there, the grooms. These were the people of rather low status in the society of the time, and he cared about them.

Humans can make changes in their lives, take an active role in paving their own ways, and contribute to influencing others and reaching out to one's nation and the world. Human actions are the guiding force toward abiding by heavenly order or achieving one's goals (人能弘道).[13] In contrast, a goal or the heavenly order per se could not make humans better without any action done by humans (非道弘人).[14] Humans need to take the initiatives in a proactive way to control the path that leads to better lives.

While humans are at the center in classic Confucianism, the good virtues can move outward to make a better world. Confucius' well-known concentric circle of human influences is described in the *Great Learning* 《大學》 (*Daxue*). One needs to begin by developing in the self the abilities to (a) distinguish human relationships and behaviors and human relationships with matters (格物); (b) understand what ultimate kindness is (至知); (c) practice a sincere mindset (誠意); (d) be righteous (正心); and (e) refine speech and behaviors (脩身). The circle then extends beyond the self to unify the family (齊家), lead the nation (治國), and bring peace to the world (平天下).[15] It is clear that the concentric circle begins with the individual's cognitive, reflective, and behavioral efforts, before any influence can take effect on others, on the family, and then on fellow citizens and the broader humankind.[16]

The outward-moving relation relies heavily on interactions among individuals in various situations in different timing. It aligns with ideologies suggested in *Yijing*, emphasizing synchronicity in time (時 *shi*) and position or role (位 *wei*). For Confucius, social roles are clearly marked. Individuals in each role should behave accordingly. While the *Analects* highlighted only the dyadic roles of ruler and officials (君臣 *junchen*) and father and son (父子 *fuzi*),[17] Mencius elaborated on these roles as he described the expectations between husband and wife (夫婦 *fufu*), between the older and the younger (長幼 *zhangyou*), among friends (朋友 *pengyou*),[18] among brothers (兄弟 *xiongdi*),[19] and between host and guest (賓主 *binzhu*).[20] These relationships and expectations recur prominently, some with further extensions to other relationships, in various parts of *Liji*. One obviously plays different roles at different times; for example, an official can be a son, a husband, and so forth at different times. Understanding social roles at different times and behaving accordingly, with respect and *li*, are keys to building belated relationships, called "brothers."[21] Zixia (子夏), a student of Confucius, described it as a principle that works anywhere (*Analects* 12.5; 君子敬而無失，與人恭而有禮。四海之內，皆兄弟也。).[22] This is a characterization of an exemplary person (*junzi* 君子).

Mencius unequivocally highlights the synchronicity of time and position in human relationships. He states that opportunities are everywhere, but that it is more important to be in an advantageous position. For Mencius, being in an advantageous position is not as important as having harmonious relationships with people (*Mencius* 4.1; 孟子曰：「天時不如地利，地利不如人和。」). He further explains that various human relationships are not isolated relationships. Aligned with the organismic worldview presented in *Yijing*, relationships are all connected. Mencius presents an example in a political context, stating that talented officials cannot manage well without the support of their superiors. To gain the support of their superiors, they need to be able to gain the trust of their friends first. To be trusted by their friends, they need to be able to gratify their parents first. To gratify their parents, they need to reflect on their own sincerity (*cheng* 誠) first. To reflect on their own sincerity, they need to understand what kindness (*shan* 善) is first.[23] Mencius not only consolidates the interconnectedness of human relationships; more important, he turns all relationships to the internal impetus of individual persons: sincerity and kindness. He establishes that sincerity is a heavenly way of operation (天之道), and that to reflect on sincerity is the proper way of humans (人之道).[24] He also uses kindness as a focus of his ideologies. Sincerity and kindness become essential elements of benevolence, which is an expectation of an exemplary person. This is suggested by Confucius and clarified by Mencius.

CHENG (SINCERITY 誠)

Sincerity is a key impetus within an individual that needs to be preserved and properly expressed. It naturally flows from many expressive channels, such as speech, behaviors, poems, and songs. Regardless of education, ethnicity, social status, social role, nationality, or musical training, everyone has something to express through these channels. While sincerity is valued, Confucius admits that disingenuity exists. In *Yizhuan*, Confucius states that one needs to maintain sincerity by preventing the invasion of evil thoughts (閑邪存其誠).[25] He further suggests that one needs to refine one's words, so sincerity can be ascertained by others (脩辭立其誠).[26] These ideas are consistent with the classic Confucian emphasis on the proactive role of humans, in this case, while ensuring sincerity.

The importance of sincerity is also presented in the core of Confucius' teaching. Like *Yijing*, *Shijing* 《詩經》, a collection of sung poems, was already extant by the time of Confucius. *Shijing* was a compulsory text in Confucius' teaching. Considering the education of *li* (禮) and *yue* (樂) as the focus of Confucius' teaching, *Shijing* does not seem to offer much. The collection of poems has little direct reference to *li* or *yue*. However, for Confucius, the poems provide an understanding of sincere expressions of true emotions and feelings across a wide range of contexts. These poems help to broaden one's perspective about people, beauty, and the world as they come from various strata and locales of the society. They collectively tell the truth (真 *zhen*) of being humans. Confucius commented on the common qualities of the collection of the diverse poems: all of them come from true expressions, without any corruption (*Analects* 2.2; 子曰：「詩三百，一言以蔽之，曰：『思無邪』。」). Literally, the poems are "without evil thoughts" (*si wu xie* 思無邪).[27] People should be stimulated and motivated by the sincere expressions of these poems so they are excited about life (興於詩). Through learning about the rules and rituals (*li*) of the society, they establish themselves (立於禮). And finally, studying *yue* (commonly translated as "music") makes people complete (成於樂).[28] On the surface, poetry, *li*, and *yue* form the core of Confucius' teaching. It is crucial to consider the underlying purpose of studying the poems, which is to understand, resonate, enjoy, and internalize the sincerity manifested through the expressions in these diverse poems. Sincerity is the foundation for the development of *li* and *yue*.

Like Confucius, Mencius regards sincerity highly. It is a source of great power to move others. He states that there is never anyone who is not moved by perfect sincerity and that those without sincerity can never move anyone (*Mencius* 7.12; 至誠而不動者，未之有也；不誠，未有能動者也。). He also feels that having everything he needs in his life is not enough. As he reflects on his life and determines that he has done everything with sincerity, it is only until then that it gives him the greatest happiness (*Mencius* 13.4; 萬物皆備於我矣。反身而誠，樂莫大焉。). However, sincerity alone does not guarantee greatness in classic Confucianism, because it can be applied in malicious acts, which is a distortion of what sincerity means. Sincerity must be coupled with kindness.

SHAN (KINDNESS 善)

In classic Confucianism, kindness (*shang* 善) is a maneuverable potent quality within humans.[29] Simply put, humans can choose to be kind or unkind. However, being kind is aligned with the natural inclination of human's preference for beauty. Confucius clearly states that exemplary persons would like to see all things beautiful (*mei* 美) and dislike all things evil (*è* 惡). Beauty here parallels the notion of kindness, as beauty disapproves of evil. Therefore, beauty is a manifesto of kindness.[30] No beauty is without kindness.

Mencius explains the directional potency much more intricately. Humans' natural tendency to be kind, rather than unkind or evil, is analogous to how water flows. This idea is reflected in a debate between Mencius and Gaozi (告子) (420–350 BC).[31] Gaozi describes how a body of water could rush to the east or to the west, depending on where the opening of the outlet is. He is trying to point out that humans do not have a natural inclination to be kind or unkind. Then Mencius posits his view in that humans have a natural potency to be kind. He states:

> Water *per se* indeed does not have a difference between east-flowing and west-flowing, but doesn't it have a distinction between upward-moving and downward-moving? Human's tendency to be kind is like water's natural potency to move downward. There is not a human without kindness, just like there is no water without a natural tendency to move downward. Now if one uses a hand to splash the water, it could go up above one's head. If we put barriers and make the water reverse its course, we can guide the water to go up a high mountain. Is that the natural character of water? These are caused by situations created by

humans (i.e., the splashing and the barriers). When humans perform unkind acts, they are in similar circumstances (i.e., in situations created by humans).[32]

This explanation clearly illustrates that kindness is an act that follows the natural, innermost, and definite drive. It is not an inherent human quality but an inherent human potency. Human's tendency for being kind or unkind is not indefinite, as Gaozi believes.

When the state of Lu (魯) was considering Yuezhengzi (樂正子) as a candidate to lead it, Mencius was so happy that he could not sleep. This was so not because Yuezhengzi was strong, intelligent, or knowledgeable, but because he liked to know about kind deeds. Then Gongsunchou (公孫丑) became curious about why Mencius was so excited about Yuezhengzi being a potential leader of the state just because he liked to know about kind deeds. Mencius explains, "Like to know about kind deeds exceeds the ability to lead the world [i.e., beyond the state]" (「好善優於天下」), because people from afar would be eager to visit and tell him about their kind deeds. "If not, people from afar would not want to visit and tell him about their kind deeds, and people would only come with words of slander flatter. Do you think he can lead well if he hears mostly words of slander flatter?"[33] These dialogues clearly show that in the classic Confucianism of Mencius, (a) kindness, rather than evil or being unkind, is a natural potency in every human; (b) sincerity is a source of utmost satisfaction in life; and (c) sincerity and kindness must work together in each individual, so the social institution, be it a family, a nation, or the world, can prosper. Sincerity and kindness are the foundations for all individuals for any community to flourish with peace. They are the initial steps on a path to meaningful and satisfactory lives (see Figure 3.1). As sincerity is associated with truth, and kindness is associated with beauty, hence there are Chinese expressions of truth and sincerity (真誠 zhencheng) and kindness and beauty (善美 shanmei). The former in each pair implies a source and the latter implies a consequence. In a Chinese idiomatic sense, truth leads to sincerity, and kindness leads to beauty. Together they form an idealistic ambience, not only for artistic pursuits, but for life in general also.

REN (BENEVOLENCE 仁)

While Figure 3.1 presents an epitome of a life philosophy, it is far from clear. The key to understand the path suggested in classic Confucianism is to figure out the path and walk on it. We now know that sincerity and

```
┌─────────────┐      ┌─────────────┐
│     誠      │      │     善      │
│   Cheng     │      │    Shan     │
│  Sincerity  │      │  Kindness   │
└─────────────┘      └─────────────┘
            ╲            ╱
             ╲          ╱
              ▼        ▼
         ┌──────────────────────────┐
         │ Path to a Most Satisfactory Life │
         └──────────────────────────┘
```

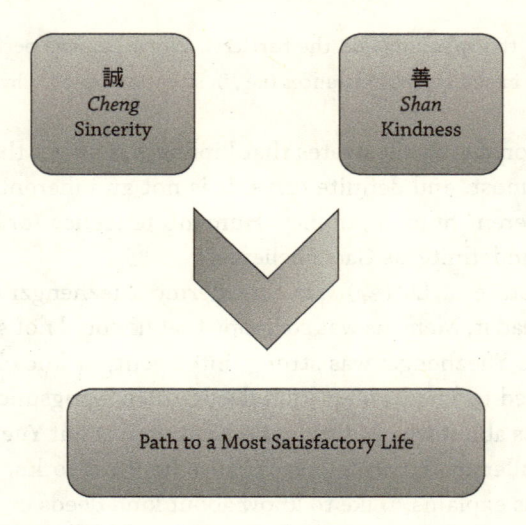

Figure 3.1: Sincerity and kindness being initial steps on a path to a most satisfactory life.

kindness set off the initial steps. Together they are key ingredients of an absolutely desirable quality: benevolence (*ren* 仁, also translated as humanity,[34] which has connotations of compassion, altruism, generosity, magnanimity, and the like). Both Confucius and Mencius are proponents of *ren* for individuals, so the society can be peaceful and harmonious, and for leaders, so they become models for general citizens.

As Confucius posits the importance of *li* (禮 ritual) and *yue* (樂 music),[35] the practice of *li* and *yue* is meaningless without *ren*. He says, "For humans without benevolence, what is the purpose of practicing *li*? For humans without benevolence, what is the purpose of practicing *yue*?" (*Analects* 3.3; 子曰：「人而不仁，如禮何？人而不仁，如樂何？」). Whatever people do, *li* or *yue* (i.e., the core of education and much of life for the educated of the time), without *ren* it is meaningless. His conviction of the need for *ren* in humans gets even stronger when he pairs *ren* with living. He says, "Those who are determined and those who live with *ren* would not desire to give up *ren* to live on. Some would even be willing to give up life to perfect *ren*" (*Analects* 15.9; 子曰：「志士仁人，無求生以害仁，有殺身以成仁。」). Those who already have *ren* in their lives would not give it up. Although not everyone will give up their life for *ren*, some would. These statements again are extremely glaring. They illustrate the importance of *ren* in practicing Confucian ideals as humans are firmly grounded in the center.

Mencius offers adamant support. He says, "those with benevolence are humans; humans and benevolence combined is the proper way of life"

(*Mencius* 14.16; 孟子曰：「仁也者，人也。合而言之，道也。」). This statement indicates that (a) *ren* is applicable to humans only, not animals or other creatures or objects; (b) it is a privilege for humans to have *ren*; (c) without *ren* is not a proper way of life; (d) achievement of *ren* comes only through human practices; (e) *ren* does not come naturally if nothing is done; and (f) most important, humans with *ren* is the *dao* (道), which we must interpret within the context of classic Confucianism and not confuse it with the distinctively different meaning of *dao* in classic Daoism (see Chapter 4). The *dao* here refers to the proper way of humans as achieved by having *ren*.[36] The classic Confucians have elevated *ren* to a highest status in human lives. *Ren* clearly takes a further step from *cheng* (sincerity) and *shan* (kindness). It involves practicing them and putting them in actions in relation to others.

The prominence of *ren* in classic Confucianism is so unshakable that it appears as a quality that permeates across various social strata with the same expectation. Regardless of one's status, ruler or layperson, parent or child, husband or wife, the older or the younger, superior or subordinate, host or guest, and so forth, all have an expectation to have *ren*. Even between teachers and students, teachers are not necessarily ahead of their students in the practice of *ren*. Confucius says, "when it comes to *ren*, the student should not go behind the teacher" (*Analects* 15.36; 子曰：「當仁，不讓於師。」). Both the teacher and the student should be at the forefront of practicing *ren*. It has nothing to do with knowledge, skill, or intellect of any sort. This is an exceptional scenario among classic Confucian thoughts where the boundary between the student and the teacher is broken.

While *ren* is expected of everyone, Mencius puts more emphasis on its importance for rulers, which is more in line with his proposition of *ren zhe wu di* (those with benevolence will not have enemies 仁者無敵) and his *ren*-based political and management style. He says, "only those with *ren* should be high in the ruling class. If those without *ren* are in the ruling class, they will spread their evil deeds to the people" (*Mencius* 7.1; 「是以惟仁者宜在高位。不仁而在高位，是播其惡於眾也。」).

In brief, *ren* is at the center of the path to a most satisfactory life. Figure 3.2 has further clarified this path. *Ren* is a path based upon the foundations of *cheng* and *shan*. While *cheng* and *shan* remain internally within the individual, *ren* is a manifesto of *cheng* and *shan* in action in relation to others. It puts the path into motion in any human interactions. In fact, the Chinese character *ren* (仁) itself is the best illustration of this quality in individual's actions in relation to others. The left side of the character comes from the character for human or person (人), and the right side comes from the

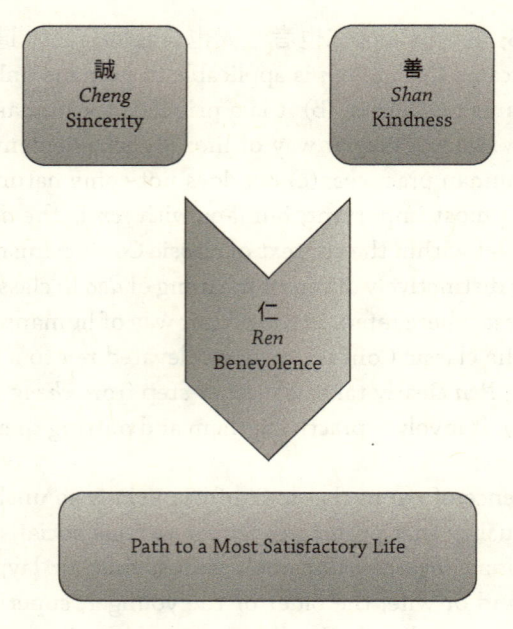

```
┌─────────────┐      ┌─────────────┐
│     誠      │      │     善      │
│   Cheng     │      │    Shan     │
│  Sincerity  │      │  Kindness   │
└─────────────┘      └─────────────┘
           ╲            ╱
            ╲          ╱
          ┌──────────────┐
          │      仁      │
          │     Ren      │
          │ Benevolence  │
          └──────────────┘
                 │
                 ▼
        ┌──────────────────────────┐
        │ Path to a Most Satisfactory Life │
        └──────────────────────────┘
```

Figure 3.2: Benevolence puts the path to motion.

character for two (二). Putting the two together—*ren* (仁)—is clearly an enactment between two (or more) persons.

The motion of *ren* (benevolence 仁) can be set off by *cheng* (sincerity 誠) and the natural potency of *shan* (kindness 善). If one is *committed* (立志) to practice *cheng, shan,* and *ren* consistently, making them a living habit and setting a lifelong goal to perfect this practice, then one has begun the journey of becoming an exemplary person (*junzi* 君子).

JUNZI (THE EXEMPLARY PERSON 君子)

The term *junzi* (君子) originated prior to the Zhou Dynasty (1059–255 BC) when describing the noble class. During the Zhou Dynasty, it was reserved for the sons of the feudal lords (君之子), who were generally well educated. In the hands of Confucius, the meaning of *junzi* was reset to include anyone who was well educated, practicing high humanistic standards, and, ideally, behaving as role models for others. Therefore, the translation of *junzi* used in this text—the exemplary person—is applicable only in the context of classic Confucianism and thereafter. *Ren* (仁) being the ultimate humanity standard, *junzi* are those committed to practice *ren* constantly. Confucius says, "When *junzi* is without *ren*, what could give them their name? *Junzi* does not go against *ren* for a split second at any time, whether they are in a hurry, or whether they are in danger" (*Analects* 4.5; 子曰：「... 君子去仁，惡乎成名？君子無終食之間違仁，造次必於是，顛沛必於是。」). There are numerous passages in the *Analects, Mencius,* and other Confucian texts that explain the expectations of *junzi*. These passages are most often focused on the implementation of *ren* or *ren*-related qualities of *junzi*.[37]

Confucius speaks of the three *daos* of *junzi* (君子道): *ren* (benevolence 仁), *zhi* (wisdom 知 or 智), and *yong* (courage 勇).[38] These three qualities appear to be distinct and isolated on the surface. A deep analysis suggests that they are intricately connected and still centered on *ren* (仁). *Zhi* is the wisdom to understand what *ren* is. Without knowing what *ren* is, one is not able to become a *junzi*. He says, "those with *ren* will walk with *ren* and be settled; those who understand *ren* will see its importance and walk with it" (*Analects* 4.2; 子曰：「... 仁者安仁，知者利仁。」). Confucius refers to *yong* as courage to act on *ren*. He says, "seeing a righteous way and not taking any action is weak with no courage" (*Analects* 2.24; 子曰：「... 見義不為，無勇也。」). He further illustrates that "those with *ren* must have courage; those with courage do not necessarily have *ren*" (*Analects* 14.4; 子曰：「... 仁者，必有勇。勇者，不必有仁。」).[39] These passages demonstrate that, for Confucius, without the wisdom to understand *ren* and the courage to carrying it out, there is no *junzi*.

Mencius posits that the nature of *junzi* is rooted in *ren* (benevolence 仁), *yi* (righteousness 義), *li* (courteousness 禮), and *zhi* (wisdom 智) (*Mencius* 13.21; 孟子曰：「... 君子所性，仁義禮智根於心，...」). These four philosophical roots of *junzi* resonate with Confucius' three *dao* for *junzi*. In *Liji*, they are described as the human *dao* (*ren dao* 人道)[40] (*Sangfusizhi, Liji*: 禮記：喪服四制; 仁義禮智，人道具矣。). In *Mencius*, they have appeared in different orders,[41] but *ren* is always first, reaffirming its centrality in classic Confucianism. Mencius explains, "*ren* begins with compassion, *yi* begins with shame on evil, *li* begins with civility, and *zhi* begins with a sense of right and wrong" (*Mencius* 3.6; 孟子曰：「... 惻隱之心，仁之端也；羞惡之心，義之端也；辭讓之心，禮之端也；是非之心，智之端也。」). While he uses very strong language to confirm that compassion, shame on evil, civility, and a sense of right and wrong are all inherent human qualities,[42] he also confirms that every human can achieve *ren, yi, li,* and *zhi*.[43] In other words, every human can be a *junzi*.

As seen from above, *junzi* must be committed to *ren* (benevolence 仁) and practice it along with its associated qualities (i.e., *zhi* 智 wisdom, *yong* 勇 courage, *yi* 義 righteousness, and *li* 禮 courteousness). To practice *ren*, one must be sincere and persistent in choosing kindness, and work toward its perfection (*Great Learning* 《大學》 1; 止於至善). A passage from *Zhongyong* 《中庸》 brings the practice of *ren* back to the individual's efforts in sincerity and kindness. "To allow sincerity to work is the human way [*ren dao* 人道].... To allow sincerity to work is to choose kindness and be persistent in it" (*Zhongyong* 20.5; 誠之者，人之道也。... 誠之者，擇善而固執之者也。). The act of "choosing kindness" involves wisdom; the "persistence" of the act involves courage. This is especially important for those who live in a world surrounded by many choices and who need courage to be persistent in being kind in a way that is different from others.

To be persistent in the practice of *ren* (benevolence 仁) in *junzi*, Confucius and Mencius emphasize self-cultivation and self-reflection. In his response to a student's question on what makes a *junzi*, Confucius says, "Self-cultivation so everything can be dealt with respectfully" (*Analects* 14.42; 子曰：「脩己以敬。」). He also points to the need to read widely and control oneself within the parameters of *li* (禮), so one will not be derailed from the proper way (*Analects* 6.27 and 12.15; 子曰：「君子博學於文，約之以禮，亦可以弗畔矣夫！」). More specifically at the behavioral level, Confucius proposes nine types of self-reflection for *junzi*: reflect on whether what one sees is understood, whether what one hears is clear, whether the facial expression is mild, whether the appearance and attitude are respectful, whether the words are sincere, whether affairs at hand are being appreciated, whether questions should be raised if there is doubt, whether there are consequences after rage, and whether it is right to possess the desirables (*Analects* 16.10; 孔子曰：「君子有九思：視思明，聽思聰，色思溫，貌思恭，言思忠，事思敬，疑思問，忿思難，見得思義。」). Constant contemplation on one's own behavior is expected of *junzi*.

Mencius takes self-reflection to another level. In *Mencius* 8.28, he begins with an affirmation that the difference between *junzi* and others rests upon their internal drive for their actions. *Junzi* are driven by *ren* (benevolence 仁) and *li* (ritual 禮). Those with *ren* love others, and those with *li* respect others. Those who love others would be loved, and those who respect others would be respected. If someone does not love and respect in return, *junzi* must reflect on themselves (i.e., self-reflection, 自反 *zifan* or 自我反省 *ziwofanxing*), whether they have *ren* and *li*. It is probable that they must not have done their best in *ren* and *li*. After the self-reflection and if the person still does not love and respect in return, *junzi* must reflect on themselves again. If that person still does not love and respect in return, then *junzi* may say, "This is a barbaric person like a beast. What difference does this person have compared to a beast? What can we blame a beast for?" Therefore, *junzi* have to be concerned about a lifetime of self-improvement but not worry about the trouble of the moment.⁴⁴ This passage indicates that Mencius does not take self-reflection lightly or casually, nor would he come to a judgment impulsively. The self-reflection, action, and response have gone through two cycles in this incidence before a conclusion is made. More important, *junzi* need to focus on what they should be worrying about in the long term rather than concerning short-lived issues with a beast-like being.

In addition to the persistent practice of *ren* and self-reflection for self-cultivation and improvement, there is one other important expectation for *junzi*: helping others to be *junzi*. In other words, *junzi* should teach. When there are people in the nation, what should we do with them? "Teach them," Confucius says.⁴⁵ For Confucius, teaching should not be selective or discriminatory. His famous motto for education is *"you jiao wu lei"* (teaching everyone irrespective of the learner's background 有教無類) (*Analects* 15.39). This way, *junzi* carries a mission of cultivating others.

Although teaching is listed toward the end in describing the qualities of *junzi* in this text, it is not additional but essential to being *junzi*. Mencius states this clearly by quoting a dialogue between Confucius and his student Zi Gong (子貢):

> Zi Gong once asked Confucius, "Do you believe you are a sage?" Confucius replied, "I can never be a sage. I am only never tired of learning and never weary of teaching." Zi Gong said, "Never tired of learning is wisdom; never tired of teaching is benevolence. Having wisdom and benevolence, you are a sage."⁴⁶

The word "sage" (聖人 *shengren*) is used to describe someone who has achieved an acme of perfection that is above *junzi*. Neither Confucius nor Mencius claim to be a sage themselves. Instead, they claim to be ever improving throughout their lives. Many of these improvements are attributed to their lifelong teaching and learning, as teaching is an act of *ren* (仁) and learning is an act of wisdom.

Mencius further describes that the opportunity to teach talented students (*Mencius* 13.20; 得天下英才而教育之) is one of the biggest happinesses in life, more so than being the ruler of a kingdom. He specifically lays out five methods that *junzi* should use to teach.⁴⁷ First, he catches the moment of opportunity in teaching. It is important to consider the context here, because students of that time often followed the teacher all day long. When an opportunity arises, the teacher should grasp it and make it a teachable moment. Second, he targets the students' learning of virtues, so students can work toward perfection. Third, he cultivates the students' competencies in various abilities. Fourth, he answers questions, so the students' knowledge base can be expanded. Fifth, he disseminates his teaching so those who cannot study with him in person can study on their own. It is remarkable to see that these five "methods" are still applicable in contemporary educational contexts.

Based on what has been presented thus far, an update of the previous figure might look like Figure 3.3. The path to a most satisfactory life fits the description of *junzi*, which is not only a noun but a path or a way of living, expecting continuous self-cultivation, reflection, and improvement throughout one's life. Becoming a sage is the destination of *junzi*, but even Confucius and Mencius did not claim to have achieved that. Although *junzi* is at the end of the diagram, it is not an end but a continuous process. There is always a better *junzi* somewhere. While *ren* plays a central role in a *junzi*'s way of living, its associated qualities (*zhi, yong, yi,* and *li*), self-reflection, and lifelong teaching and learning are very important in fulfilling the humanly *dao* (人道). It begins with the initial determinations of using sincerity from the heavenly *dao* (天道) and taking kindness as the natural human potency. In summary, based on the ideologies of classic Confucianism, everyone could be, and should strive to be, an exemplary person. An exemplary person should be a model for others and to help others to be an exemplary person also.

誠
Cheng
Sincerity

善
Shan
Kindness

仁
Ren
Benevolence

君子
Junzi
Exemplary Person

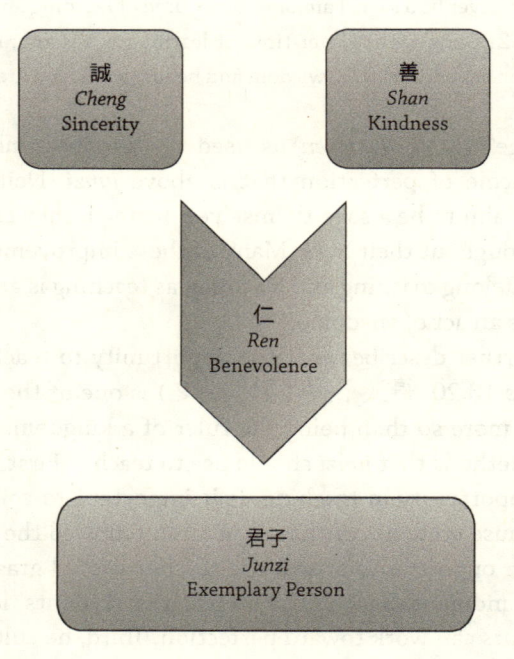

Figure 3.3: The path to a most satisfactory life becomes a way of *junzi* living.

MUSICAL NOTES: A HAPPY CONNECTION

As in any historical, philosophical, and cultural ideologies, interpretation must take the context into consideration. A mere linguistic translation is often semantically incomplete. The idea of *yue* (樂), as in classic Confucianism, being translated to "music" is a widespread example of such incompleteness. While *yue* is commonly translated as "music," the meaning of *yue* during the time of Confucius and Mencius in China is quite different from the meaning of the word "music" in contemporary English. The same Chinese character (樂) can be pronounced in two different ways: *yue* or *le*. When pronounced as *yue*, the closest English word one can find is "music." When it is pronounced as *le*, it means "happiness" or its synonyms (e.g., happy, glad, joy, enjoy, etc.). These meanings of *yue* and *le* are intricately connected within Confucius' core teaching areas: poetry, *li*, and *yue*. Poetry, to be sung, presents sincere expressions of all sorts. *Li* is to maintain order in the society, so that life is happy for everyone. When people are happy, they express it through sound and movements. What they create in these circumstances is called *yue*.[48] Music making behaviors and the state of being happy are intricately connected. Based on the literature from the Warring States period, it is not difficult to figure out that *yue* encompasses instrumental music, songs, poetry, and movements in contemporary terms. In contemporary English, however, there is no word with the same range of coverage. Therefore, readers should keep in mind the meaning of *yue* when the word "music" is used henceforward.

The connection between *yue* and *le* is exemplified in Confucius' singing behaviors as observed by his student. On the day when Confucius has cried,[49] he is not going to sing (*Analects* 7.10; 子於是日哭，則不歌。). On a sad day after he cried, it's not a day for Confucius to sing. Put it another way, he sings regularly on days that he is not sad, which is described by his students also: Confucius sings with others joyfully. He surely will make his company sing again, then he and others will sing together yet again (*Analects* 7.32; 子與人歌而善，必使反之，而後和之。). While no one should represent the full range of human emotions as merely happy or sad, nor should musical expressions be limited to the dualistic emotions, these snippets of documentation support the etymological link between *yue* and *le*.

Figure 3.3 is one way, but by no means the only way, to understand the classic Confucianism of Confucius and Mencius. As the model presents a path to work toward an exemplary person, it provides a frame of mind for anyone to make excellent music. It begins with sincerity (*cheng* 誠) and kindness (*shan* 善); through the *practice* of benevolence (*ren* 仁), one becomes an exemplary person (*junzi* 君子). This section offers an explanation of what these mean in musical experiences.

To begin, one must have something to express; that something needs to be true and sincere. To make music with sincerity, Confucius has made it clear that music is not about the musical instruments or their sounds. It is about the truth and sincere expression behind the musical sounds.[50] Be it an emotion, a story, or an abstract idea, whatever is being expressed should come from real-life experiences and be presented sincerely so it can be shared and received with respect. The expressive quality of the music must be true to the music maker before it can be presented sincerely. Most important, the expressive quality must not have been corrupted by any evil thoughts (as in *Analects* 2.2 when describing the poems in *Shijing* 《詩經》: *si wu xie* 思無邪). Confucius describes the expressive qualities of a well-known poem *Guanju* as happy but not licentious, sorrow but not hurtful (*Analects* 3.20; 子曰：「《關雎》，樂而不淫，哀而不傷。」). Clearly, happy and sorrow are appropriate expressive qualities, but licentious and hurtful are not.

From a music listening perspective, one must be sincere while listening to music or it would make the experience meaningless. Sincerity in music listening might be parallel to sincerity in listening to others talk. The listener needs to pay attention with open ears and respect. If people are listening to others' speech with sincerity, they would try very hard to understand it. If they don't understand, they would try harder. If they disagree with it, they would still respect it. They may ask questions about it. The same is true in music listening, in that if listeners do not understand or agree with the meaning of the music, they would still try their very best to understand it and to respect it. They should ask questions about the music too.

At various decision points, music makers will make choices that are going to affect the quality of the music. If the choices are made based on kindness, the music is likely to sound beautiful. The act of choosing kindness as a basis is to follow the natural human potency for kindness and beauty. Just like Mencius' analogy of water, the natural potency of downward movement in water is like human's natural preference for kindness and beauty.

"Extreme kindness and extreme beauty" in Chinese (*jin shan jin mei* 盡善盡美) is often translated as "perfect." In commenting the "perfect" type of music heard under the regime of Shun (舜), this is how Confucius describes it: "extremely beautiful, and extremely kind" (*Analects* 3.25; 子謂韶，「盡美矣，又盡善也。」).[51] He immediately follows with a comment for the music heard under the regime of Zhou Wu Wang (周武王) that is quite good but not perfect by saying that it is "extremely beautiful, but not extremely kind" (*Analects* 3.25; 謂武，「盡美矣，未盡善也」。). To compare the two types of music, the difference is attributed to the *duration* of their honorable rules.[52] Shun's honorable rule lasted for more than fifty years, but Zhou Wu Wang's honorable rule lasted for only six years. One might deduce from this comparison that being kind requires a higher level of persistence than being beautiful and that it takes a longer period to reach perfection as reflected in the music.

For music to be meaningful, there must be *ren* (benevolence 仁) in the music (*Analects* 3.3). As explained in the benevolence section above, *ren* by definition involves interaction between two or more individuals. Therefore, music is not an isolated entity or activity. Music is inherently interactive. In a classic Confucian sense, music is connected among individuals and with the society from which they come. Music is meant to be shared and is reflective of the characteristics of the society. Mencius suggests that sharing music with more people is happier, especially for those who are in the ruling class. This is reflected in a dialogue between Mencius and Qi Xuan Wang (齊宣王 350–301 BC), who reigned Qi 319–301 BC:

> Mencius asked, "Enjoying music alone or enjoying music with others, which one is more enjoyable?" Qi Xuan Wang responded, "With others." Mencius asked again, "Enjoying music with a few people or enjoying music with many people, which one is more enjoyable?" Qi Xuan Wang responded, "With more people."[53]

Then Mencius continues to explain that enjoying life (including music) with the citizens is a key element of being a ruler of integrity.[54] Sharing music and other enjoyable experiences with others allows for more happiness. Although sharing music for greater enjoyment is not a novel idea in the contemporary musical world as music is shared in more different ways than any other time in history, live and recorded, acoustic and electronic, synchronous and asynchronous, and in person and via the Internet, this is one of many pieces of evidence that show the perspicacity of the classic wisdom.

Having *ren* (benevolence 仁) in the musical process and product is not enough. In fact, musical process and product should be outcomes of *ren*. Those involved in music need to *practice ren* consistently, so the music they make or the musical activities in which they participate are aligned with the ideology of the classic Confucianism. *Ren* is the lifelong practice of *junzi*, and it is expected of all involved in music. It is no different in music making, music listening, or any type of musical or artistic endeavor. Knowing, practicing, and refining *ren* are critical in any musical interactions. These have tremendous implications on, say, how composers choose their ideas for a new composition, how performers interact with their audience and vice versa, how performers interpret the composer's work, how composers tailor the techniques involved for specified performers, how music participants respect and abide by the "rules" of the musical tradition, and so forth. There is much self-reflection and consideration for others involved. Practicing *ren* is a way of living; it is also a way of musical involvements. It requires persistence in pursuing knowledge and skills (i.e., *zhi* 智 wisdom). At times, one needs to be brave in setting a new model that could change the mentality of the field or simply "doing something different" that is well-informed, righteous, kind, and cordial (i.e., *yong* 勇 courage). Based on one's role in the musical involvement, interactions with others should be cordial and orderly (i.e., *li* 禮 courteousness). This holds true for all participants to include the traditionally musician roles (e.g., composers and performers) as well as listener and analyst roles (e.g., audience, critics, theorists, musicologists, and historians) and mediator roles (e.g., educators, sound engineers, stage managers, instrument makers, disc jockeys, and producers). All thoughts and actions of an evil nature should be excluded (i.e., *yi* 義 righteousness). These parallel the expectations of *junzi*. If all those in contact with music could interact with others while practicing *ren*, then the music from that community will be filled with qualities of *ren*. If everyone in that community could extend their way of musical involvement with *ren* to their way of living, then the entire community will be filled with qualities of *ren*. This cannot be achieved without the act of teaching, which is also an important expectation of *junzi*. In classic Confucianism, all *junzi*, musicians or otherwise, carry a mission of helping others to become *junzi*.

NOTES ON MUSIC EDUCATION: MUSICIANS AS MUSICIAN-EDUCATORS

It is important for readers to be aware that the contemporary notion of music education did not exist during the time of Confucius and Mencius; instead, *yue* education (樂教) was pervasive. *Yue* (樂) has a distinctive identity that approximates the contemporary notion of "music" in that it (a) includes poetry and movement, as well as singing and instrumental music; (b) has a much more intricate connection with social order through its pairing with *li* (禮); and (c) has a much heavier emphasis on the reflection of individual human characters. In contrast to *yue* education, contemporary music education in Western contexts tends to cover vocal and instrumental music with only occasional association with other areas under interdisciplinary initiatives, such as those with other art forms (e.g., visual arts, media arts, theater, and dance) or other academic subjects (e.g., English language and literature, physics, math, and social studies). Other than advancing studies of music in social context, contemporary music education rarely considers music's connection with social order. Furthermore, contemporary music education treats music mostly as a performing art, a creative art (as in composition or improvisation), or an academic subject (e.g., history and theory). Contemporary musicians do not always reflect on music as a medium to cultivate human character.

While I do not intend to take contemporary music education back to the *yue* education practice of Confucius' and Mencius' times, there is still much to learn, borrow, or even repossess from classic Confucianism. As mentioned in Chapter 1, classic Confucianism is among the earliest pinnacles of human philosophical accomplishments that have prevailed throughout the millennia and is still seriously being sought after, just like some ancient religious texts around the world that are still providing guiding principles in many people's lives. In the context of classic Confucianism,[55] being a *junzi* is the pursuit of a lifetime. It entails all the qualities and expectations described in this chapter. *Junzi*, in Confucian context, is a loaded term, in referring to those who practice *ren* (仁) consistently and trying to perfect it throughout their lives.

The expectations for all involved in music based on classic Confucian principles remain precious. As teaching is an expectation of all *junzi*, all musicians should be teaching to some degree. In this sense, it may be appropriate to address all musicians as musician-educators. They are music makers and scholars, carrying the teaching mission of a *junzi*. For the sake of explanation, let me put all musician-educators on a continuum with two extreme ends: on the one end, they dedicate all their time and conscious efforts in teaching music; and on the other end, they dedicate the all their time and conscious efforts in musical or non-musical activities that are seemingly non-teaching-related. Let me call the former *explicit* music educators and the latter *implicit* music educators. The valuation at both ends of the continuum is equal, and most people fall somewhere in between.[56]

Explicit music educators are those who teach music in school settings, private studio settings, or any social or community settings, in person or online. Just because they are teaching, it does not mean that they should stop learning. Just because they are explicit music educators, it does not mean that they are committed to doing so. Being an insincere and non-compassionate music educator is not on the path of a *junzi*. Sincere dedication, continuous self-reflection, and self-cultivation is a way of *junzi*. Areas of improvement should focus on *ren* when making all decisions and in all interactions with others. As one makes policies, designs curricula, plans lessons, grades assignments, meets parents, discusses issues, advocates for music, and so forth, the qualities of *junzi* are expected. Questions to reflect on include whether one is dedicated to and compassionate about teaching (i.e., sincerity), whether the act of teaching is kind to the learners and those around them (i.e., kindness), whether one is courageous to be righteous in the act of teaching (i.e., courageous and righteous), whether one has the proper knowledge and skills to make appropriate decisions in the teaching practice (i.e., wisdom), and whether the learners and those around them are treated with courteousness and respect (i.e., *li*). If there is any negation in these reflections, then one should find a way to work toward improvements. Furthermore, the teacher needs to be alert and sensitive so they will not miss any teachable moment (*Mencius* 13.40).

Implicit music educators are those who compose music, perform music, improvise music, analyze music, or study music in historical and social contexts. Their teaching is revealed in two different ways: (a) the musical work they produce (i.e., the composition itself or the product of the performance) and (b) the writing about the music. In the former, the teaching is manifested in the interactions between the composer and the performer, between the performer and the audience, or between the composer and the audience. For instance, the composer is teaching the performer and the audience something about music expressivity and the time in which they live. Likewise, the performer is teaching the audience. At the same time, the audience is teaching the composer and performer about the collective social reaction to their work. Throughout these interactions, all the qualities of *ren* are expected. These include stage etiquettes, appropriate social behaviors, and the like that accompany the musical event, be it a staged concert, a social gathering, or even private interactions among the composer, the performer, and the audience, such as backstage conversations, online blogs, personal emails, or social media postings. If the teaching is through written work or recorded performance, then it is similar to Mencius's fifth teaching method: disseminate the work so learners can study on their own (*Mencius* 13.40). Although the teaching of the implicit music educators may not be a primary goal, the teaching is still there regardless. Whoever is exposed to the performance or the written work, they are learning from it.

For both explicit and implicit music educators, they need to strive to live lives as models, so others can follow, from perfecting the skills of the trade to perfecting the desirable characters of the *junzi*. They should turn away from anything of an evil nature, so their sincerity, kindness, and benevolence can be preserved, as humans and participants in musical activities.[57] They should be ready to answer questions from any learner. It implies a need for an open channel of communication with any curious individuals. This goes hand in hand with Confucius' motto of teaching without discrimination (*you jiao wu lei* 有教無類). In a classic Confucian sense, there is no such thing as purely musicians, but all musicians are musician-educators. And all musician-educators are *connected* with the rest of the society, not an isolated group of professionals. Composers should be able to compose for anyone, and performers should be able to perform for anyone; composing and performing are ways of teaching.

CHAPTER 4

⚜

Foundations of Classic Daoism

Wuwei *(Non-egoistic Action)*, Guan *(Observation)*, Qiwu *(Equality)*, and Rou *(Softness/Flexibility)*

BACKGROUND OF DAOISM

There is little doubt that Laozi (老子) (b. ca. 570 BC)[1] is the founder of Daoism. His ideologies predicate Daoism as a major philosophical school that is distinctively different from Confucianism. Historical documentation in *Shiji* (*Book of History* 《史記》) by Sima Qian (司馬遷) (145–86 BC) suggests that Confucius had met Laozi once and then told his students how he was amazed by his wisdom.[2] Furthermore, Sima Qian wrote:

> Laozi is a person who practices *dao* (道) and *de* (德). His doctrine aims at a latent life. He has lived under the Zhou regime for a long time and has witnessed its decline. He departed Luo Yang (洛陽) and went westward toward Han Gu Gate (函谷關). The gate officer Yin Xi (尹喜) was pleasantly surprised to see him and said, "You are going to retire and live in seclusion. Please leave me with a book." Then Laozi wrote *Daodejing* 《道德經》 in two parts, mainly addressing *dao* and *de*, together in about five thousand words. Hence, no one has ever heard from him again.[3]

This description clearly shows that Laozi was known for his wisdom during his lifetime. The gatekeeper recognized him and knew that he was a man of great wisdom and virtue. It also reveals that he aspires to live as a hermit who looks to a natural way of living, as outside the gate is wide-open wilderness. While he has given up hope on the regime of his time, he was willing to leave with the gatekeeper the work of his life.[4] Contemporary literature also refers to *Daodejing* 《道德經》 as *Laozi* 《老子》. The two parts of the book focus on *dao* (道) and *de* (德virtue). *Dao* suggests a heavenly way that follows a natural path. *De* is the way to fulfill *dao*. All beings, objects, and phenomena have *dao* and *de*. Laozi took on the organismic view found in *Yijing* and developed a complete philosophical system (*dao*) regarding a worldview, its relationship with humans, and desirable ways of living (*de*).[5]

Zhuangzi (莊子) (368–288 BC) was a successor of Laozi. He took Laozi's ideas and developed them further, unleashing the power of *dao* and reaching for ultimate freedom. His ideologies are found in the book with the same name, *Zhuangzi* 《莊子》. However, during the Qin (221–206 BC) and Han (206 BC–AD 220) periods, Daoism had begun to divert into many branches,[6] including a religious branch with influences from folk religions and other branches with different emphases, notably politics, and influences from different ideologies, such as Legalism, Confucianism, and Buddhism. This chapter, however, focuses on the classic philosophical Daoism of Laozi and Zhuangzi, prior to the Qin Dynasty.

An organismic view is a hallmark of classic Daoism. *Dao* is the origin of all matters. It reveals itself in two opposites: *yin* and *yang*, within which they interact and generate a harmonious ambience for all matters to exist. The universe is considered as an organism in which all elements are connected. Different entities appear to be disconnected but indeed they are connected. Fu Pei-Rong's illustration puts it exquisitely: cows take in grass and produce milk, children drink the milk and grow up to be humans.[7] This illustration describes how humans are connected with the grass without taking it in directly. It also demonstrates how children grow up to be humans, not to be cows, although the milk comes from the cows. I would push this illustration further by including the sun and the rain that nurture the grass, and therefore they are connected in this chain of events as well. In addition, after humans have passed on, their bodies are naturally integrated with the soil, which again contribute to the growth of the grass (although this is not always the case anymore in contemporary contexts). In this sense, classic Daoist view is so all-encompassing that a view of the universe is prominent. The existence or change in any element affects the rest of the organism. Humankind is part of this nature and appears to be small in the universe. An orientation toward nature and its operation has a notable presence throughout the classic Daoist thoughts.

THE SIGNIFICANCE OF LAOZI AND ZHUANGZI

In a milieu of social disorder during the Spring and Autumn period (771–476 BC), the Confucians advocated *li* and *yue* to bring order and peace, so humans could be back on track to satisfactory and rewarding lives. The ever-improving *junzi* working through acts of *ren* is a desirable way of life. Laozi saw something different. He found little hope in focusing on human interactions. He looked further, much further, beyond the complex layers of social roles and human relationships and connections. He stepped back, observed, and reflected. He found another way out. His revelatory insights from *Yijing* took him to a breakthrough, seeing a much bigger picture. Humans are parts of a huge system—the universe. There is a heavenly way for everything, tangible or non-tangible. Anything done in a humanly (and egoistic) way is an obstruction of the heavenly way. Humans should try to understand it, observe it, and be an integral part in it. Being frugal, soft, and flexible, as observed in many matters in nature, is a way that leads to a satisfactory life. His propositions become the backbone of classic Daoism. These views are in stark contrast to those of the classic Confucians, yet his ideas as documented in *Laozi* have received worldwide attention. *Laozi* (or *Daodejing*) is the second "most translated work in world literature," behind only the Christian Bible.[8] Unfortunately, there is much uncertainty about his personal background and life stories. It is deemed more important to examine his philosophy found in *Laozi* than to verify any biographical details.[9]

Like Mencius, Zhuangzi lived during the Warring States period (476–221 BC), but there is no record of them meeting. During this time of political turbulence, Zhuangzi was trying to survive with his family, like most others. What makes him stand out is his extraordinary wisdom and his knowledge gained by reading broadly and deeply into the extant literature. He also traveled extensively, especially throughout the southern part of China. Using Laozi's ideologies as a foundation, he advanced his conviction on the same thread. His book, *Zhuangzi* 《莊子》 (sometimes referred to as *Nanhuajing* 《南華經》), written by Zhuangzi and his students, is filled with fables written in some of the most eloquent writings of their time. The book makes his ideologies approachable yet profound. He is able to relate the abstract concepts associated with *dao* to a personal, soulful, and practical level. Some suggest that Zhuangzi's philosophy is most mature among Daoists in the pre-Qin period (i.e., prior to 221 BC) and that he perfected Daoism as a doctrine.[10]

DAO-CENTRIC IDEOLOGY

The center of Daoism is the *dao* (道), which is often translated literally as "the way." However, Laozi explicitly stated that *dao* is not describable in words.[11] However one puts it, it is still incomplete in explaining *dao*. Readers are encouraged to shape their own apperceptions of *dao* after reading original classic Daoist texts[12] and the writings of those who study them. This and the following paragraphs are merely a synthesis of what it appears to me.[13] It is the source, the nature, the way, and the destination of all matters. It is both transcendental and immanental.[14] It is the basis of how nature works and the explanation of all phenomena and events. It includes the principles, the rules, and the ways of all entities and their movements and interactions. It is non-describable, untouchable, and invisible. A key passage in explaining *dao* is found in *Laozi* (25):

> There is an entity with everything in it. It appeared before heaven[15] and earth. It is quiet without a sound. It is empty without a shape. It is independent and never changes. It works in cycles and never stops. It can be the mother of heaven and earth. I don't know its name, and I reluctantly label it *dao*. More reluctantly, I call it "big." It is so broad that it does not have boundaries nor does it rest as it flows from one place to another, reaching everywhere. It reaches everywhere and returns to its source. . . . Human depends on the earth, the earth depends on heaven (the sky), heaven (the sky) depends on *dao*, and *dao* depends on its natural way of operation.[16]

This explanation suggests that *dao* is the only entity that never changes while everything else change constantly. *Dao* is everywhere and in everything. It is everlasting. It rules the sky (mainly through the seasons), which rules the earth (mainly through weather patterns), which rules the human realm (mainly through sources of food coming from the ground and the provision of habitat and mobility). This passage presents an important view of the universe: *dao* is one entity before anything appears. Heaven and earth are already two entities that appear after *dao*. Note that heaven and earth is represented by *yang* and *yin* respectively in *Yijing*. It follows that *dao* exists prior to *yin* and *yang*. In *Laozi* 42, *dao* is described again as one entity. That single entity comes out as two *qi* (vital energies 氣): *yin* and *yang* (see Figure 4.1). They interact and make three: *yin*, *yang*, and *he* (harmony 和) (see Figure 4.2). These three vital energies create all matters (see Figure 4.3) (*Laozi* 42; 道生一，一生二，二生三，三生萬物。).[17]

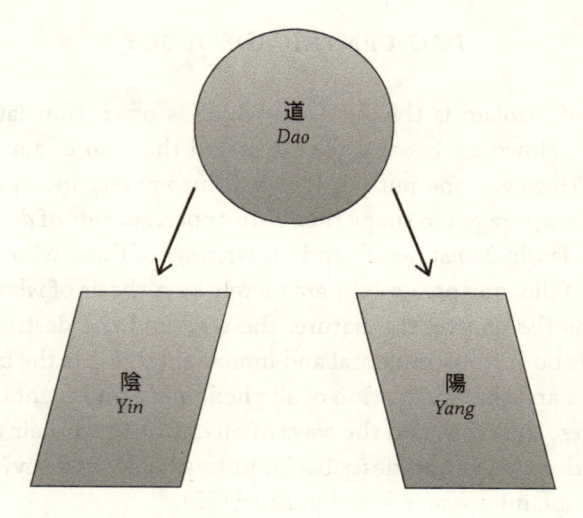

Figure 4.1: *Dao* comes out as *yin* and *yang*.

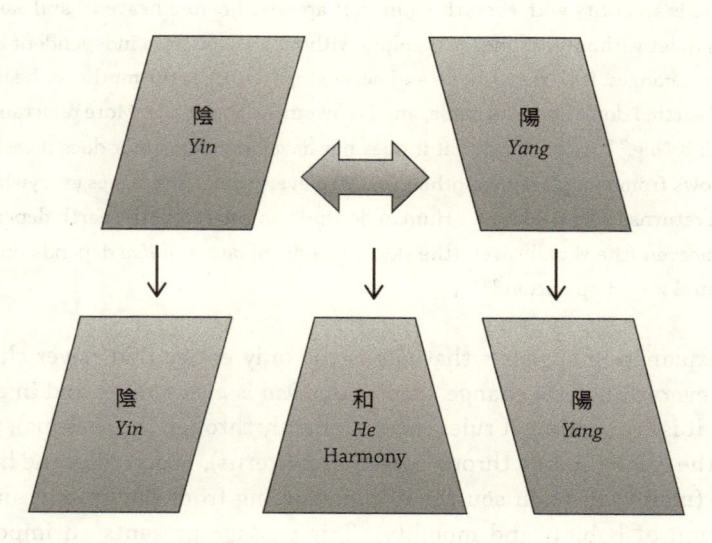

Figure 4.2: *Yin* and *yang* interact and make three: *yin*, *yang*, and *he* (harmony 和).

Zhuangzi clarifies further and connects *dao* with *de* (德) most explicitly. "At the very beginning, only 'nothing' exists. There is no 'existence' and no name. This is the source of one unified entity. Everything is in it and nothing is formed. Everything needs it to be formed. This process is *de*" (*Zhuangzi* 12.8; 泰初有無，無有無名，一之所起，有一而未形。物得以生，謂之德；...). In other words, *de* is a process that accompanies *dao*. Loazi's support is obvious: "Everything honors *dao* and values *de*. *Dao*

```
       ┌─────┐     ┌─────────┐     ┌─────┐
       │ 陰  │     │   和    │     │ 陽  │
       │ Yin │     │   He    │     │Yang │
       │     │     │ Harmony │     │     │
       └──┬──┘     └────┬────┘     └──┬──┘
          ↓             ↓             ↓
       ┌─────────────────────────────────┐
       │             萬物                │
       │            Wanwu                │
       │          All things             │
       └─────────────────────────────────┘
```

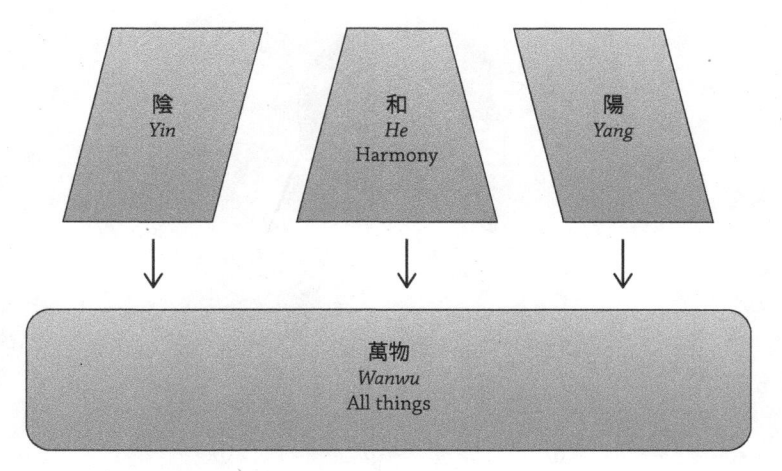

Figure 4.3: *Yin, yang,* and *he* create all things.

is honored and *de* is valued; no entity is giving an order to do so, but this is always the natural way" (*Laozi* 51; 是以萬物莫不尊道而貴德。道之尊，德之貴，夫莫之命常自然。). It is easier to understand this statement from Laozi if one thinks of *dao*, for example, as the everlasting principle of various life stages (i.e., birth, growth, sickness, and death). This is a principle that everyone has to honor and respect regardless. Going along with this natural principle is a way to live with *de*. If one could observe and understand all the natural principles of *dao* and engage with them in a *dao*'s way, then *de* is achieved.

Zhuangzi further explains that the enigmatic *de* at its highest level (*xuan de* 玄德) is to harmonize with heaven and earth, integrating with *dao* without a trace (*Zhuangzi* 12.8; . . . 與天地為合。其合緡緡，若愚若昏，是謂玄德，同乎大順。). The greatness of *dao* lays in that it is honorable yet not possessive. "[*Dao*] creates all things but without owning them, cultivates all things without relying on its own strength, and develops all things without controlling them. This is the enigmatic *de* at its highest" (*Laozi* 10 and 51; 生而不有，為而不恃，長而不宰，是謂玄德。). It is clear that Zhuangzi is in perfect alignment with Laozi, from what *dao* is to what it does. *Dao* makes two (*ying* and *yang*), and two makes three (*ying*, *yang*, and *he*), which create everything (see Figure 4.4). Most important, the achievement of *de* is to walk the path of life with *dao*. Figure 4.5 depicts this process with the complete cycle of *de* as everything is on a path with *dao*. Everything is going to return to *dao*.

To walk the path of life with *dao*, one needs to develop an apperception of *dao* through keen observation and profound understanding. Life

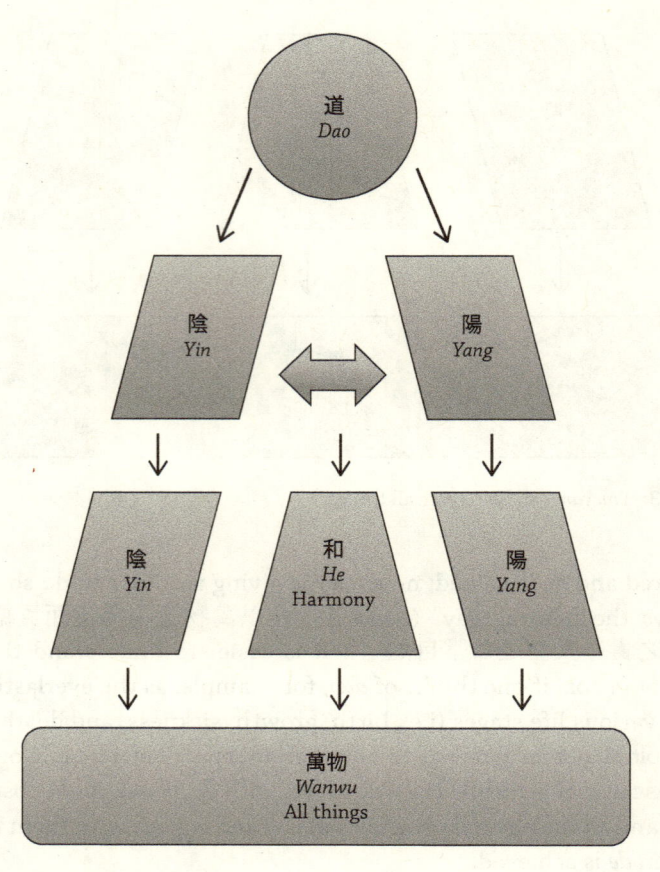

```
              道
              Dao
             ↙  ↘
         陰  ⇔  陽
         Yin    Yang
          ↓  ↓  ↓
         陰  和  陽
         Yin He  Yang
            Harmony
          ↓  ↓  ↓
            萬物
           Wanwu
          All things
```

Figure 4.4: From *dao* to all things.

on earth is part of a bigger order, humans and others alike. It is important to know the principles of *dao* and what humans should do with them. In the following four sections, I have highlighted a key *dao* principle in each: *wuwei* (無為 non-egoistic action), *guan* (觀 observation), *qiwu* (齊物 equality), and *rou* (柔 softness/flexibility). They, among other priniciples, give *dao* a unique identity as a classic philosophical school.

WUWEI (無為 NON-EGOISTIC ACTION)

Wuwei (無為) is often translated as "doing nothing," "non-action," "non-striving," or "inaction," all of which I am reluctant to adopt, because I find these translations lack a vital element. "Effortless action"[18] is better, but it still does not capture the needed essence in the current discussion. When

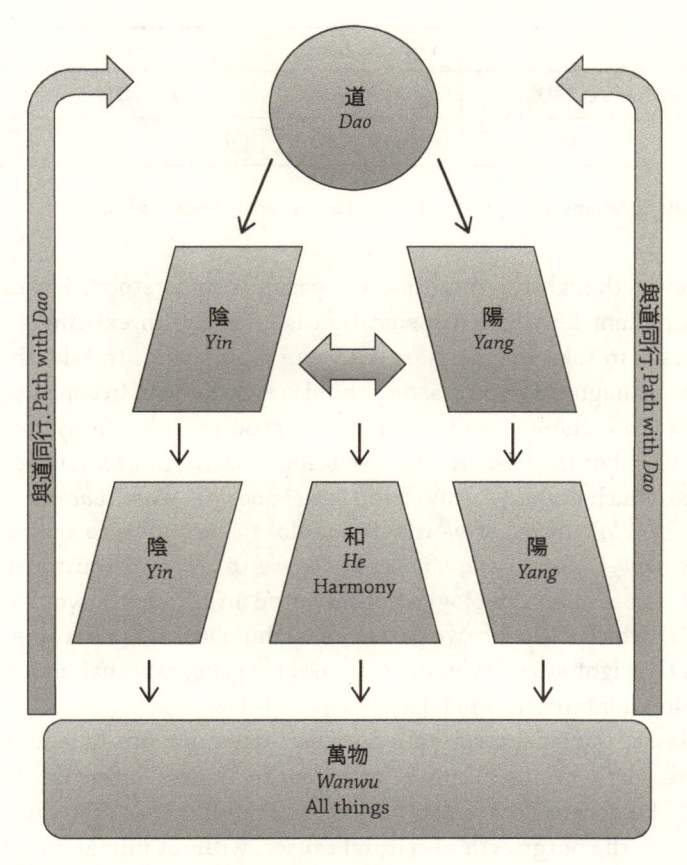

Figure 4.5: The complete cycle of *de* as everything is generated from *dao* via *yin*, *yang*, and *he*; is on a path with *dao*; and returns to *dao*.

the meaning of *wuwei* is focused on the action portion of the expression, the critical element of intention and reason behind the action becomes lost in the translation. *Wuwei* carries a notion of effortlessness, being at ease, or following the natural flow, but not without action.[19] To understand *wuwei*, it is helpful to begin with a Chinese linguistic approach. The word *wei* (為) refers to actions *with human intention or reason*, which could be virtuous or wicked, coming from humans, not in the purview of *dao*. *Wu* (無) is an expression of negation that connotes emptiness or absence. When *wu* and *wei* are put together, it means taking actions but that the intention or the reason does not come from the human mind (i.e., empty). In Chinese, there is another word for negation: *bu* (不), which is similar to the English adverb "not." *Wuwei* and *buwei* (不為) can easily be confused. In a sense, *buwei* is an opposite of *wuwei*. Figure 4.6 illustrates the relationships between action and intention for *wuwei* and *buwei*. *Buwei* denies the

	Action	Intention
Wuwei (無爲)	Yes	No
Buwei (不爲)	No	Yes

Figure 4.6: Relationship between action and intention in *wuwei* and *buwei*.

action even though the intention or reason is understood. For example, when a patient knows that medication is good for an existing symptom but refuses to take it, that is *buwei*: there is no action to take the medicine even though the good reason behind is fully known. In contrast, *wuwei* has action but there is no intention or reason initiated from the human ego. To be rid of the human intentions and reasons, one should be aligned with *dao*, which is always *wuwei*, and *buwei* does not exist (*Laozi* 37 and 48; 無為而無不為). In other words, if *dao* does everything to maintain the state of *wuwei*, there is no chance for *buwei* to come forward. It is interesting to note the etymological observation in a Chinese word for false (*wei* 偽),[20] which contains two parts: *ren* (人 human) on the left side and *wei* (為) on the right side. Etymologically, *wei* (偽) suggests that actions come from human intentions are false.

In classic Daoist interpretation, *wuwei* does not preclude actions. In fact, it requires actions to engage with *dao*. The human intention or reason needs to be absent so *dao* can become the guiding force for the actions. Actions are the outgrowth of natural causes, without human intention or reason. Fu Pei-Rong interprets the Daoist *wuwei* as *wuxinerwei* (無心而為, literally "taking actions without heart"),[21] meaning that actions should not be based on human reasons, and it implies that actions should be based on *dao*. In other words, *wuwei* in the classic Doaist context should be understood as taking no egoistic actions from the human perspective but taking actions to go along with *dao*. Therefore, I adopt "non-egoistic action" as the translation of *wuwei* to focus on the non-existence of the human ego in the intention and reason for the action. Humans should not interfere with *dao* by doing something to obstruct the natural cause of matters and phenomena. Otherwise, actions would become human (not *dao*) endeavors, *renwei* (人為) or *wei* (偽)—false.

Laozi suggests that *wuwei* should be a principle for a sage to rule. If the ruler is not doing anything with an egoistic intention, the citizens will cultivate on their own (*Laozi* 57; . . . 我無為而民自化 . . .). He furthers with similar statements and ends the section on one regarding selfish desires, "[when the ruler] does not have selfish desires, citizens will pursue a simple life" (*Laozi* 57; . . . 我無欲而民自樸). Throughout classic Daoist texts, emphasis on *dao* and de-emphasis on humanly ways (i.e., desires, intentions, and reasons) could not be missed. Ronnie L. Littlejohn sums it up in this way: "moving naturally along with *dao* . . . is the way out of the tangles we have created for ourselves by the institutions, rules and distinctions that clutter our minds and generate tension in our life together" (2009, p. 18). Turning to a natural way of living, reverting back to simplicity, and doing nothing based on egoistic intentions and reasons to obstruct the natural cause of matters and phenomena are at the heart of *wuwei*.

GUAN (OBSERVATION 觀)

Although observation (*guan* 觀) is a behavior described in both classic Confucian and classic Daoist texts, the classic Daoists present a unique view about observation and how it is related to *dao*. For classic Daoists, observation is an important way of understanding *dao*. Regardless of the existence of human desires, intentions, or reasons, observation would allow for an apperception of the wonders and mysticism of all matters (*Laozi* 1; 故常無欲，以觀其妙；常有欲，以觀其徼。). Laozi explains how he knows the world: "observe individuals from an individual's perspectives, observe families from a family's perspective, observe villages from a village's perspective, observe nations from a nation's perspective, and observe worlds from a world's perspective" (*Laozi* 54; 以身觀身，以家觀家，以鄉觀鄉，以國觀國，以天下觀天下。). Individual, family, village, nation, and world are all perspectives that humans are able to experience, through which one can observe and gain knowledge.

Zhuangzi extends from this concept and applies it to experiences that humans cannot have, introducing the idea of *wuhua* (物化 materialization). He explains it through Zhuangzhou's dream of becoming a butterfly, feeling so happy and free and forgetting about the existence of the self. When he wakes up, lying on his stiff body, he is not sure whether he has been dreaming of becoming a butterfly or the butterfly has been dreaming of becoming Zhuangzhou.[22] He swiftly clarified that there is certainly a distinction between Zhuangzhou and the butterfly. That is the same distinction between humans and all other beings and matters: only humans can develop an apperception of *dao*.[23] Humans can be materialized (物化 *wuhua*). This idea is a key foundation for the classic Daoist view on observation.

If humans can be materialized, then humans can understand all beings and all matters from the standpoints of being observed. Zhuangzi (*Zhuangzi* 17.5) confirms that regardless of how any beings or matters appear to be, they all have their values, perspectives, sizes, strengths, weaknesses, functions, and perceptions by others. All are relativistic. If beings and matters are viewed from their own vantage points, they all assert themselves and question others, and they all see that they are important and valuable and that others are not as important or valuable (*Zhuangzi* 17.5; 以物觀之，自貴而相賤。). When observing others, it is important to observe from the perspective of the subject or object involved (i.e., *yiwu guanwu* 以物觀物). This is how one should understand all beings and matters.[24]

QIWU (EQUALITY 齊物)

The principle of *qiwu* (equality 齊物) is based on the unifying nature of *dao*. It is most clearly illustrated in the chapter on *Qiwulun* (齊物論, Theory of Equality) in *Zhuangzi*, where Zhuangzi suggests a state of selflessness is important so biases would not be in the way of making judgments (*Zhuangzi* 2.1). It is also important to understand how *dao* has allowed humans to coexist with heaven and earth, and all matters and the self become one (*Zhuangzi* 2.9; 天地與我並生，而萬物與我為一。). When all has become one and all things have opposing ends, it is meaningless to argue for either side of the dyad. Everything and all perspectives are valuable, meaningful, changing, relative, and connected. Right and wrong, big and small, good and bad, and so forth, are not the nature of being but are subjective evaluations. One being or its perspective could become its opposite when the context or condition changes. There is no absolute objectivity. Any stratification or value judgment is hollow and ungrounded and should be avoided. All matters, beings, and their opinions should be treated equally without human biases.

Zhuangzi (*Zhuangzi*, 2.6) clearly states that every being (including non-humans and objects) has a *self* (此 *ci*) and an *other* (彼 *bi*). The *other* has a right or wrong, and the *self* has a right or wrong (彼亦一是非，此亦一是非。). Due to this relationship between *self* and *other* and the existence of the *other* is unavoidable, no one is able to tell what absolutely right or absolutely wrong is. The *self* and the *other* are equally important, and therefore the right could be wrong and vice versa, depending on the context and perspective of the *self* or *other*. To align with *dao*, the *self* and the *other* should not be opposites. Making the *other* non-confrontational with the *self* is mastering the pivot of *dao* (彼是莫得其偶，謂之道樞。). Grasping the pivot of *dao* is to place the *self* at the center of a circle, where things can go in any direction equally well, and one could adapt to indefinite *changes* (樞始得其環中，以應無窮。). He suggests that the best strategy is to observe the nature of the being or matter to clarify our understanding (莫若以明), which implies avoiding the biases of the *self* or the *other*. Therefore, all matters, beings, and their opinions should be treated equally. It is through this equality that harmony is possible.

Zhuangzi uses a fable of feeding a monkey to demonstrate how one should care less about certain right or wrong arguments, as the outcome is the same (*Zhuangzi* 2.7). A monkey keeper suggested feeding the monkey three units of chestnuts in the morning and four in the evening, but the monkey was mad about this plan. Then the keeper suggested four units of chestnuts in the morning and three in the evening, and the monkey was very happy. The fact is that both plans would yield the same outcome as a whole, seven units of chestnuts for the day. The trick is that the manipulation of the two plans could alter the emotion of the monkey, from mad to very happy, as the keeper is going along with the natural inclination of the monkey. One could extract two layers of meanings from this fable. First, humans should not be too uptight about a specific way of life. Being flexible to accommodate the natural way is more important. In a lifespan, someone might be successful early in life, and others might prosper later, but life as a whole is more or less equal. There is no need to push too hard so the effect becomes sad, hurt, ill, and so forth. It is more important to go along with *dao*. The second layer contains a much deeper meaning. The monkey keeper's actions are analogous to those of a sage, who has the ability to *harmonize* right and wrong and let them be settled according to a natural share. The strategy is to allow right and wrong to coexist in harmony (*Zhuangzi* 2.7; 是以聖人和之以是非，而休乎天鈞，是之謂兩行。). Equality is an essential quality of harmony.

The significance of *qiwu* is not only in its central locus in Zhuangzi's writing; the principle of *qiwu* is rooted in *dao* and is linked to the important concept of harmony.[25] The equality does not only concern humans; it includes non-humans, objects, and opinions as well.

ROU (SOFTNESS/FLEXIBILITY柔)

The quality of *rou* (柔 softness and flexibility) clearly belongs to the *yin* side in the *yin* and *yang* dyad. The *yang* side would be characterized as strong, stiff, and rigid. This places classic Daoism as a philosophical school in direct opposition with classic Confucianism, in which the emphases on *cheng* (誠), *shan* (善), *ren* (仁), and *junzi* (君子), who is supposed to carry out *li* (禮) all the time, are relatively strong and rigid, positioning it on the *yang* side in the philosophical milieu.[26] In classic Daoist's view, *rou* has superiority over rigidity or stiffness. Between softness and rigidity, only the former could allow room to bend and be flexible. As the world is constantly changing, flexibility is much desirable in response to the changes. The idea of softness having an edge over rigidity is described multiple times in *Laozi* (e.g., 36, 43, 76, and 78). Laozi believes that the softest element of all is water, which is the best in attacking the strongest. Nothing can replace water with the same power (*Laozi* 78; 天下莫柔弱於水，而攻堅強者莫之能勝，其無以易之。). Water is so flexible that it can be in any shape and state, from steam to ice, and can work in any quantity, yet it could be penetrating and powerful, as in eroding the hardest of stones through long periods of drips or in flooding and destroying an entire village in severe rain or a tsunami.

Simply declaring that classic Daoism glorifies softness and flexibility is an understatement. The repeated mentioning of how *rou* has an edge over rigidity in *Laozi* could give that misperception. While it is true that *rou* has an edge over rigidity, the refreshing view of how the softness of water generates renewed livelihood is often overlooked. The ability to remain still in turbid water so the water becomes clear is found in those who can renew liveliness in stability. Those who live by this principle know that perfection is unachievable. This is how life can be renewed continuously, by striving toward perfection.[27] Stillness, as in turbid water, avails renewed livelihood. While the quality of *rou* suggests a strong flavor of *yin*, it still has to work in a proactive mode—a renewed livelihood, a *yang* quality—to keep moving forward. This is in perfect alignment with the nature of *dao*, in which it keeps cycling and moving forward with no rest (*Laozi* 25; 周行而不殆).

The quality of *rou* has opened up a lot of possibilities. Softness suggests the ability to adapt to changes. There is room for flexibility, freedom, and choices. As time and situation is synchronized, *rou* could be in an advantageous position to capture the moment and exert a renewed livelihood.

MUSICAL NOTES: MUSIC AS A STATE OF MIND

In the classic Daoist literature, both music and sound are described as *lai* (籟). There is *lai* coming from the sky (*tian lai* 天籟), humans (*ren lai* 人籟), and the earth (*de lai* 地籟). However, they do not always refer to the contemporary understanding of sound and music. They are described metaphysically to align with the classic Daoist ideologies. Music of the earth (*de lai* 地籟) is made by wind and all types of orifices found in nature, including spaces among trees and grass. It merely refers to the multiplicity and irregularity of the sounds and is hard to compare or grasp meaning.[28] Music of humans (*ren lai* 人籟) comes from measured pipes, which infers regulated tunes, techniques, and intent. Therefore, it can be compared and has varied qualities. This *ren lai* is closest to the contemporary concept of music because it contains intentional tuning by humans. However, this is not the most valued in the classic Daoist's view, as suggested in Laozi's axiom "great music contains few sounds" (*da yin xi sheng* 大音希聲) (*Laozi* 41), for which the annotator Wang Bi (王弼) (AD 226–249) explicitly states that tuned sounds such as *gong* (宮) and *shang* (商) should be few and far between in great music.[29] Music of the sky (*tian lai* 天籟) is the most metaphysical of all. It is the type of music that can be heard only through a specific mindset, attitude, self-cultivation, and philosophical attainment. Listening of *tian lai* requires the ability to hear beyond the physical sounds and beyond comparative qualities, but to understand and accept all possible sounds as conditions are synchronized to produce the music. The underlying meaning is that there is an acceptance of all beings and phenomena as they are outcomes of *dao*.

Combining the descriptions of the three types of *lai* and the broader classic Daoist principles, I venture to extend a few notes on music. First and foremost, based on the classic Daoist principle of *guan* (observation 觀), music should be understood from the standpoint of its indigenous perspective. This should occur at the level of a musical piece, a musical style, or a musical tradition. In light of the world of multiple musical heritages, the development of comparative musicology in the early twentieth century, evolving into ethnomusicology as a field in the mid-twentieth century, testifies to the desire to fulfill this need. Contemporary musicians have a far greater understanding of this need than their counterparts did a century ago.

Again, in light of the contemporary awareness of multiple musical heritages, musicians should respect and value all musical traditions equally (*qiwu* 齊物). No one is better or more valuable than the other. It is a matter of time, space, and synchronicity that one would encounter a musical tradition. Musicians should acknowledge the *self* and the *other*, while not holding onto biases induced by either. The same ideology should be applied to various musical styles and musical pieces.

Among *tian lai, ren lai*, and *de lai, ren lai* is the type of musical sounds that is closest to the contemporary understanding of music. However, musicians should not be limited to making the *ren lai* type of music. While *de lai* is rather irregular and unpredictable, musicians might want to contemplate its synchronicity and randomness, and perhaps incorporate it into a type of *ren lai*. While some twentieth-century composers have already experimented with it, it doesn't mean that twenty-first-century composers cannot do it anymore. Contemporary composers can always find a renewed way to do it. *Tian lai* metaphorically refers to a state of mind, which I believe musicians and non-musicians alike should try to aim at achieving as well. It involves careful listening, being open to possibilities, and getting rid of evaluative judgments. It is a constant cultivation process. While accepting *ren lai* as a normal musical practice, understanding and being open to *de lai* and *tian lai* are critical in cultivating a harmonious relationship among human, nature, and *dao*. Musicians have the privilege to be pioneers to bridge these arenas, as they have the natural inclination to listen carefully and to work with musical sounds from various sources.

NOTES ON MUSIC EDUCATION: WALKING WITH *DAO*

While the contemporary notion of music education did not exist during the time of Laozi and Zhuangzi, their ideologies are so penetrating that they have many rich implications for music educators. I am highlighting just a few most obvious ones. The principle of *wuwei* suggests that nothing should be done to stop learners from learning music if they are naturally inclined to learn it. Anyone who has spent a significant amount of time with young children would be quick to agree that it is hard to encounter a child who does not enjoy music or wouldn't be eager to learn a song or to move to music. In the spirit of not interfering this natural inclination, music should be at the core of education for young children.

Furthermore, nothing should be done to obstruct young learners' natural way of learning music. Our knowledge in psychology today has informed us that children are naturally inclined to like musical activities. It has provided support in developing teaching strategies that are child-centered. Music educators should go by what is most natural for the learners at each of their learning stages. By the same token, music educators should use the types of music that are most natural in the learners' setting.

Based on the classic Daoist principle of *guan*, we should put ourselves in the same position as the music learners whenever we observe music learners, whether for teaching or for research purposes. This way, the understanding is genuine. Learning from the subject is critical in deciding on a course of actions that are most appropriate and effective in that particular setting. When studying a musical tradition, an indigenous view is a must.

There is no doubt that music educators will come into contact with music of various traditions and learners of different strata. Musical traditions, music teachers, and music learners are fluid organisms that are intricately connected. They progress with influences from within, among, and outside themselves. The principle of *qiwu* suggests that music educators should respect the *ways* musicians and their musical traditions are progressed. Regardless of personal preference, all *ways* are valuable and important.

The principle of *rou* suggests that music educators should remain flexible as they practice in the field. There are many ways to help learners to achieve musically. There are many ways of teaching music. In some situations, one way is better, and in other situations, another way is better. To be flexible, educators should be prepared with multiple ways of thinking about and teaching music. It allows room for creativity in teaching and making music.

When music educators apply these principles in their practice, learners would learn in their most natural ways; music, musicians, and learners would be understood from their own perspectives; all perspectives are treated equally; and educators would be so flexible that they need not worry about what is forthcoming. When music education is conceived as part of the organismic universe, it should be seen as part of life, not a separate entity. Music educators should learn to understand and practice with many changing and interconnected parts, notably music, culture, humans, nature, and life in general.

PART II

Complementarity and a Trilogy

CHAPTER 5

∽

Complementary Bipolar Continua in Music Education

The previous three chapters present *Yijing*, classic Confucianism, and classic Daoism as an emphatic triad in the classic Chinese philosophical milieu. With *Yijing* being the root of the triad, Confucianism and Daoism built upon it amid some of the most turbulent environments from the mid-sixth to the mid-third century BC China, making them among the strongest, lasting, and profound philosophical schools in history. They have become a foundation for much of the philosophical development in China and many parts of Asia thereafter, some of which are in line with the classic milieu, while others have substantially derailed from it or have mixed in influences from different sources. They have also made important contributions to the world of philosophies.[1] This harmonious triad provides a mystical mix of philosophical pitches and overtones that have permeated gradually in an expanding way to a substantial part of the world for two and a half millennia.[2] The construction of a philosophical frame of reference based on an understanding of this classic Chinese philosophical milieu in contemporary musical and music educational context is long overdue. This chapter and the three that follow are an attempt to present such a frame of reference.

The musical and music educational interpretations of the triad presented in the previous three chapters are starting points that illuminate how music and music education can be philosophized in a way that transcends across time and space. An underlying principle throughout this book is that ideologies are presented as resources available for consultation. There is no forceful choice of any sort. Anyone is free to take any portion of the ideologies as long as there is relevance, value, and use. One is unlikely to put these ideologies into practice without developing an apperception for them. It is important for music educators and others to make judgments based on their unique circumstances, values, and beliefs. The approach suggested here is simply offered as considerations. Once they are understood, I am confident that relevance, value, and use will emerge in part or as a whole, because of the inherent connections in the organismic world and the human-centric nature of music and music education.

COMPLEMENTARITY ACROSS *YIJING*, CLASSIC CONFUCIANISM, AND CLASSIC DAOISM

The previous three chapters demonstrate that classic Confucianism and classic Daoism stand on their own as two distinctive philosophical schools inspired by *Yijing*.[3] The sheer connections among these three sources, each with a unique set of ideologies, that are settled and vitalized (or resettled and revitalized in the case of *Yijing*) in close geographic and cultural proximity within the same time frame, suggest an intricate collection of ideologies characterized as *classic Chinese wisdoms* in this book. The interplay among the uniqueness, the relevance, the practicality, and the shared ambience across the three philosophical sources have made the classic Chinese wisdoms profound for two and a half millennia and doubtless for many more years to come.

If one were to identify a common thread that runs across *Yijing* and the classic texts from both philosophical schools, it is not difficult to see the prominence of human (人 *ren*) and *dao* (道) cutting across all three sources. Although classic Confucianism emphasizes more on humans, the human-centric perspective on and the reference to *dao* are also pervasive. The same is true in classic Daoism, in which the emphasis is on *dao*, but its relation to humans is prevalent. The words *ren* (人) and *dao* (道) appear 215 times and 106 times respectively in *Yijing* (in combination with *Yizhuan*). The same words appear 219 times and 90 times in the *Analects*, 39 times and 10 times in *Great Learning*, 52 times and 54 times in *Zhongyong*, 611 times and 150 times in *Mencius*, 85 times and 77 times in *Laozi*, and 1,003 times and 368 times in *Zhuangzi*, respectively. Although these statistics do not inform readers about the aspects of human being referred to and the mystical meaning of *dao*, they confirm a common interest in the human and *dao* across the classic Chinese thoughts and draw readers' attention and attempt to explore and clarify their meanings.

Since *Yijing* is purported to describe all sorts of phenomena, everything, including humans, has a *dao* attached. In *Yijing*, *dao* is associated with heaven, earth, humans, *junzi*, *xiaoren*,[4] sage, friends, family, *qian*, *qun*, *yin* and *yang*, change, food and drink, and so forth. Two directions in interpreting *dao* arise as the two schools emerge. The Confucian *dao* emphasizes the path that one should follow to become an exemplary person (i.e., *junzi*), and therefore it is "the process of generating an actual order in the world."[5] In contrast, the Daoist *dao* refers to an indescribable entity that is both transcendental and immanental, a path that naturally occurs in all beings and things. These directions support Confucius' and Mencius' emphasis on values and Laozi's and Zhuangzi's emphasis on existence. On the one hand, classic Confucians are interested in clarifying the relationships across people with different roles, taking responsibilities in the society, and thereby having a clear separation between class, role, and social strata. The humanly *dao* and the heavenly *dao* seek to work together (天人合德 *tian ren he de*). On the other hand, classic Daoists are interested in blending in, following along with the natural way and find homage in a state of quiescence with no human desires. Humans should be flexible to go along with changes in nature as they unify with nature in peace, calmness, and tranquility (天人合一 *tian ren he yi*).

Representatives from both schools admit their differences. Confucius recognizes the difference in *dao* and says, "our *dao* is different, there is no need to discuss" (*Analects* 15.40; 子曰：「道不同，不相為謀。」). While he is convinced that his way is the right path, he does not see a need to debate with those who believe in a different path. He allows that different path to co-exist without being confrontational. Elsewhere in *Analects*, Confucius makes it clear in stating that humans are not meant to live with wild animals, referring to those who avoid human entanglements and trying to blend in with nature. Humans are meant to be with humans, even with the need to take our society to a proper path, not to avoid the society altogether (18.6; 鳥獸不可與同群，吾非斯人之徒與而誰與？天下有道，丘不與易也。). Zhuangzi, after Laozi, takes a step further to delineate two different types of *dao*: heavenly *dao* (天道) and humanly *dao* (人道). The former is the thrust of the Daoist *dao* achieved by *wuwei* and going along with the natural way, and the latter is the thrust of the Confucian *dao* achieved by ruling as a *junzi*. There are big differences between the two *dao*s and they should be observed (*Zhuangzi* 11.11; 何謂道？有天道，有人道。無為而尊者，天道也；有為而累者，人道也。主者，天道也；臣者，人道也。天道之與人道也，相去遠矣，不可不察也。).

The ideological differences between classic Confucians and classic Daoists do not preclude their complementarity. In the contrary, they support a good deal of complementarity because of their differences. The two schools are addressing different human needs, the Confucians mainly for social relationships and the Daoists mainly for a relationship with the natural world. Each school presents humans with a different role, in the society or in the universe. At different times, humans have different needs, much like the need for different foods for different meals. No one should take the same food for every meal if a healthy well-being is desired. The two schools are offering different types of philosophical foods.

The complementarity between classic Confucianism and classic Daoism can be explained in six perspectives.[6] The two schools influence each other and provide momentum for each other. The strength of one is the weakness of the other. First, Confucianism has a strong and masculine (i.e., *yang*) quality, while Daoism has a soft and feminine (i.e., *yin*) quality. This is reflected in Confucians' emphasis on the strength of humans as they fulfill various social roles. In contrast, Daoists emphasize softness as being advantageous over rigidity because of the needed flexibility in encountering changes. Second, Confucianism tends to advocate a more proactive mindset to make improvements in the society, while Daoism tends to promote retreat as a strategy. Third, Confucian ideologies support individuals to fulfill their responsibilities for their societies, oftentimes serving the community or becoming involved in politics. Daoist ideologies, however, encourage individuals to stay away from human entanglements and to blend in with nature. Fourth, Confucian doctrines assume socialization at the center, but Daoist doctrines glorify independence based on the individual's relationship with nature. Fifth, Confucians focus more on the lasting principles that contribute to improving the human spirit for the long term, while Daoists assume that everything is constantly changing and demands flexibility. Sixth, the Confucian approach is to affirm social roles, values, and proper behaviors, but the Daoist approach is to negate the rules and confidence created by humans in pursuit of something bigger. The two schools seem to work well together, which could be the reason why they have co-existed for two and a half millennia as the two most significant philosophical lineages[7] in Chinese communities throughout the world.

The complementarity between classic Confucianism and classic Daoism could be analogous to how vegetables and meats are used to nourish the human body. Although no direct parallel is drawn here, being a vegetarian and a meat-eater is like being a dedicated classic Daoist and a dedicated classic Confucian. Each individual decides on the type of food she takes to maintain a healthy diet and be able to accomplish various tasks. Some decide to be extreme vegetarians, while others decide to be heavy meat-eaters. Most would like to maintain a balance in between the two diets and allow the complementary natures of the foods to work so that an optimum health benefit is achieved to meet individual needs. The primary principle for vegetarians is that there is no meat consumption. However, there are various levels of vegetarianism as determined by the abstinence of meat by-products (e.g., animal broths, gelatin), animal by-products (e.g., eggs, dairy, honey), fish, or seafood. Furthermore, the frequency of such abstinence is governed by health, dietary, cultural,[8] religious (e.g., Buddhism or Hinduism), social, or personal needs, which can range from always to only one day per year. While vegetarians and meat-eaters seem to suggest a dichotomy, most people are benefited by a combination of both, utilizing the complementary nature of the two diets. Classic Confucianism and classic Daoism can be conceived in a similar way, in that one can be a dedicated classic Confucian or a dedicated classic Daoist, just as one can be an extreme vegetarian or an extreme meat-eater. Elements of both seem to benefit most people, especially when different circumstances are considered. There may be a need for a different degree of each, depending on the time of day, stage in life, context, and need. Ideologies of each can be found in the same person, just as different type of foods are taken by the same person. The different perspectives and emphases of the two schools do not eliminate the possibility of each other, unless an individual decides to be an extremist of one. Even in an extreme classic Confucian or an extreme classic Daoist, there are still traces of the other. A total dedication to human values cannot be void of thoughts about existence, and a total dedication to human existence in nature cannot be void of value judgments. Despite their complementary differences, the two schools are not totally exclusive of each other.

As one is open to accepting the complementarity between classic Confucianism and classic Daoism, more common grounds could be unfolded. Both set goals to observe, understand, monitor, and improve the self, with concentric circles expanding outward to impact the family, the nation, and the world.[9] It is clear that the classic philosophical schools emphasize self-reflection and self-cultivation as a starting point, and in the end they aim to achieve a better world. Borders of clan, race, or nationality should eventually disappear. The philosophies are aimed at the furtherance of *tianxia* (天下), which literally means "everything under the sky," interpreted as the world or universe. The Confucian and the Daoist pursuance of a sage carry similar expectations of continuous self-cultivation and equal treatment regardless of background. When the sage reaches the highest level, sagehood becomes unknowable and indescribable. Laozi states it most concisely: "If one can speak of *dao*, it is not the *dao*" (Laozi 1; 道可道，非常道。). Mencius has a more elaborated explanation on how the highest-level sage is so mystical, from kindness, to sincerity, to beauty, to great, to sage, and to the (godly) unknowable.[10] Since no one claims to have reached the highest level, it remains unknowable and indescribable. Regardless, the pursuit of a better world as a united entity is essential, even vital, as the world is more connected than ever, not just for the Chinese but for everyone.

TOWARD COMPREHENSIVE HARMONY

While harmony and *dao* are shared ideas with different interpretations across the classic Chinese thoughts, *he* (和 harmony) is a highly desirable quality that permeates all layers in life, from within the individual, to between humans, and between human and nature (including heaven and earth, 天地). As Chenyang Li puts it:

> harmonization generates order; generated order in turn becomes an element of continuous harmonization. . . . the ancient Chinese concept of harmony is best understood as a comprehensive process of harmonization, as "deep harmony." It encompasses spatial as well as temporal and metaphysical as well as moral and aesthetic dimensions. It is a fundamentally open notion in the sense that it does not aim to conform to any pre-set order. This broader, richer, and more liberal understanding of harmony has had a profound influence on Chinese culture as a whole over its long history.[11]

Classic Daoism congenitally presents a macrocosmic view of harmony. The interaction between *yin* and *yang* creates *he*, and the three together create all matters (see *Laozi* 42, and Figures 4.2 and 4.3 in chapter 4). Everything is generated through a harmonization process. The pursuit of harmony is a constant long-term endeavor, not just a moment of compromise. As Laozi states, "understanding harmony is everlasting, understanding everlasting is wisdom" (*Laozi* 55; 知和曰常，知常曰明。). All matters are created upon the changes in energy between *yin* and *yang* along with harmony. Therefore, harmony is above all matters like *yin* and *yang*. The role of humans is to harmonize *with* all matters, most notably the natural world. Classic Confucianism also puts harmony on a pedestal but with humans and socialization at the center. "Harmony is the way to reach everywhere worldwide" (*Zhongyong* 1; 和也者，天下之達道也。). When humans are harmonized with heaven and earth in their proper positions, all things would flourish (*Zhongyong* 1; 致中和，天地位焉，萬物育焉。). The state of harmony is ideal in all human interactions. This is a more proactive view of harmony in which humans are taking actions, through social interactions, to transform the world in achieving harmony.

To understand harmony in a characteristically Chinese way, one must depart from the common notion that it is conformity to, agreement with, compromise with, or in accordance with a predetermined order. Zhuangzi suggests that achieving harmony involves the actions of *jun* (均) and *tiao* (調).[12] The former, *jun*, refers to equalizing or making even. Entities involved in harmony must be treated on equal footing; not one is more valuable than another. The latter, *tiao*, means adjusting or reconciling. Description of harmony in *Zhongyong* focuses on human emotional expressions while interacting with others, which should fulfill principles of sincerity and *li* (禮), implying that the adjustment should not lead to extreme or overboard expressions.[13] Although Chenyang Li argues for a definition of harmony from a Confucian standpoint, his proposed characteristics of harmony are helpful for anyone interested in delving deep into its meaning in a classic Chinese context. He suggests that heterogeneity, tension, coordination and cooperation, transformation and growth, and renewal are characteristics of harmony.[14] Heterogeneity implies that two or more different entities are involved in harmony. Various levels of tension arise as the entities are different and interacting. In coordination and cooperation, harmony "involved parties make allowances for one another and preserve their soundness. . . . Through coordination, tension is transformed and conflict is reconciled into a favorable environment for each party to flourish. In this process, involved parties undergo mutual transformation and form harmonious relationships."[15] Since achieving harmony is an ongoing process that never ends, "a harmonious relationship is maintained through continuous renewal."[16]

Clearly, the harmony described here is quite comprehensive. It is not just harmony for an incident based on any preconceived notion; it is macrocosmic, temporal, lateral, vertical, social, and personal in an organismic world of metaphysics and change. To put it in an individual's perspective, harmony is a pursuit of a lifetime in relation to other humans and the natural environment across various life stages. It constantly demands for change, flexibility, coordination, adjustment, equalization, reconciliation, self-cultivation, and conviction (denial of disharmony). To understand how comprehensive harmony works in music education, I must first explore how *yin* and *yang* work in the field.

TOWARD *YIN* AND *YANG* IN MUSIC EDUCATION

The concept of *yin* and *yang* found in *Yijing* is a foundation for both classic Confucianism and classic Daoism.[17] It has also been applied to a great variety of fields in the contemporary world, from architecture,[18] to biochemistry,[19] to business communication,[20] to geometry,[21] to pathology,[22] and to psychology,[23] to name just a few. In music, as far as can be determined, there are two elaborated systematic uses of *yin* and *yang* principles in music composition[24] and in some wellness and therapeutic applications.[25] It is surprising that, despite the all-pervasive potential of *yin* and *yang* principles, I find no major systematic philosophical application in music education,[26] which is a field dominated by aesthetics, social interactions, and a temporal dimension.

To fulfill expectations of principles found in *yin* and *yang*, there needs to be two bipolar entities showing the following qualities:

1. Energy transmission. One entity must be transmitting energy to the other. Energy may take the form of sound, movement, momentum, change, idea, effort, knowledge, or authority.
2. Continuum. The two entities should represent a continuum to reflect various gradations in between them. They should not be dichotomies or binary opposites.
3. Non-judgmental. The two entities must be equally valuable. Belonging to a specific entity does not infer any value judgment.
4. Indexical. The two entities must be indexical. One may become the other due to change or transformation. Reference to an entity is changed as a situation changes. For example, the entity "student" may actually mean the teacher when the teacher is taking a class from another teacher.
5. Complementarity. The two entities must be complementary to each other. The strength of one is the weakness of the other. One is perpetuating the other. The existence of the two entities represents a form of perfection and completeness.
6. Concomitance. The two entities must be mutually dependent, concomitant to each other. They are non-exclusive of each other. One must contain a bit of the other.
7. Forward moving. The two entities work together to create change, so the involved domain moves forward.

Rather than making an unwieldy term to include all seven criteria to label pairs of entities as I work toward the *yin* and *yang* of music educational experiences, I simply use the abbreviated term *complementary bipolar continua* to capture the most outstanding qualities of the *yin-yang* dyad.

COMPLEMENTARY BIPOLAR CONTINUA IN MUSIC EDUCATION

The practice of music education inherently encompasses the subject of music, the teacher, the learner, and the interactions among them. Implicit to this is the context where music education takes place. It can take place anywhere, within or outside educational institutions, in person or online, or in families or in community organizations. Music education is not only an experience of the moment in a defined space. There is also a temporal element in which the present would become the past, and the recent past would become a distant past, which may become the present (e.g., as in performing music from hundreds of years ago). At any given moment, events are synchronized with or without meaning. Based on the principles of *yin* and *yang*, I propose four complementary bipolar continua to address elements inherent in music education practices.

The first continuum is active musical motions and passive musical motions. As music is made or heard, the nature of music has a direct influence on the music education experience. The musical motions refer to sonic activities in any musical elements, namely dynamics, rhythm, tempo, pitch, melody, harmony, and timbre. The adjectives "passive" and "active" are directed to the *yin* and *yang* qualities, respectively. Energies are weighted heavily on the active side, and there are gradations of different energy levels in a continuum. The active and the passive are equally valuable. For example, slow music is as valuable as fast music, or a melody with few movements is as valuable as one with many changing pitches. As musical motions change, the passive can become active, and vice versa. For example, in musical ensemble dynamics, a *mezzo piano* part is passive in relation to a *fortissimo* part, but the same *mezzo piano* part would become active if the *fortissimo* part is changed to *pianissimo* or a rest. Music makers make changes across all musical elements and synchronize each moment with musical meanings, sometimes well planned, and at other times on the spur of the moment.

In other words, musical elements may each form a sub-continuum between passive and active, again representing qualities of *yin* and *yang*. They each can change, switch roles, coordinate, and work in a complementary way. Most important, they work together to move forward as the

| **Active Musical Motions** ←————————————→ | **Passive Musical Motions** |

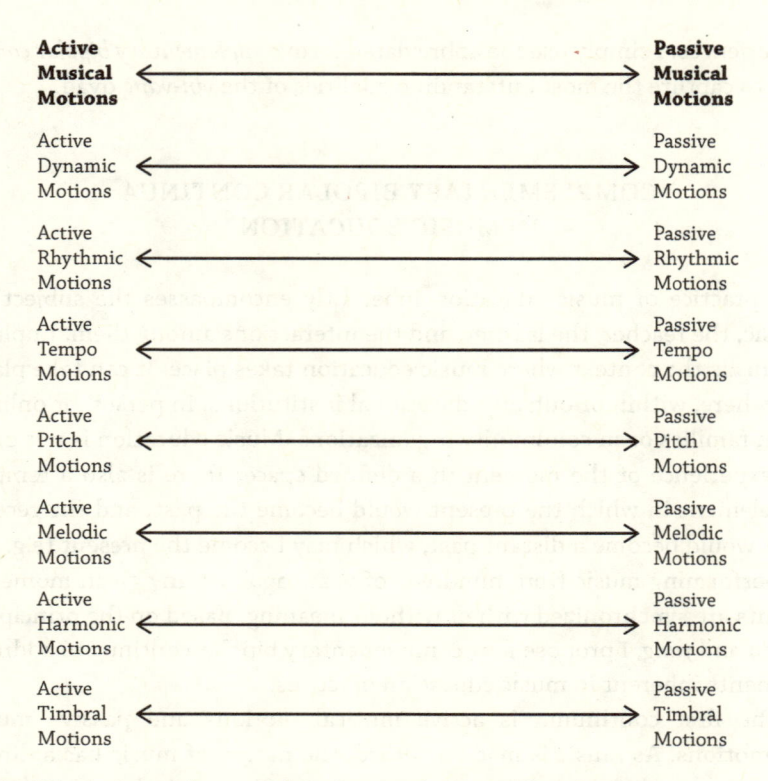

Active Dynamic Motions ←————————————→ Passive Dynamic Motions

Active Rhythmic Motions ←————————————→ Passive Rhythmic Motions

Active Tempo Motions ←————————————→ Passive Tempo Motions

Active Pitch Motions ←————————————→ Passive Pitch Motions

Active Melodic Motions ←————————————→ Passive Melodic Motions

Active Harmonic Motions ←————————————→ Passive Harmonic Motions

Active Timbral Motions ←————————————→ Passive Timbral Motions

Figure 5.1: Active-passive musical motions continuum and its sub-continua.

music progresses. Figure 5.1 is a visual representation of this continuum and sub-continua. The number of sub-continua should remain open as musical elements may be viewed in different frameworks.

The second complementary bipolar continuum is teacher and learner. This continuum is based on the assumption that the role of the teacher is to teach and of the learner to learn. However, in reality, the teacher almost never just teaches, and the learner almost never just learns. Without learning, one could not be a teacher. The learner is constantly teaching the teacher how to teach without being aware of it, and sometimes the learner may share with the teacher what the teacher does not know.[27] The complementary and concomitant nature of the relationship is inevitable. Teaching and learning are necessary for anyone to grow.[28] In this continuum, the teacher is on the *yang* side, because the teacher is the one who holds the thrust of the energy, in the form of knowledge, skill, or wisdom. The level of energy the teacher has varies depending on the mode of teaching. For example, the lecture mode is more of an authoritarian mode of teaching, where knowledge (energy) is supposedly transmitted from the teacher to the learner. In a discussion mode where the teacher and learner may ask questions of each other, then, the energy of the teacher is much reduced, because the learner is sharing the energy in the form of questions. The other side of the phenomenon is that the learner is on the *yin* side, where more likely, energy is received. From the standpoint of music education or any form of education, the teacher and the learner are both valuable. There will be no music education without any one side, and their co-existence makes music education possible. Because of interactions between the teacher and the learner, music education may move forward. Depending on the dynamics of the interactions between the teacher and the learner, the teacher may become the learner and vice versa. The role switching is more probable in a different context, for example, when the teacher takes a class for professional development or when the learner is teaching a sibling at home.

The teacher and learner roles can be used implicitly to depict any musical situation where there is interaction, or energy exchange, between an energy-emitting party and an energy-receiving party. For example, for presentational music in a recital or concert setting, the performers are emitting energy received by the audience. In other words, the audience is *learning* about the performance, the pieces, and the performers. Without being consciously thinking about the teaching role, performers are actually *teaching* the audience about the music, the composers, and themselves through the performance.

One sub-continuum may evolve from the teacher-learner continuum. To be a teacher of a specific knowledge or skill area, she is expected to have a higher-level expertise in that specific area than the learner. It is probable that the learner might have a higher-level expertise in another specific area, but that would be a role switch if that other specific area is engaged in a teaching and learning setting. Therefore, expert and novice could be a sub-continuum under teacher and learner. As with the previous continuum, the number of sub-continua should remain open as new concepts may evolve from the teacher-learner continuum that fit the criteria of *yin* and *yang*. Figure 5.2 presents the teacher-learner continuum and its sub-continuum.

The third complementary bipolar continuum is high-energy activities and low-energy activities. It is directed toward the activities that occur in the music education process. High-energy activities are those that are

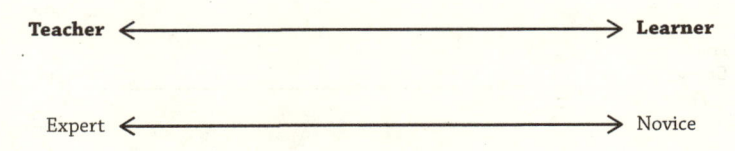

Teacher ←——————————————→ Learner

Expert ←——————————————→ Novice

Figure 5.2: Teacher-learner continuum and its sub-continuum.

active and engaging. Low-energy activities are those that are relatively passive and less engaging. In music education settings, high-energy activities are likely to include performing, improvising, composing, or moving along with the music (including marching in a marching band). Low-energy activities are likely to include analyzing, responding to music with minimal motions, listening, and the most passive and unengaging of all, which is to listen to the music in the background without even paying attention to it. Both types of activities are valuable, indexical, and complementary to each other. As in a normal cycle of activities, they are concomitant to each other, as rest is needed in preparation for the higher-energy activities. After a period of high-energy activity, there is a high demand for low-energy activity.

The varying energy level activities can be teacher-directed or learner-directed, notation-driven or sound-driven, or in a structured setting or an unstructured setting. No matter how the activity comes to place, the teacher and the learner are always involved. Therefore, two sub-continua are included within this continuum, one for the energy level involved in each of the main roles in music education practices (see Figure 5.3).

The fourth complementary bipolar continuum is familiar musical experience and unfamiliar musical experience. It focuses on the temporal aspect of music education as all things unfamiliar can become familiar if they are exposed, taught, or practiced. As a broad definition of music education suggests, the exposure, teaching, or practice may occur within or outside an educational institution, in families and in communities. In this continuum, the energy is shown in the (un)familiarity of the musical experiences. This is not just about the familiarity with the music per se, but more important, with the entire musical event, which engage all perceptual senses and cognitive avenues. When a familiar musical experience is presented, more information is transmitted, but less effort (i.e., energy) is required to process the information. When a completely foreign musical experience

High Energy Activities	← →	Low Energy Activities
High Energy Teacher Activities	← →	Low Energy Teacher Activities
High Energy Learner Activities	← →	Low Energy Learner Activities

Figure 5.3: High- and low-energy activities continuum and its sub-continua.

is presented, little information transmission is involved, but more effort is required to gain from the experience. As a musical experience is exposed, taught, or practiced repeatedly, it becomes a familiar experience.

The opposite can occur too, when a familiar experience is being forgotten[29] or being situated in a different context; a familiar experience can become unfamiliar. As one learns more about the music, some unfamiliar elements of the music can be uncovered. The familiar and the unfamiliar create a dyad that is in line with the principles of *yin* and *yang*. There are varying degrees of familiarity in all musical experiences. Both ends are valuable, indexical, complementary, and concomitant. As a result of their interactions, music education moves forward.

In educational settings, the familiarity-unfamiliarity dyad can be explained by exposure, teaching (and learning), and practice. They would naturally form three sub-continua: exposed musical experience and unexposed musical experience, taught (and learned) music and untaught music (i.e., music not learned), and practiced musical experience and unpracticed musical experience. In a micro-musical perspective, energy transmissions in the musical elements are already explained in the active-passive musical motions continuum. In a macro-musical sense, it is appropriate to explain the energy transmissions in terms of familiarity with the musical structure and the musical style. Both involve a combination of musical elements and offer some relevance to the overall musical event, such as the reason or the socio-musical context for creating the musical event. In a social-geographical view, familiarity with musical experiences can be due to the places where one has been: local and foreign. "Local" refers to wherever the individual has been in the past, and "foreign" refers to places where she has never been, in person and in cyberspace. Therefore, the local-foreign dyad is not just physical, but also psychological and virtual.

And finally, discussions in familiarity with musical experiences cannot avoid a focus on its temporal aspect. From a macro-social viewpoint, music with long-standing traditions remains recognizable and familiar to those who have been exposed to it. The more widespread and the more stable the tradition, the more people are likely to be familiar with the experience of it. In contrast, contemporary and new musical experiences with a lot of changes and new elements are likely to be on the unfamiliar side. Figure 5.4 presents a visual representation of the familiar musical experiences and unfamiliar musical experiences continuum and its seven sub-continua.

The number of continua and sub-continua presented above is not definitive. Although they all fit the criteria for the *yin* and *yang* dyad, flexibility should remain to allow room for new developments in understanding the philosophical ideologies and the field of music education. There could be

Familiar Musical Experiences	←——————————→	Unfamiliar Musical Experiences
Exposed Musical Experiences	←——————————→	Unexposed Musical Experiences
Taught Music	←——————————→	Untaught Music
Practiced Musical Experiences	←——————————→	Unpracticed Musical Experiences
Familiar Musical Structure	←——————————→	Unfamiliar Musical Structure
Familiar Musical Style	←——————————→	Unfamiliar Musical Style
Local Musical Experiences	←——————————→	Foreign Musical Experiences
Traditional Musical Experiences	←——————————→	Contemporary Musical Experiences

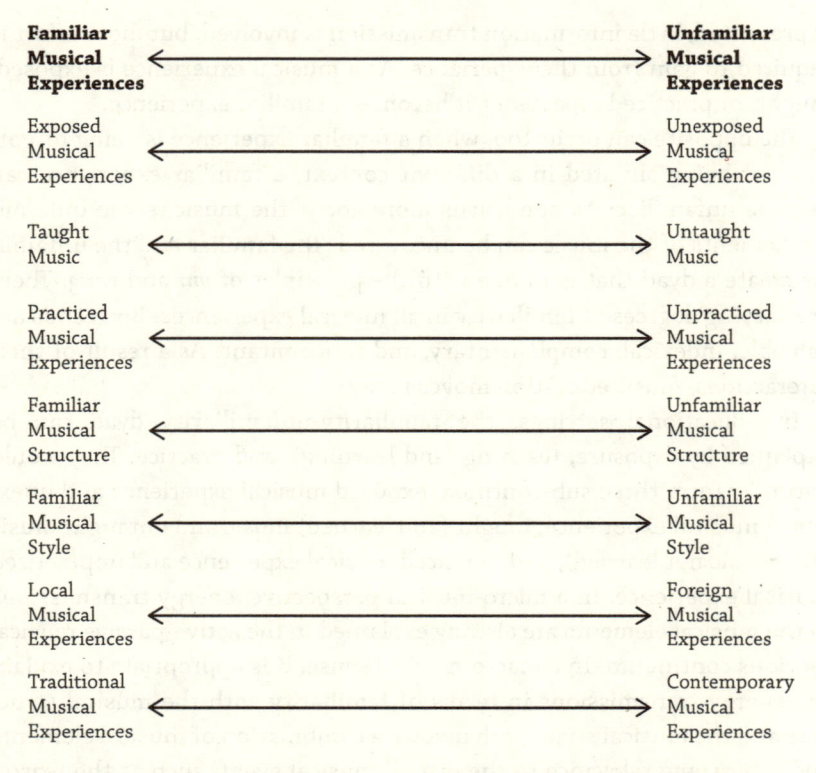

Figure 5.4: Familiar-unfamiliar musical experiences continuum and its sub-continua.

room for more continuum and sub-continuum, but it is important to maintain its consistency with the principles of *yin* and *yang* as suggested in *Yijing*.

CIRCULARITY AND CHAOS IN THE CONTINUA

A continuum is generally understood as two poles with extreme and distinct differences, while the gradation in between them contains minute differences. This is a rather straightforward linear psychometric view, in which the two extremes are opposing poles with variations between them. It is effective in indicating the state of a matter. However, in *Yijing* and in classic Daoist view, *yin* and *yang* is more than that. They are in circular motions, meaning that the subject on one extreme could become the other extreme, due to changes in situations. There is always a continuous perpetuation, as one propels the other. In the active-passive musical motions continuum, music is almost never constantly active in all elements or constantly passive in all elements. After a period of active motions, a period of passivity is expected, and vice versa. In the teacher-learner continuum, one goes in circular motion back and forth as a teacher and a learner. In the high-low

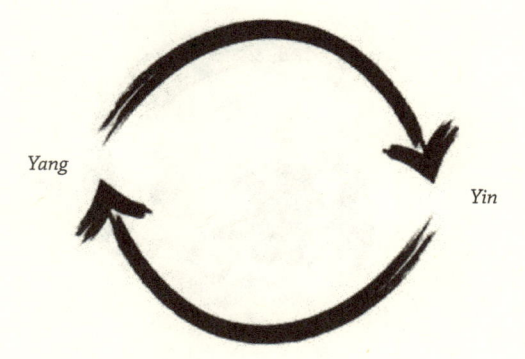

Figure 5.5: *Yin* and *yang* in a circular continuum.

energy activities continuum, music education activities are almost never constantly high energy or low energy. One would return to the other in different settings or for different needs. In the familiar-unfamiliar musical experiences continuum, the unfamiliar will become familiar through time as music education progresses, but one would not be settled with the familiar. One would likely seek out more unfamiliar musical experiences as music education moves forward. One could not miss the circular characteristic of *yin* and *yang* in classic Daoist texts. Before the appearance of *yin* and *yang*, Laozi describes *dao* as "a mass of everything mixed together" (*Laozi* 25; 有物混成) "in circular motion that never ends" (*Laozi* 25; 周行而不殆). As *yin* and *yang* are spin-offs from *dao* in circular motion, they continue the same motion, not independently but co-dependently, as they generate all matters and move forward. The concept of *hundun* (混沌 chaos) is not only found in *dao*, but it is in between *yin* and *yang* also.

To incorporate the ideas of circularity and *hundun* in each continuum (Figures 5.1 through 5.4), their visual depiction should depart from the traditional linear format. It is more appropriate to use two arrows that form a circle (see Figure 5.5) to represent each continuum. I would go even further to incorporate the non-exclusive nature of *yin* and *yang*, that is one always includes the other, and put a dot of *yin* in the *yang* arrow and a dot of *yang* in the *yin* arrow. Figure 5.6 presents such a depiction, and it begins to look like the early Ming Dynasty (1368–1644) interpretation of *yin* and *yang* in a *taiji* circle (see Figure 2.1). There can be multiple routes for the motions that go between *yin* and *yang*, as the route should be flexible to adjust to the changing situations. Another dimension of the multiple routes is that there can be multiple sub-continua running simultaneously. The use of a three-dimensional space is necessary to represent these tracks. As presented in Figure 5.7, each of the continua shown in Figures 5.1 through 5.4 should look like a ball, rather than a two-sided arrow, with continuous motions running between the two poles on multiple tracks.

Figure 5.6: *Yin* and *yang* continuum with a dot of *yin* in the *yang* arrow and a dot of *yang* in the *yin* arrow.

Based on the parallels between the continua and the *taiji* circle, the continua are more accurately represented with a *taiji* circle in between the two extreme ends. This is to ensure that the meanings of the continua entail the principles of the *yin-yang* relationship, not the typical linear relationship found in modern psychometric continua. Figure 5.8 presents such a representation for the four main continua. The same representation for the sub-continua is subsumed within the main continua in a similar fashion. All continua presented in this text hereafter should be understood as such.

CONNECTIVITY AMONG THE CONTINUA

The four complementary bipolar continua presented in this chapter are built upon the essential aspects of music education practices: the music,

Figure 5.7: *Yin* and *yang* continuum with multiple tracks represented in three-dimensional space.

Active Musical Motions ☯ Passive Musical Motions

Teacher ☯ Learner

High Energy Activities ☯ Low Energy Activities

Familiar Musical Experiences ☯ Unfamiliar Musical Experiences

Figure 5.8: Complementary bipolar continua with *yin-yang* relationship.

the teacher, the learner, and their interactions along with a temporal consideration. They concern active and passive musical motions, the teacher and the learner roles, high- and low-energy activities, and familiar and unfamiliar musical experiences. The four continua may seem separate and distinct, but in fact they are tightly connected in music education practices. Their connection is so tight that music education cannot occur with any one of the four continua missing. Each continuum constantly moves in circular motion and is connected with the other three. The design of a contemporary tennis ball is a good representation of a continuum, because of the tightly woven dyadic pattern that appears on the ball, similar to that of *yin* and *yang* in the *taiji* figure (see Figure 5.9).[30] When all four continua

Figure 5.9: Connection of the four complementary bipolar continua as represented by four tennis balls.

are in motion simultaneously, they generate a complex web of influences and tensions. The influences can explain a synchronicity of events, and the tensions call for a desire for harmony.

Motions in the four complementary bipolar continua in music education are not isolated from the rest of life. They are organically in contact with changes in other aspects of life. The constant motion of each continuum is surrounded by constant changes in the person, the culture, the environment, and nature. These changes set up a synchronized situation in music education for every individual, who makes decisions and takes actions continuously. The following chapter focuses on change, which is the first in a trilogy of thinking about music education.

CHAPTER 6

Change

Change (*bian* 變) is a universal phenomenon that has received tremendous attention, from the East to the West, from antiquity to contemporary, and from artists and humanists to scientists, social scientists, economists, and business managers. The earliest documentation of its interest is found in the Chinese civilization, dating back to the origin of *Yijing* from the 29th–28th century BC. The ancient Greek philosopher Heraclitus (535–475 BC) also has a well-known doctrine of change that is being central to the universe.[1] Although they are apart by millennia and by geographic location, ideas found in *Yijing* and Heraclitus are in agreement, in that change is a constant and is part of life. It is a natural phenomenon found across all elements and all aspects of the universe.[2] They suggest that no one can go back in time to make a change, but they leave open regarding the role humans can play in forthcoming changes. In other words, everyone must accept the inevitability of change, so life and its meaning can be situated, and at the same time human actions *may* have an impact on upcoming changes.

Change is often perceived in its totality, meaning a full replacement, a dramatic transformation, or a complete turnaround. The bigger the magnitude of the change, the more noticeable it is. Smaller changes are less noticeable and require more attention, sensitivity, and reflection. A slight modification or a slow and gradual progression tends to receive less immediate attention in everyday life, if at all. Furthermore, many changes are so minuscule that they are unperceivable by humans yet they are pervasive throughout everyone's life.³ The changes discussed throughout this book are all-encompassing, regardless of their magnitude and perceptibility. They are a nature of the universe and all of its elements. All beings must accept and learn almost simultaneously about these changes, simply for survival, to say the least.⁴ To sustain life and be meaningful in it, change must be part of it.⁵ Even stagnancy on a surface level infers lifelessness; at the same time, absolute stillness is next to impossible in everyday life. As humans, we must accept the fact that we are living in a system in which there are constantly changing elements that are not maneuverable by humans, for example, the rite of passage and the change of seasons. These are the same elements that contribute to the eternity of *dao*.⁶

The more one learns about changes, the better positioned one is in making decisions to promote prosperity and to avoid adversity.⁷ Confucius is quoted in *Yizhuan* as stating, "for those who understand the *dao* of change, they should also understand the mystical way" (*Jicishang, Yizhuan* 《繫辭上》；子曰：「知變化之道者，其知神之所為乎。」). In the same essay, change is described as the phenomenon of interactions between advance and retreat (變化者，進退之象也。), hard and soft (剛柔相推而生變化。), and open and closed (一闔一闢謂之變). Energy is flowed from one side to another, back and forth in self perpetual motions.

In the Chinese language, change (*bian* 變) and cultivation (*hua* 化) are often grouped together in one expression (*bian hua* 變化). *Hua* acts like a suffix in English, meaning -ify, -ize, or -ization. The grouping of *hua* with *bian* has been evident from antiquity through contemporary. In *Yizhuan* alone, this expression appears twelve times. This does not account for the two Chinese characters appearing separately in proximity. *Yizhuan* offers an explanation between *bian* and *hua* using the sky and humans to represent nature and human behaviors, respectively: in observing the sky, there is an understanding of changes (*bian*變) of seasons or time; in observing humans, there is an awareness of cultivation (*hua* 化) to allow success in all (*Ben, Tuanchuan, Yizhuan* 《易傳》《彖傳：賁》；觀乎天文，以察時變；觀乎人文，以化成天下。). This statement helps to clarify how change is a partnership between natural phenomena and the roles of humans. Change does not stand alone, nor apart from humans, to be meaningful. In the midst of incontrollable change (e.g., time and seasons), humans are the ones to use it and to act upon it, hoping for a fulfilling experience.⁸ Since change is viewed from a human perspective, "*bian*" and "*bian hua*" can be considered as synonyms. They usually have the same translation: *change*. The slight distinction between them is that *bian hua* has an added emphasis on the change being cultivated, progressed, transformed, or integrated, implying a state of becoming and being acted upon.

SIGNIFICANCE OF *TONG* (通)

Like *hua* (化), *tong* (通) requires human participation in the advent of change. According to *Yizhuan*, it is important to pair *bian* (變) and *tong* (通 or flowing through) so the change is sensible. When describing open (as in split) and closed (as in united) as change, going back and forth *endlessly* is described as *tong* (*Jicishang, Yizhuan* 《易傳》《繫辭上》；一闔一闢謂之變；往來不窮謂之通). Furthermore, while cultivation and justification (by *dao*) is change, pushing (*dao*) into operation is *tong* (化而裁之謂之變，推而行之謂之通).[9] The pairing of *bian* and *tong* is inevitable to put change in the context of the moving universe. Semantically, *tong* has the connotation that the operation has to be sensible and coherent, not forceful, reluctant, or far-fetched in any way.

In *Jicixia, Yizhuan* 《易傳》《繫辭下》, *bian* (變) and *tong* (通) are explicitly tied to the concepts of time and eternity. Those who know how to act with *bian* and *tong* know how to coordinate with the forward motion in time (變通者，趨時者也。). This is in accord with the assumptions that change is temporal and that there is no return. A principle found in *Yizhuan* states that when one is out of options, change is going to occur; when change occurs, *tong* follows; when there is *tong*, there is eternity (窮則變，變則通，通則久。). In other words, change should not occur just for the sake of change; change without *tong* is not going to last and prosper. The pairing of *bian* and *tong* provides further support for the embedded meaning of eternity in *bian*.

The idea of *bian* (change) and *tong* (flowing through) together is in concurrence with music making and music education. On the one hand, parameters for music making (e.g., pitch, tonality, rhythmic structure, timbre, and dynamics) and for music education (e.g., developmental appropriateness, roles of teacher and learner, and evaluation) can be changed instantly. On the other hand, music making and music education actions reside within a musical system and a social system, each with an established framework. Simply put, the framework for each musical and social tradition provides avenues for *tong* in music making and music education actions, and *bian* occurs within the parameters provided by the musical and social framework. Humans are obligated to make *tong* occur regardless of *bian*, so there is a greater likelihood of lasting prosperity.

FROM ORGANISM TO ECOLOGY: TOWARD A MEGASYSTEM

The notion of *tong* has a strong undercurrent of connectedness. If there is no connection, there can hardly be any *tong*. An important premise of this book is that the universe is an organism in which all elements within it are organismic. Every phenomenon (*xiang* 象) has an explanation and a reason (*li* 理).¹⁰ The explanations and the reasons are illustrative of the connections of elements and entities. While music and music education are the foci in this writing, they are not detached from other aspects of life. As demonstrated in the previous chapter (see Figure 5.9), the four complementary bipolar continua are in contact with each other. Beyond the continua are connections with other aspects of life. Beyond one's life, there are other people's lives; all are linked, some directly and others indirectly.

The Russian-born American psychologist (1917–2005) Urie Bronfenbrenner's model from the 1970s is of some relevance here. Like music and music education as presented in this book, Bronfenbrenner's model is a human-centric model with a global appeal and implications for the entire lifespan. It is an ecological model of human development, in which the individual is at the center, living within a "microsystem," which is "a pattern of activities, roles, and interpersonal relations experienced by the developing person in a given setting with particular physical and material characteristics."¹¹ Humans grow in the context of "the *changing* [emphasis added] properties of the immediate settings in which the developing person lives, as this process is affected by relations between these settings, and by the larger contexts in which the settings are embedded."¹² The embedded settings are connected to what he calls a "mesosystem," an "exosystem," and then a "macrosystem." A mesosystem contains the interrelations among two or more settings such as home, school, and peer groups for a child or family, work, and social life for an adult.¹³ An exosystem includes "one or more settings that do not involve the developing person as an active participant, but in which events occur that affect, or are affected by, what happens in the setting containing the developing person."¹⁴ He cites examples of a parent's workplace and the parent's circle of friends for the child. Changes in the non-participating systems (e.g., parent's workplace) are not only connected to the individual but are affected also. A macrosystem "refers to consistencies, in the form and content of lower-order systems (micro-, meso-, and exo-) that exist, or could exist, at the level of the subculture or the culture as a whole, along with any belief systems or ideology underlying such consistencies."¹⁵ Using venues such as a classroom or a post office as examples, he states that there are consistencies in how they look and function in France but differ from their counterparts in the United States. He further states, "it is as if in each country the various settings had been constructed from the same set of blueprints."¹⁶ The blueprints or the principles found in a macrosystem are characteristics of a setting within a larger frame of reference, which often times is a (sub) culture, a society, or a nation. The interrelations across the micro-, meso-, exo-, and macro-systems are viewed like layers of Russian dolls, with the microsystem nested in the innermost layer and the macrosystem as the outermost. Each layer is connected and influenced by the other layers. This model reveals that the human connection with the environment plays a key role in realizing one's genetic potential. Within his model, "an ecological transition" may occur when "the ecological environment is altered as the result of a *change* [emphasis added] in role, setting, or both."[17] According Bronfenbrenner, ecological transition occurs throughout one's lifespan and is marked by events such as a newborn in the family, a child starting school, job promotion, relocation, marriage, emigration, illness, and retirement. All ecological transitions are directly linked to a *change* in role, setting, or both.

Bronfenbrenner's model is relevant here not only because it is human-centric, but it also points to the importance of *change* in the environment within an organic system in which layers of subsystems are interrelated. *Ecological transition* frees the individuals from systemic boundaries, availing them to flow from one (sub)system to another, which in itself is a type of change. In other words, change in the environment is the change that occurs in the system, and ecological transition demands for change in the person. Environmental changes and ecological transitions are ways of looking at change as life progresses. However, Bronfenbrenner's model does not address a view beyond the macrosystem to include human characters that are consistent across cultures, belief systems, or ideologies. This is a limitation that the classic Chinese philosophies may fulfill, with their foci on the human spirit and *dao*, which can form an all-encompassing system that transcends time and space, a "megasystem" that promotes better lives for everyone.

OPTIONS FOR HUMANS

As change is a given within and across various systems and layers, humans have two basic options. One may *ignore* it, meaning that one would continue to behave as if changes do not occur. This is an extremely passive and ignorant option. Depending on the circumstances, this option may lead to catastrophe quickly. Even if by chance the ignorance avoids immediate adversity, it will eventually lead to obliteration. This ignorance could be viewed as *bian* (變) without *tong* (通 flowing through). The change in the environment is disconnected with the human behavior. There is no flowing through, and there is no channel that connects change with the human. If humans choose to ignore change persistently, they are destined for troubles.[18]

The other option is to take action to go along with the changes so they make sense (i.e., *bian* with *tong*) to the individual taking the action. For the sake of explanation, I present these actions in three alternative groups: (a) *avoidance*: act deliberately to avoid direct contact with the changes; (b) *passivity*: react to changes by exerting minimal efforts just to get by in the short term without being hurt; or (c) *proactivity*: make proactive moves to induce another change for prosperity in the long term (see Figure 6.1). Any of these action alternatives can be sensible if they are properly contextualized.

The first alternative, *avoidance*, suggests a choice to retreat from the impending changes, which is sometimes necessary. However, doing so consistently for an extended period will likely lead to devastation. For example, one might avoid playing a note in an ensemble setting or avoid participating in a musical activity, such as a class or a concert. These actions may not cause severe harm when they occur for a good cause (e.g., illness). Consistent avoidance of such actions, however, is going to jeopardize her ensemble or class membership. The second alternative, reacting

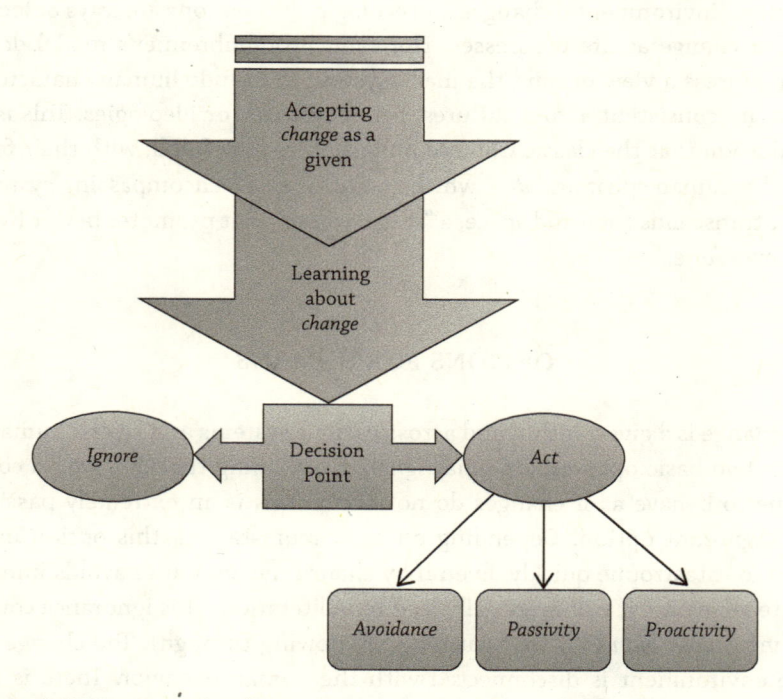

Figure 6.1: From accepting change as a given to options humans have.

to changes with minimum effort, may sustain survival but it is in a passive mode. One is to go along with no novel acts. This passive reaction may be appropriate for changes that do not affect the high-priority aspects of life. For example, one may play the correct note in an ensemble setting but with minimal expression, or participating in a musical activity without making the effort to attend to the details or to excel. The third type, inducing a new change, is the most proactive. It can change the course of events by creating a different path that not only avoid adversity but, more important, promote prosperity. One would tend to choose this alternative in dealing with changes in a high-priority aspect of life, such as survival, safety, and satisfactory life experiences. Preventive measures are in place to avoid unsafe conditions, and career decisions are made to promote a more satisfactory life. In other words, if music and music education is a high priority, one would induce changes in their lives to promote prosperity in it. For example, one would attend to the details of the notes being played in an ensemble or musical activity when music is one's activity of choice. While all types of actions contain elements of *yin* and *yang*, proactivity tends to be dominated by qualities of *yang*. More energy is required in proactive actions. There is room for all types of actions depending on the situation and the persons involved. No one is expected to act in the same way in dealing with all types of changes, because not everyone has the same priority.

In music and music education, change is a natural phenomenon of the local setting and is a part of a meaningful musical experience. It engages musical sound, the teacher, the learner, the activities, and the experience of the musical event in a complex web of energy exchanges. All involved must accept and learn about the changes, systematically or implicitly, within and around them to make the musical experience meaningful. While *bian* is inevitable, *tong* is not necessarily present in all cases when humans make their decisions in music or music education. While *dao* is there to cultivate and justify *bian* (change), humans are the ones to make *tong* happen so that music and music education may persist into eternity. In exploring the ideas of *bian* and *tong* in music and music education, I use the options and alternatives presented above to serve as reference points to the changes found in the complementary bipolar continua. The two options (ignorance versus acting with three alternatives) are presented in order from the one with the most resistance to change to the one with the most acquiescence to change. Although much of the current discussion is about music and music education, readers should maintain an organismic worldview in mind, in which changes in music and music education are connected to changes in other aspects of life.

Ignorance

The first option humans have after acknowledging and learning about change is to *ignore* it. Although it is possible to have good intentions with this approach, knowing of the occurrence of change but behaving as though change does not occur is essentially self-centered, inconsiderate, careless, uncaring, and negligent. The change may be perceived as indirect, so indirect that it is almost irrelevant; therefore there is no immediately need to pay attention to it. The decision to ignore change downplays the organismic view in which all things are connected. The choice to ignore changes in music and music education is destined for random chaos. *Ignorance* represents scenarios where human actions do not correspond with changing situations. Random chaos is a characterization. Music and music education is doomed to failure when ignorance to musical changes persists. It is hard for trained musicians to imagine that changes in musical motions are ignored when making music. The music would not make sense if the "musical" sound is irrespective of any musical structure or tradition. Tonality and metric structure are expected in many musical traditions. Making random sounds without a reason creates confusion. Manipulations in timbre or dynamics regardless of changes in the overall musical setting could be disruptive. Ignorance also implies no intention to improve. In the case of early music learners, some ignorance is expected, but there should be an intention to improve in music teaching and learning settings. If there is enough encouragement and curiosity, early music learners should take actions in response to the changing musical environment, which is described in the following subsection.

Ignoring the roles of the music teacher and the music learner would lead to another set of random chaos. Without the roles of the music teacher being a role model, a leader, a facilitator, an organizer, a producer, a counselor, a conductor, a director, or a lecturer, music learners are not able to recognize and respect the underlying framework of the music learning. In the recent advent of informal learning,[19] autonomous learning, student-directed learning, or learner-centered learning, the roles of the teacher and learner are still clearly recognized; the teacher is still the one providing the underlying framework, guidelines, and criteria. Ignorance of the teacher-learner role leads to fuzziness in the direction of the learning and leaves learning to chance. It is important to distinguish between the teacher-learner *role* and the teaching-learning *activity*. They are not direct parallels; the teacher does not only teach and the learner does not only learn. In fact, a teacher should learn from the learner while teaching, and the learner should be given opportunities to demonstrate (or teach) what they have learned. The teaching and learning activities should be complementary so everyone involved can improve.[20] This paragraph is about the teacher-learner role, not the teaching-learning activity, which is addressed in the following paragraph.

Ignorance in musical activities, regardless of energy level or direction of energy flow, leaves the outcomes of the activities to chance. Musical activities may lead to musical or non-musical outcomes. Likewise, learning may or may not occur if a music educational activity is ignored. Since music making and learning requires concentration, ignoring musical activities would more likely lead to non-musical outcomes, even if the activities are intended to be musical or educational. When ignorance is found in a musical activity, or any type of activity, it is perceived as disorganized. If the teaching and learning activity is ignored, there is little chance to follow up or realize development on any teaching or learning moment.

Ignorance in musical experiences can be revealed when one is situated in a musical event and there is no attention to the overall experience. Inappropriate behavior at the event is an indication of inattention and ignorance. One may clap, shout, talk, or walk around in a musical event at specific times, but not in all musical events and at all times. Again, random chaos would occur when there is ignorance that leads to a clash between the person involved and changes in the musical event. The experience becomes perplexed. It can happen to musicians too when a new type of musical event in a foreign tradition is introduced. For example, when Western-trained musicians attend a *noh* performance in Japan, their Western concert hall etiquette does not totally transfer to a Japanese *noh* theater, making them feel somewhat ignorant. The occasional shouting or calling out from the audience during the performance appears to be confusing to Western-trained musicians unfamiliar with the *noh* tradition. However, those with sincerity, kindness, benevolence, the spirit of a Confucian *junzi*, and a Daoist sense of observation, equality, and flexibility would turn the ignorance into a learning opportunity and act upon it in a constructive way. In brief, the ignorance laid out in this text is an ignorance in the Confucian *dao* and the Daoist *dao*. While everyone carries this ignorance to some degree, it is not to be promoted but to be recognized and to be acted upon to bring about improvements.

Act

The second option humans have is to act in recognition of change. Before deciding on an action, the change is acknowledged. Individuals learn about the change in relation to their lives, then they determine an action. Different actions reveal idiosyncrasies in each person's priorities, life stages, and situations. They may act in avoidance, passivity, or proactivity. These are not discrete categories but a way to conceive of alternatives to the action. One can move from one way of acting to another when change occurs in one's priorities, life stages, situations, musical genres, personalities, personal needs, and so forth. Furthermore, *Yijing* reminds us through the interaction between *yin* and *yang* that there are gradations of possibilities depending on the levels of energy exchange in various elements.

Act in Avoidance. One may deliberately avoid musical motions by removing oneself from environments where there is music. In avoiding musical motions, one would not choose to listen to music, let alone making music. If avoiding musical motions persists over a long period, music could become a remote phenomenon, and various types of adversities may occur. An important component of being humans becomes missing. As an individual, life would be less meaningful, less interesting, less healthy, and less social; as a species, humans would not be as wise as they are. This may seem negative, but avoiding musical motions *briefly* may be necessary on occasions, such as during moments of activities when music becomes a distraction or an undesirable intervention. The challenge, however, is to make these moments brief and not to allow them to extend beyond a transitory period.

In avoiding the music teacher-learner role, one would stay away from any setting where there is an identifiable music teacher or learner. For example, one may avoid taking a music class in an educational institution. Some music learning may still occur, but the learning would be limited, less organized, and more likely left to enculturation and acculturation.

In avoiding musical activities, there is a lack of participation in any musical activities, be they institutional, communal, or social. One might shy away from, say, singing "Happy Birthday" when a group of friends or family members are doing so. There would be no extracurricular activity or community group participation in music. Regardless of the energy level or the form of the activity, one would try to escape from it. Again, musical learning is likely deferred to enculturation and acculturation.

Avoiding musical experiences is to avoid experiencing any musical events, whether they are familiar with them. Such musical events include a concert or karaoke evening. Those who avoid these experiences would lack musical experiences in any organized way, be they social or institutional. Avoidance in taking part in a musical event may be related to other non-musical priorities. Consistent avoidance in having contacts with musical motions, the music teacher-learner role, musical activities, and musical events are unlikely to acquire any musical or music educational outcomes. It leads to a musical adversity, which is a barrier to moving music forward. In an organismic world, musical adversity is connected to other aspects of life, which are likely to induce an adversary effect also, namely psychological and physical well-being. In other words, the state and effort of the person's affairs are intentionally mismatched with changes in the four complementary bipolar continua. If any musical actions are avoided, it should only be temporary so no one is void of musical experiences for too long. Momentary avoidance of musical actions may still lead to a long-term appreciation in music.[21] Extended avoidance may turn into a regret later in life.

Act in Passivity. Acting in passivity in music and music education depicts a compromise between non-musical priorities and the ubiquity of music. Actions are taken in recognition of the changes found in the continua only to get by without any immediate adversity, including the feeling of guilt, shame, inferior, underprivileged, degraded, dissatisfaction, dishonor, discomfort, disadvantaged, dysfunction, disenfranchised, being outcast, disappointing others, and so forth. Acting passively in response to changes in musical motions may occur in a situation where one is in an inescapable musical setting, such as a required music class, and at the same time music is not a priority. When the class is making music, one may play the right notes in the right timing but with no passion or interest. This is simply to get through the class without any negative consequences. In such conditions, music may be made intermittently or "as required."

As the roles of the teacher and the learner are exchangeable but distinctive, it is appropriate to present their passive actions separately. Acting passively as a music teacher would characterize those who teach reluctantly. One may not find a better alternative than to teach music since they might have decided on their career path years ago, possibly at a time without a full comprehension about the profession or when influenced by one or more peers or authority figures before an independent judgment was developed. In such situations, the music teacher is merely getting by without falling into an adversary condition. Even though such teachers may feel stuck in the teaching position, they still perform their responsibilities adequately. The downside of this type of action is that the teacher is not realizing his or her full potential as a music teacher. From curricular development and lesson planning to lesson implementation and assessment, to caring for music learners' futures, mediocrity may be commonplace.

As music learners, acting passively makes the learning not much beyond a time-filler, doing the minimum work without making new initiatives or connecting the music learning to life experiences. They mainly follow directions as needed. They may still learn something musically in a situation where they have to learn (e.g., in a required music class). Minimum efforts are made just to avoid adversity (e.g., disappointing a parent or a teacher). The potential of music learning is not fully explored. There is no enthusiasm in learning music.

Acting passively in musical activities naturally leads to participation at low energy levels, which goes more in line with low-energy activities. As in *yin* and *yang*, the lowness of energy is relative to the overall activity. Among all musical activities, listening while sitting is a low-energy level activity, compared to, say, wearing a drum on a strap while drumming and moving with large body movements. The latter is a much higher-energy level musical activity. At the same time, listening to music while sitting can involve low energy or high energy;[22] one may engage the music minimally by paying little attention to the sound (i.e., low energy), while another may engage the music fully by analyzing the melodic contour, harmonic structure, rhythmic patterns, dynamic variations, timbre exchanges, thematic development, structural layers, musical form, historical and cultural relevance, and so forth (i.e., high energy). If one chooses to act passively, a lower-energy option would be more favorable.

Similar to how passivity favors low energy musical activity, passive actions in musical experiences would favor familiar musical experiences over unfamiliar ones. Doing minimal work to avoid adversity is a foundation for the decision to act in passivity. Familiar musical experiences tend to require less cognitive effort than unfamiliar ones. There is less "new" information to receive and process. Familiarity may be found in any musical parameters (e.g., timbre, tonality, rhythmic structure, texture, style), context (e.g., rituals, events), format (e.g., presentational, participatory, small group, large group), or a combination of these. If there is unfamiliarity in the musical experience, more energy is required in receiving and processing the experience.

Consistent passive actions allow one to get by to avoid major adversity. Following the flow in musical motions with the least efforts, doing bare minimum work as music teachers or learners, and sticking to low-energy musical activities and familiar musical experiences would help individuals to get by with some music in their lives. Musical gains from passive actions prevent individuals from entering a musical destitution. It is certainly better than not having any music at all. To make musical lives prosper, however, one must act proactively.

Act in Proactivity. Acting proactively in music would release one from the limits of avoiding adversity. It promotes musical prosperity and represents the highest level of *meaningful* synchronization between change and human actions. Musical prosperity is a state where music is explored, created, recreated, grown, expanded, developed, spread, transmitted, taught, learned, and used in daily lives with much propensity. There is a sense of direction, meaning, and purpose in the music. In other words, *bian* and *tong* are aligned in perfect coordination in the world of music. Acting proactively in musical motions does not only make the right sound that fits, but it also has the extra zest to make the sound alive, with a sense of direction and moving forward, like the interactions between *yin* and *yang*. Even in quiet, slow, and steady musical moments, one would still feel the intensity and enthusiasm in the music. One would actively seek out opportunities to practice and to make the music happen. Whether the music is original or recreated, it is situated perfectly, be it in a microsystem, mesosystem, exosystem, or macrosystem, in Bronfenbrenner's terms, but they are not the limits. Music is a phenomenon that occurs across and beyond macrosystems; I call this a megasystem, which is a human endeavor that is transcultural, transnational, and therefore trans-systemic.

Acting proactively in the music teacher-learner role means that the teacher and learner are fully engaged in the teaching and learning. The role of the teacher is fully explored. All efforts are made to bring about the most effective teaching. The role of the learner is fully engaged. All efforts are made to ensure optimal learning. The teacher and the learner work together in a complementary condition so music and music education move forward and prosper.

Acting proactively in musical activities allows for a full range of musical experiences and development. One can participate in low- and high-energy musical activities freely and with great enthusiasm. The musical energy is so flexible in a controlled way that musical expressiveness is freed from any technical limitations. In group settings, activities are set to aim at well-rounded musical development, beyond activities catered for those who act in passivity. All facets of music are addressed, explored, learned, and developed. These facets include all types of musicianship, all aspects of music, and all musical parameters, traditions, and techniques. These are summarized in Table 6.1. While this is not an exclusive list, no one is expected to be fully developed in all of them. However, musical activities with all energy levels, low and high, should aim at developing all these facets. The outcome of such participation through an extended period would be a well-rounded musician who feels comfortable in engaging in a wide range of music activities, not limited to specific musical techniques, traditions, parameters, types of musicianship, or level of participation, nor would they feel uneasy discussing various aspects of music.

To be proactively involved in musical experiences, one would have a continuous curiosity in all types of musical experiences, regardless of one's level of familiarity with these experiences. There are always new elements, aspects, or perspectives in experiencing a familiar musical scenario, because every time the same music is made it creates a different experience. Furthermore,

Table 6.1. FACETS OF MUSIC

Facets of Music	Ingredients
Aspects of music	Philosophical, historical, contextual, acoustical, psychological, behavioral, cultural
Musicianship	Analogic, digital, aural, theoretical, analytical, notational, evaluative
Musical parameters	Pitch, melody, harmony, rhythm, timbre, loudness, texture, structure
Musical traditions	Cultural, social, geographical, national, religious
Musical techniques	Improvisation, performance, technology, keyboard, composition

there is always a new type of musical experience to explore, considering the rich and diverse musical traditions that humans have generated. For example, when one travels to a foreign location, that foreign musical experience may be preferred over a non-musical experience. Experiencing the foreign musical event may entail attending a musical performance, visiting a musical landmark, or shopping for a unique folk musical instrument or recordings of foreign artists. Even without the travel, one can still find excitement and curiosity in local and neighboring musical events. Exploration of musical experiences in local neighborhoods, migrant groups, and transient cultures should be commonplace. Although with limited depth, the Internet can expose one to a dramatically diverse range of musical traditions and practices. Through time, one would have accumulated a broad view of musical possibilities across all systems, each embedded with kaleidoscopic changes. Proactive actions in response to all aspects of change in music and music education contribute to a comprehensive understanding of music. This understanding is beyond the artful production and reproduction of musical sounds. It is an understanding of how music relates to humans, physically, psychologically, philosophically, contextually, and spiritually, making life more meaningful, enriching, and prosperous. A musical prosperity contributes to the overall quality of life for the individual and for the human race. Table 6.2 presents a summary of possible outcomes as humans respond to changes in the four complementary bipolar continua.

Disposition of Actions

Although the action alternatives above (i.e., avoidance, passivity, and proactivity) seem to be discrete, it is illusive to assume a straight path for anyone in response to changes in the music, the teacher-learner role, musical activities, and musical experiences. There are varying degrees of avoidance, passivity, and proactivity within each alternative. One would be expected to experience a path that goes back and forth across one or more types of actions and in and out in any of the action alternatives. The back-and-forth and in-and-out motions might be fast or slow and last for any length of time. They might be stable or dramatic throughout one's lifetime. While it is desirable to take proactive musical actions throughout one's lifetime, it is generally not practical.[23] At the same time, it is beneficial to experience more than one type of actions for short periods. Zhuangzi suggests throughout his *Theory of Equality* (*qiwulun* 齊物論) that holding one viewpoint firmly at all times would displace other perspectives, leading

Table 6.2. EXAMPLE OF OUTCOMES IN MUSICAL AND EDUCATIONAL SETTINGS AS HUMANS RESPOND TO CHANGES IN THE FOUR CONTINUA

Human Options	Changes in Complementary Bipolar Continua in Music Education			
	Active Musical Motions ☯ Passive Musical Motions	Teacher ☯ Learner	High-Energy Activities ☯ Low-Energy Activities	Familiar Musical Experiences ☯ Unfamiliar Musical Experiences
Ignore	Random chaos: Making wrong or inappropriate sounds	Random chaos: Role confusion	Random chaos: Disorganized activities	Random chaos: Inattentive and perplexed experiences
Act:				
Avoidance	Lack of music making	Lack of organized teaching or learning	Lack of participation in activities	Lack of organized musical experiences
Passivity	Making music intermittently, as conditions call upon it	Barely getting by and not realizing a full potential of teaching or learning	Some participation in activities; gravitate toward low-energy activities	Some musical experiences; gravitate toward familiar musical experiences
Proactivity	Making music properly and diligently, actively seeking out opportunities	Fully engaged teaching and learning, aiming at reaching a full potential of teaching or learning	Well-rounded musical development; engaged in all music parameters and open to all types of activities	Comprehensive understanding of, and continued curiosity in, all types of musical experiences

to a biased view. The experience of all types of actions makes the chosen action an educated choice. In addition to the flexibility needed to adapt to the changes, observations and experiences from other perspectives would allow for a comprehensive understanding of the phenomenon. Therefore, moving across different types of actions is not only expected, it is more robust if proactivity dominates over, but does not exclude, the others.

As music has an imprint on humans,[24] music has a disposition to bring prosperity in human lives. Without music, life would be incomplete.[25] However, humans have the option of changing this prosperous disposition, for better or for worse, from the point when they were born. If individuals are too young to make decisions regarding their musical actions, typically their parent, guardian, or caregiver does it for them.[26] Humans may act upon musical changes to make life *more* prosperous, to *maintain* an inherent level of prosperity, or to turn prosperity into an adversity.[27] Figure 6.2 presents a conceptual diagram that shows the point of human birth, when music is meant to contribute to a prosperous life, as a starting point. That is the same point when humans and their parent, guardian, or caregiver begin to have options in response to musical changes. An outcome of actions based on these decisions would place one on a musical prosperity-adversity continuum (i.e., between points "X" and "Y" in Figure 6.2) at a given moment in life. If one consistently takes proactive musical actions, then the level of prosperity would remain high, above the point of birth. In contrast, if one consistently avoids musical actions, then the level of prosperity would be marginal or even become an adversity. A middle section on the continuum represents outcomes of consistent passive musical actions. This middle section is on the prosperous side by a narrow margin but not going into the area of adversity. Where one falls on this prosperity-adversity continuum (i.e., on a point between "X" and "Y" in Figure 6.2) at a given moment depends on the type of musical action they are taking.

Musical Zones

Just as there are varying degrees of avoidance, passivity, and proactivity, their state of prosperity falls in a range, from great prosperity to great adversity. Based on these ranges, I call them the *zone of musical avoidance*, *zone of musical passivity*, and *zone of musical proactivity* (refer to Figure 6.2). Each zone refers to an intention to act with its prosperity-adversity outcome. The *zone of musical avoidance* represents an intention to deliberately avoid changes in the music, the music teacher-learner role, musical activities (especially the high-energy activities), and musical experiences

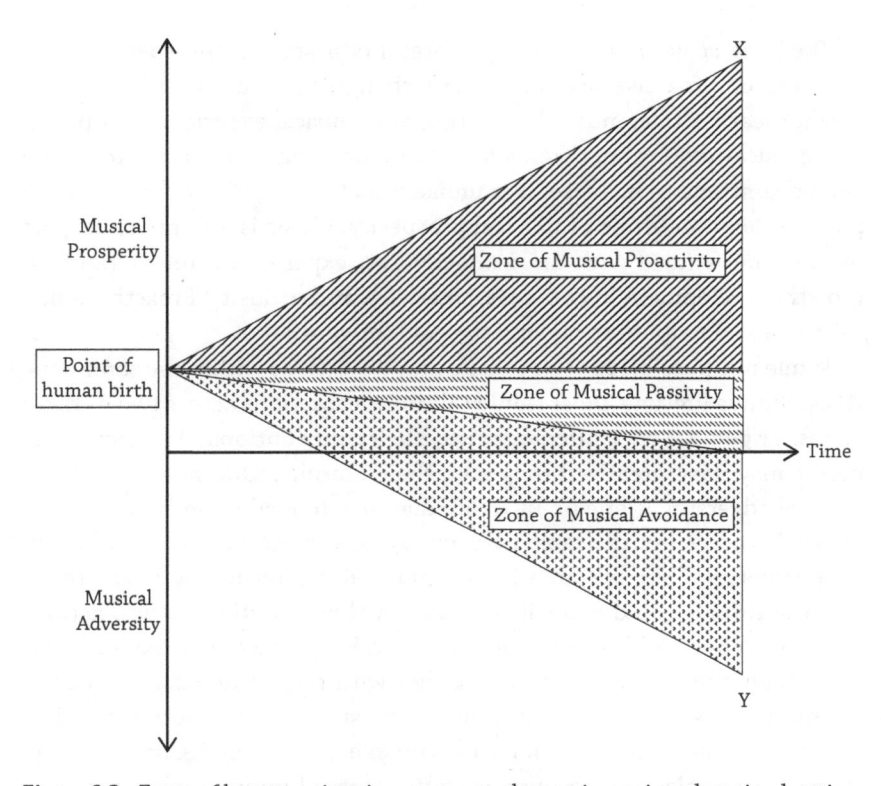

Figure 6.2: Zones of human actions in response to changes in music and music education.

(especially experiences in unfamiliar musical events). If one stays in this zone for a short time, it may not do any immediate harm, as it remains at a nominally prosperous state. If one stays in it for an extended period, however, the individual may start to experience a sort of adversity, which could be psychological (such as intellectual and emotional), physical, social, or even spiritual. Within this zone, adversity can be understood as an incomplete human with some essential elements missing. The longer one stays in this zone, more elements may be missing, which presents a trajectory of worsening adversity.

The *zone of musical passivity* represents a state of prosperity as an outcome of passive actions toward changes in the music, the music teacher-learner role, musical activities, and musical experiences. These actions are aimed at making minimal efforts just to avoid adversity. At the same time, no special effort is made to promote greater prosperity. It is likely that nominal prosperity is maintained at a level around or below the point at birth, but it is unlikely to enter an adversary zone, which is deliberately evaded.

The *zone of musical proactivity* represents a state of prosperity as an outcome of proactive actions toward changes in the music, the music teacher-learner role, musical activities, and musical experiences. If proactive musical actions are taken since the point of birth, musical prosperity should continue to increase. It is unlikely that one would go far below the point of birth in terms of musical prosperity. Music is an important part of life. Life is filled with musical activities, experiences, understanding, growth, development, techniques, creativity, and curiosity. Proactive musical actions contribute to moving the field forward.

While it is possible for one to take musical actions within the same zone throughout a lifetime, most would take musical actions across two or three zones. By going across different zones, their contributions to musical prosperity may vary greatly throughout their lifetime. One may experience musical adversity at one point in life due to extended periods of avoiding musical actions, but the same person may experience a high level of musical prosperity if she becomes proactive in taking musical actions later in life. The reverse could occur if one takes highly proactive musical actions early in life but avoids musical actions later. Everyone's life experience has some high points and low points, either within the same zone or across different zones. The transition from one musical zone to another could be attributed to many reasons, some explainable, others not.[28] Changes in life stages, social roles, socioeconomic status, state of mind, priorities, and so forth could explain some of the transitions across different zones. There is also a need to be aware of the unexplainable connections. Concepts of *shi* (勢) and synchronism help to explain these connections in change, leading to an amalgam of changing needs.

SHI (勢)

From an individual's perspective, change is both a given and a maneuverable. Humans are responsible for the maneuverable portion of the change. The given is typically perceived as uncontrollable by the involved individual, but it may be negotiable or symbiotic depending on what the given is.[29] The weather, for example, is a factor that affects human lives and that humans typically feel that they are not able to control as an individual. However, through the collective efforts of many humans and through an extended period, weather patterns may change.[30] Similarly, culture is typically not controllable by an individual, but an individual could negotiate with it symbiotically through an extended period to make a change.

This explains why human actions do not guarantee immediate specific outcomes in a field such as culture or music; actions are only an effort to move a phenomenon in a certain direction. The connected beings have to be involved. The outcome could be minuscule, gradual, substantial, or even unexpected. To promote prosperity and avoid adversity, some decisions, followed by corresponding actions and group efforts, are more likely to move toward a prosperous outcome than others. If there is no decision to take a musical action (as in *musical ignorance*), the result, be it prosperous or adversary, would be fortuitous or controlled by an entity other than the individual. When the given is on the adversarial side (e.g., bad weather or malicious culture), there is still an opportunity to take an action to move toward a prosperous direction. A requirement is that the given has to work together with the maneuverable in the right condition. To make the given and the maneuverable work together, *shi* (勢) plays a key role.

Shi can be understood as situation, condition, circumstances, tendency, state of affairs, and timing. It provides a context for a phenomenon to occur. It takes the psyche, the time, and the place into consideration. Laozi has made clear that everything must be set in the right *shi* (勢) for it to work. He states, "everything is generated by *dao* (道), governed by *de* (德 natural principles), formed by *wu* (物 materials), and complete by *shi* (勢)" (*Laozi* 51: 道生之，德畜之，物形之，勢成之。). Even with all the elements, methods, reasons, and materials, an event or an outcome will not be complete without the proper *shi* (勢). Zhuangzi provides a resounding agreement in that, if the *shi* is not right, there is no room to demonstrate one's ability (*Zhuangzi* 20.7: 處勢不便，未足以逞其能也。). The importance of *shi* (勢) is also reflected in Mencius' quote from the people of Qi (齊) during the Warring States period: "although there is wisdom, it is better to take advantage of *shi*; although there is hoe [a farming tool], it is better to depend on the right timing" (*Mencius* 3.1: 齊人有言曰：「雖有智慧，不如乘勢；雖有鎡基，不如待時。」). In 7 BC, Liu Xiang (劉向) (77–6 BC) wrote a short story describing Confucius' acknowledgment of the gifts of food and carriage he received, providing the right *shi* (勢) and in the right timing so his teaching can be spread. Without the conditions set forth by these gifts, his teaching would not have been so successful.[31]

These passages from Laozi, Zhuangzi, and Mencius and the short story about Confucius have demonstrated the significance of the conditions, situations, and timing (i.e., *shi*) for events to occur. Musical and music educational events are no different. The people and the materials need to be set in a right condition for an event to be musical and music educational. The idea of *shi* must be considered as one makes a decision to act, so the condition would be set properly for prosperity. *Shi* is the given, not something maneuverable by any one individual but that *could be* created collectively, in change. Imagine a music class, a music lesson, a music curriculum or program, a musical event, and so forth: all of them need a supportive *shi* to work toward prosperity.

The current *shi*

We now live in an era of possibilities. Social media and electronic networks grow swiftly alongside with deepening knowledge in various cultures and musical traditions, past and present. We position ourselves to become aware of all sorts of events, musical or non-musical and near or far. The *shi* (勢 situation) has become clear in that the possibilities are limitless. All known ways of music making and music teaching and learning can be applied somewhere. Anyone could possibly be making the music of the future.

SYNCHRONISM

The concepts of *shi* and synchronism are integral to an organismic way of thinking, as both rely on connections with external elements in any psychic state or event. In light of *shi* and synchronism, chance is not an option in explaining a phenomenon. It is a matter of the unthinkability and unpredictability of a cause. Synchronism refers to "the simultaneous occurrence of two [or more] events."[32] When events are synchronized, there are three key dimensions to consider: time, space, and causality. From a psychoanalytic point of view, these simultaneous occurrences may or may not be meaningful or causal. Humans, scientists in particular, are habitually interested in occurrences that are explainable by causality. For connections that do not have an explainable cause, they tend to escape human awareness and are considered as occurrences by chance. The specific concept of *synchronicity* helps to address these phenomena with unexplainable causes. Jung suggests that in those cases "a cause is not even thinkable in intellectual terms,"[33] which shares similar characteristics found in *Yijing* and classic Daoism.

Synchronicity

Synchronicity, a concept coined by the German psychologist Carl Gustav Jung (1875–1961), offers a more inclusive explanation that surpasses chance. It considers a psychic state and external events when they are acausal. Jung points to the *Yijing* and classic Daoism as the earliest references to the concept of synchronicity.[34] Jung describes synchronicity as "meaningful coincidence" and "an acausal connection."[35] It is "the simultaneous occurrence of a certain psychic state with one or more external events which appear as meaningful parallels to the momentary subjective state—and, in certain cases, vice versa."[36] In other words, synchronicity consists of a psychic state and events that are meaningfully, but not causally, connected. A psychic state is the basis of a maneuverable action (e.g., avoid, passive, or proactive). From an individual's standpoint, an external event is a key component of the given.[37] Synchronistic phenomena "prove that a content perceived by an observer can, at the same time, be represented by an outside event, without any causal connection."[38] In the current discussion, it is important to point out that Jung's definition of synchronicity contains two distinctive elements, the psychic state and the external event. Here is an example in a musical context: after a kindergartener hears a song at her school in the US, then she hears it again in a sports event with her family (i.e., two distinctively different events). Then later, she discovers that it is the national anthem as she learns about the social meaning of national anthems (i.e., a psychic state). These events and the psychic state are connected by simultaneity and meaning, but not cause. Such connections are significant for musicians and educators to recognize because they are not explainable by the direct cause-and-effect or teaching-and-learning mode of thinking. They provide an alternative to broaden our thinking and to gain deeper understanding.

CHANGING NEEDS

Considerations of *shi* and synchronism suggest that all elements with which musicians and music educators work are changing. Humans have a choice to take on a more acquiescent role (i.e., *hua* 化) in a complex network of changes or a more resistant role to defy these changes. Humans could also choose whether to allow change to go through sensibly (i.e., with *tong* 通). To couple these considerations with the given (e.g., various life stages and the environmental conditions), *shi* and synchronism position an individual for specific needs, be they musical or non-musical. Various needs arise as one goes through different life stages, transitions from one environment to another, or moves from one psychological state to another. In music, these changing needs to corroborate with variations in preferences for music listening, musical roles, musical activities, and musical events. The challenge of meeting these constantly changing needs is to develop skills in maintaining an optimal balance in every moment, which is discussed in the following chapter.

CHAPTER 7

Balance

Balance is a necessary sequel to change. Change without a corresponding search for balance creates a state of disequilibrium, which commonly causes discomfort or, worse, adversity. There is always a driving force behind the change, as explained by the Daoist *dao* (a natural or heavenly phenomenon; see Chapter 4). A privilege of being human is that the wisdom within us allows for many options in response to changes of all sorts and to influence some of the changes.[1] The Confucian *dao*, built upon desirable natures of being humans (see Chapter 3), provides sagacious guidelines for human actions. As humans respond to and influence the changes, ideologies from classic Confucianism and classic Daoism should be considered together so that the roles of humans and nature are integrated in conceiving of a way of music education.

This chapter continues as the second part of the *change-balance-liberation* trilogy in an organismic worldview, which can be considered within the world of music and music education or in broader human experiences. The balance discussed in this chapter mainly concerns the former, but it is subsumed under the latter; music and music education is part of the broader human experience. It follows that achieving a state of balance in music and music education must be connected to the state of balance in the broader life experience. I begin with a relative perspective on balance, followed by the key concept of *he* (和 harmony) and a call for flexibility in maintaining a balanced way of music education. The chapter concludes with the importance for music educators to pursue a balance and their obligation to guide others to search for that balance.

A RELATIVE PERSPECTIVE ON BALANCE

Balance may suggest a state of stability, but in the current discussion it is quite the contrary. Balance exists in the context of change. As change is a constant, the state of balance must ensue its course. In other words, humans are in a state of imbalance most of the time, which drives a pursuit for balance. In search of a state of balance, there is a constant exchange of energies, be they musical, social, psychological, physical, or in combination. The energies might be internal (i.e., within the individual such as actions and motivations) or external (e.g., from an authority figure, a parent, or a community group). The energy flows from one side to another, back and forth, sometimes to an extreme, but most of the times not so, just like *yin* and *yang*: there is *yin* inside *yang* and vice versa. It is natural for humans to explore ways of achieving balance in these energy exchanges. A state of balance can vary depending on individual circumstances—the musical motions, the teacher-learner role, the activity energy level, and the level of familiarity with the musical experience—all can affect the way to achieve it. The state of balance, if realized, is not only a natural desire, but it is also a driving force for change, as though one is walking on a moving carpet,[2] where the carpet is the ever-changing situation. A state of balance does not suggest motionlessness. Rather, one becomes more skillful in *making the next move* (i.e., change) to achieve another moment of balance. Maintaining such type of balance in motion is a basis for music educators' decision-making and actions. A series of moments of balance is desirable more often than not.

Balance is not an absolute. There is no one way of balancing for more than one person. Even within the same person, the demand for balance changes through time. Therefore, balance is relative to the moment for a specific individual. The same music or musical activity can present different perspectives to individuals. For example, two young adults are sitting next to each other in the audience in a concert hall at a performance of a Mozart's symphony. One could be in a *zone of musical proactivity* by being cognitively involved, having a desire to find out more, involving all of her senses, looking at the musicians attentively and being aware of the activities and surroundings, finding joy and great interest in the musical event. On the contrary, the other person could be in a *zone of musical passivity* by trying to get through the concert without being disruptive, not paying attention to the music or the environment, having no desire to find out more, and wishing the concert would be over quickly. At the same time she is neither creating any chaos nor disrupting others. In the former case, the individual might have chosen to be there from among many activities; the latter might have no choice but to be there to accompany someone important such as a loved one or to fulfill an academic or a social obligation.

These two individuals clearly have different needs, and balance could mean something very different. The music, the activity, the role, and the event are fulfilling the needs of the former and they propel for more. In the latter case, the music, the activity, the role, and the event are not fulfilling the needs of the person within the concert and so there is no desire for further experience. Within the concert, there is a musical imbalance: simply put, musical energies are not being received. Instead, a state of balance is sought in her broader life experience, with the concert being a part of it. While musical energies are not received, she might have received plentiful social and psychological energies surrounding the concert. This example shows that balance is not an absolute or stable concept and that it must be viewed within broader life contexts. Moving the scenario to a music classroom, students in class work in a similar way. One might find a state of balance within the music class, and another might find it in her broader life experience. Many students probably shift their balancing moments between the two at varying rates.

The relativity of balance suggests a demand for meticulous observation (*guan* 觀) and tremendous flexibility (*rou* 柔), so the *changing* situation (*shi* 勢) is noticed and utilized. In light of the diversities found in the contemporary world, all musics, learners, and pedagogical approaches must be considered equally from their own perspectives (*qiwu* 齊物). Music educators should take actions without their egoistic intentions but go along with the learners' natural inclinations (*wuwei* 無為) in developing their full potentials,[3] in performance, composition, improvisation, analysis, criticism, and other musical or non-musical abilities. Conscientious music educators must practice with sincerity (*cheng* 誠), kindness (*shan* 善), and benevolence (*ren* 仁), so that they can serve as exemplary models (*junzi* 君子) in the community. Genuine music learners must possess the same qualities as music is learned. The type of balance achieved through these means would make good humanistic sense in the changing world (*bian tong* 變通), so that humanity gets to move forward with prosperity. Classic Confucianism and classic Daoism offer the key concept of *he* (和 harmony) to substantiate this practice.

HE (和 HARMONY)

The occurrence of *he* (和 harmony) requires an interaction of two or more different elements. Classic Daoism suggests that the interaction of *yin* and *yang* produces *he*, where *yin* and *yang* are opposites yet interactive and complementary (see Chapter 4). Texts from *Yijing* suggest that *he* is a desirable outcome that involves the interaction between two sincere beings. This notion is beautifully depicted in a crane metaphor. "A crane is calling under the shade, his young crane son harmonizes in response" (*Jiuer, Zhongfu, Yijing* 《易經》《中孚》《九二》:鳴鶴在陰,其子和之,....。). It uses a call-and-response between a parent crane and his son as a metaphor for harmony. Although the literal meaning is simple and brief, its philosophical meaning is thick and deep. The crane initiating the call is clearly on the *yang* side of the *yin-yang* dyad, not only because the crane belongs to the *yang* family of animals,[4] but, more important, because it is the one emitting the energy: making the call. He is calling from the shade,[5] meaning that he is positioned in a *yin* environment. The crane being *yang* is situated in *yin*. Making the call is an act of *yang*, which is received by the young crane, who is positioned as *yin* in relation to the parent (*yang*). The young crane on the receiving end is also positioned as *yin*. Responding in harmony is an act of *yang*, as energy is released in the response.

A web of *yin* and *yang* relationships is thus tightly knit within and among the cranes, their environment, their actions, and their roles. All work together in achieving a moment of balance. The actions of the call and the response in harmony are done in the sonic world. The psyche behind this metaphor is that, when the adult crane is calling in the shade, only the sound of the call is heard and there is no other clue about who is calling. There is so much trust in the adult crane that the call is going to be heard by the young crane. When the young crane hears the call without seeing who is calling, he has so much trust in the sound of the call and he responds with a harmonizing reply. If the call were not from his parent, he could risk revealing himself to a predator. The ability to discriminate various sounds and calls is critical. This act of call-and-response shows a strong sense of mutual trust between the two cranes as they share the calling sound and communicate in harmony. The call and the response are the outgrowth of sincerity and trust,[6] which are fundamental to harmonizing acts. This is supported by the corresponding passage in *Yizhuan*: "His young crane son harmonizes in response based on sincerity. It is his wish to respond in harmony" (*Xiangzhuan, Yizhuan* 《易傳》《象傳》;其子和之,中心願也。).[7] Another important point shown in this metaphor is that *he* is not a noun but a verb. *He* is an act of *harmonizing*, not a product as in harmony. The young crane does not make just any sound to harmonize, but he has to make a judgment and adjust his responding call so it harmonizes with the initial call. It shows that an untainted relationship, parent and son, is built upon trust and sincerity.

Observing a natural phenomenon and extending its principle to a human setting is rather sagacious in classic Chinese texts. Immediately following the crane metaphor is an elaboration of how the harmonizing experience could be revealed in humans. "I have fine wine, and I share it with you" (*Jiuer, Zhongfu, Yijing* 《易經》《中孚》《九二》;... 我有好爵，吾與爾靡之。). Instead of sharing the calling sound of the cranes, humans share fine wine. The sharing is an outcome of sincere communication and trust between the individuals. This passage reflects that sincerity and trust are essential precursors for harmonizing acts to occur.

Yijing also suggests that *he* is a reason for happiness and propitiousness (*Chujiu, Dui, Yijing* 《易經》《兌》《初九》; 和兌，吉。). Its corresponding *Yizhuan* passage explains that *he* is due to unquestionable actions (*Xiangzhuan, Yizhuan* 《易傳》《象傳》; 和兌之吉，行未疑也。). Again, due to sincerity and trust, there is nothing to hide. All harmonizing actions are without doubts.

Classic Confucianism emphasizes human relationships in *he*. A precondition of *he* is *zhong* (中 middle). As shown in the classic Confucian text *Zhongyong* 《中庸》,[8] before emotions are expressed, they are positioned in the middle; when they are expressed appropriately, it is *he* (*Zhongyong* 1: 喜怒哀樂之未發，謂之中；發而皆中節，謂之和。). The idea of *zhong* here refers to a psychological space between the person expressing and the person receiving the expression. For the two persons to have a harmonious relationship, the way the expression is released must be done appropriately. It follows that everyone has a state of *zhong*, which is a basis for being humans, and that *he* is a proper way for people to act (*Zhongyong* 1; 中也者，天下之大本也；和也者，天下之達道也。). The key is that everyone should use this state and action, so that a harmonious community can be established. The challenge is that not everyone can achieve and sustain this *zhong* and *he*. If this can be achieved, then everything will be in place for prosperity (*Zhongyong* 1: 致中和，天地位焉，萬物育焉。). This idea suggests that a consistent use of *zhong* and *he* would help to sustain a continuous balance in human relationships.

Classic Daoism uses *he* not only as a way to achieving balance, but it is also a means to eternity. Laozi makes it clear: "understanding *he* is critical to endlessness" (*Laozi* 55: 知和曰常); and endlessness is a form of prosperity. Put another way, something is going to cease if there is no *he*. In terms of energy transfer between *yin* and *yang*, a certain amount of energy is lost without a perpetual motion. As *he* is an outcome of perfect interactions of various elements found in nature, embedded in *yin* and *yang*, *he* should be a way of life if harmoniousness and longevity are desired qualities of life. From a classic Daoist musical perspective, sounds from nature create the greatest harmony.⁹ This is why classic Daoists view that the greatest music contains only a few sounds.¹⁰

Zhuangzi points to the importance of understanding the operation of the natural world, so that one can live in harmony with nature. With this understanding, one can *adjust* with the natural world and live in harmony with other humans (*Zhuangzi* 13.1: 夫明白於天地之德者，此之謂大本大宗，與天和者也；所以均調天下，與人和者也。). While constant change in the natural world is a given, the *adjustment* (*juntiao* 均調) suggests that a change in the human is required to live in harmony with other humans. The idea of adjustment in the midst of different or opposing elements to achieve harmony has been documented in other classic texts also. Metaphors in culinary art and *yue* (music) provide most helpful insights in the act of *he* (和 harmony).

Culinary art. More than a millennium prior to Confucius and Laozi, Yin Yi (伊尹, ca. 1649–1549 BC) explains that the matter of adjusting for harmony (*tiao he zhi shi* 調和之事) is based on the five characteristic tastes of sweet (*gan* 甘), sour (*suan* 酸), bitter (*ku* 苦), spicy (*xin* 辛), and salty (*xian* 鹹). The timing and quantity of adjusting these flavors when cooking are subtle, but there is always a cause and effect.¹¹ Each of the five flavors is distinctively different from the other four, yet they can be mixed and adjusted to different amounts with various ingredients in good timing, producing an indefinite number of delicious foods that harmonize with the human sense of taste.

A contemporary of Confucius, Yanzi (晏子, 578–500 BC),¹² draws the metaphor from culinary art more explicitly. He states that harmony is like making a thick soup¹³ (*he ru geng yan* 和如羹焉), cooking various ingredients in water using fire.¹⁴ The master cook would adjust the ingredients to harmonize their flavors by adding what is needed and reducing what is excessive. This metaphor shows clearly that harmony in culinary art requires different ingredients and that each ingredient needs to exert its function and strength in good timing and in the right amount and condition (e.g., temperature). The natural strengths of each ingredient must be used to bring forth a harmonized whole. Cooking is a balancing act using different, if not opposing, elements. Yanzi further states that it becomes meaningless if one uses the same ingredient to remedy itself. "Who could take the food when one uses water to remedy water?"¹⁵ (若以水濟水，誰能食之？). To achieve harmony, *different* elements are not only valued but are *necessary*.¹⁶ The different elements are used to enrich each other to make a harmonized organic whole. Merely seeking agreement, or conforming to the same ingredient, is not achieving harmony.

This metaphor in culinary art shows a direct parallel to Confucius' view in that *junzi* (君子) harmonizes with others but maintains the individual differences (*Analects* 13.23: 君子和而不同). He then makes an immediate contrast by stating that villains (*xiaoren* 小人) behave in the same way but without harmony (*Analects* 13.23: 小人同而不和). In other words, achieving harmony is not about conformity or agreement, let alone force. It has more to do with utilizing the differences to the advantage of creating a bigger and stronger entity, which could be a relationship, a family, a community, a nation, or a world.

Yue. Although *yue* (樂) is commonly translated as "music," its meaning in the classic Chinese context is broader than the contemporary understanding of the word, which entails the sound, concept, or behavior of organizing sounds and silences using instrumental, vocal, technological, or a combination of media. *Yue* as evident in classic Chinese texts, however, goes beyond this contemporary interpretation to include dance[17] and social activities.[18] Technically, sounds (*sheng* 聲) and tones (*yin* 音) are subsidiaries of *yue*.[19] In classic Confucian view, *yue* is an archetype of producing *he* (和 harmony).

Chenyang Li's considerations have helped explain this phenomenon through a classic Confucian lens. His first consideration is based on the nature of *yue*, which connects various elements, including dance and social activities, to form a whole. "The etymological meaning of *he* implies bringing things (different flavors or different sounds) together. Music (*yue*) brings people together; . . . As early as the eleventh to eighth centuries BCE, China already had no fewer than seventy kinds of musical instruments. . . . We can say that the overall orientation of music [*yue*] is to gather instruments and people together, not to drive them apart. Harmony [*he*], too, implies first of all bringing various things or people together."[20]

Li's second consideration takes a step further. *Yue* "integrates various elements into relations and makes them coordinate with one another. Etymological studies show that the original meanings of *he* are 'corresponsiveness (of sounds)' and 'mingling things.'"[21] Various elements found in *yue* "come together to form a unity."[22] He further explains that:

> The production of music requires partnership between various elements. Conceptually, "corresponsiveness" implies a sense of partnership, a sense of equality, even though the parties involved are not necessarily equal to the full extent. "Mingling" implies integration; through mingling, different parties are integrated into wholeness. Both partnership and wholeness are at the core of harmony. . . . The fundamental principle of music-making is to let each component take its appropriate place, rather than allowing the components to exclude or suppress one another. This is arguably also the central characteristic of harmony.[23]

He refers to a quote from the state music officer Zhou Jiu (州鳩), who served 544–520 BC in the Zhou Dynasty:[24] "Ultimate *yue* (樂極) occurs when musical instruments are used according to their natural characters. It is a collection of musical sounds (*sheng* 聲). Each musical sound maintains its own quality is *he*, and when no musical sound is overcoming another is balance" (*Zhouyu C, Guoyu* 《國語》《周語下》: 物得其常曰樂極，極之所集曰聲，聲應相保曰和，細大不逾曰平。).[25] This description further supports the importance of maintaining the original quality of the different sounds without overshadowing others—just like in culinary art, in that the different flavors of the ingredients are maintained as delicious food is produced with a harmonizing taste. The link between *he* and balance is also revealed in Zhou Jiu's words. Not only should there be no intention to overpower, for allowing various elements to reveal their natural qualities is to achieve *he* and balance simultaneously. It is no coincidence that combining the Chinese characters of harmony (*he* 和) and balance (*ping* 平) makes the expression *peace* (*heping* 和平). This comes in close parallel with Confucius' view in that the purpose of using *li* (禮) is to achieve *he* (和).[26]

Li's third consideration is also related to Zhou Jiu's point of view, in which "music is the sounds that people produce from interacting with their surroundings and mingling together in a patterned way, which symbolizes their social co-existence and cooperation."[27] Therefore, "governing is like *yue*. *Yue* is a matter of *he*, and *he* is a matter of balance [*ping* 平]"[28] (*Zhouyu C, Guoyu* 《國語》《周語下》: 夫政象樂，樂從和，和從平。). In Li's words, "Music has been understood to symbolize good governance and good society."[29] Zhou Jiu's idea is closely aligned with that of Confucius, as he lived within the same timeframe as Confucius.

As music is an archetype of harmony in classic Confucianism, the making of music shares three more common foundations with the pursuit of harmony—sincerity,[30] kindness,[31] and beauty—which comprise three other of Li's considerations. Sincerity is an essential quality expected in *junzi* (an exemplary person; see Chapter 3). From studying sincere expressions of sung poems in *Shijing* 《詩經》 to continuous self-reflection and cultivation, sincerity is an utmost source of refined behaviors that permeates ideologies of classic Confucianism. Sincerity is the origin of sung poems, songs, and dance ([詩，歌，舞] 三者本於心). When the expressive energies are deep and abundant, the phenomenon becomes mystical (情深而文明，氣盛而化神). *He* (和 harmony) is accumulated internally and radiance is shown externally (和順積中而英華發外). The only condition is that *yue*[32] cannot be spurious (唯樂不可以為偽).[33] The requirement of sincerity in *yue* parallels the expectations of practicing *li* (禮), which is likewise expected to be sincere and be rid of hypocrisy (著誠去偽).[34]

Kindness and beauty go hand in hand in classic Confucian thoughts for harmony. Confucius' comments on the best music he's ever heard, music of Shao (韶), reflect that it is the most beautiful and the kindest (*Analects* 3.25; 子謂《韶》,「盡美矣,又盡善也。」). As Fu Pei-Rong explains, the utmost kindness is an effect of virtue.[35] This comment is in contrast to Confucius' comments for the music of Wu (武), which is the most beautiful but not the kindest (*Analects* 3.25; 謂《武》,「盡美矣,未盡善也」。). These comments show that being beautiful alone is not sufficient for the highest distinction. For Confucius, the kindness in music is a reflection of kind governing through a long period that allows the citizens' prosperity to optimize, as Shun (舜) did for over fifty years for the music of Shao to stand out. In contrast, although Wu Wang's (武王) governing is virtuous, only six years of ruling is not long enough for its kindness to show in the music of its people. The kindness in ideal musical harmony is deeply ingrained in the state of the society and requires decades to achieve. Confucius further comments on the effect of hearing the music of Shao in that his sense of hearing the music overrides his other senses, numbing his taste.[36] On his remark for a well-known sung poem from *Shijing* 《詩經》 titled *Guanju* 《關雎》, he states that it is happiness but not indulgence and sorrow but not hurtful (*Analects* 3.20; 子曰:「《關雎》,樂而不淫,哀而不傷。」). The virtue and beauty found in *he* (和 harmony) involves a balance between various qualities. An extensive description of balanced qualities in great music is found in the historical document *Chunqiu Zuozhuan* 《春秋左傳》, where the prince from the State of Wu (吳) comments on a performance of sung poems from the *Song* (頌) section of *Shijing* 《詩經》 during his visit in the State of Lu (魯) in 544 BC. (Xianggong year 29, 襄公二十九年):

> This is the most beautiful [music]. Straightforward but not arrogant, euphemistic but not subservient, intimate but not offensive, distanced but not alienating, various but not unruly, recurrent but not boring, sorrow but not misery, cheerful but not indulgent, frugal but not stingy, rich but not extravagant, charitable but not wasteful, profitable but not greedy, restful but not stagnant, and progress but not profligate. The five sounds are harmonized, and the eight winds are coordinated. The measurements are regulated, and the order is managed. These are the common characteristics of great virtues.[37]

These descriptions further support the connection among kindness, beauty, and *he* (和 harmony). A classic Chinese interpretation of *he* is much deeper than the common understanding of harmony, which usually infers notions of compromise, agreement, or conformity. To borrow Li's concept, it is "deep" harmony,[38] which extends to the broader experience of sincerity, kindness, and beauty. It suggests a creative tension of different or opposing elements that are mutually supportive, enhancing, and beneficial. It is multifaceted, dynamic, and self-renewing rather than linear, sequential, or static.

DYNAMIC FLEXIBILITY FOR CONTINUOUS BALANCE

The previous section shows that *he* (和 harmony) is key to achieving balance, admitting a creative tension among different elements yet producing a bigger benefit as a whole. The multidimensional and dynamic nature of *he* calls for a high degree of flexibility (柔 *rou*) in constant motion. Imagine a physical activity that requires balance to move forward, such as cycling or skateboarding. It can be a challenge to maintain a balance by adjusting one's body posture while moving. The external elements, such as the strength and the direction of the wind or the hardness and the slope of the road, are constantly changing and form a series of situations (*shi* 勢). One has to be skillful in *adjusting* the body posture and movement to maintain a *continuous* balance. It is this type of dynamic flexibility that music educators should develop in dealing with changing situations. Simultaneous manipulations of back-and-forth, up-and-down, left-and-right, and in-and-out motions and interchanges may be necessary to adapt to the multidimensional and changing situation. Just like *yin* and *yang*, they set themselves up for a perpetual motion in moving forward by constant exchanges and adjustments of energies. I use the four complementary bipolar continua (Chapter 5) and the three musical zones (Chapter 6) as two frameworks to illustrate a dynamic flexibility that could help working toward a continuous balance.

Balancing across Four Complementary Bipolar Continua

The multidimensional nature of *he* (和 harmony) suggests that different dynamic flexibilities are expected at various levels in relation to the complementary bipolar continua. Each continuum and its sub-continua call for different types of skills to maintain a continuous balance with the presence of various external elements. The first continuum, on active musical motions and passive musical motions, concerns the music. The musical motions occur in parameters such as dynamics, rhythm, tempo, pitch, melody, harmony, and timbre. It may seem that composers would manipulate these parameters the most. Naturally, composers should have the facilities to use them flexibly in achieving a dynamic and continuous state of balance within a musical piece. Musical energies go back and forth between the active and passive across these parameters in concept. A composer's collection of works throughout her career is an indication of a balancing act within her life. Each composer maintains a balance that draws from a mixture of large-, medium-, and small-scale works in conjunction with a metamorphosis of compositional styles through a flexible manipulation of various musical parameters. The way of achieving balance varies from one composer to another, depending on the larger context of the composer's life. As long as there is sufficient flexibility in the composer, dynamic manipulations are exercised to fulfill the composer's desire for continuous balance.

In the Western classical tradition, performers are the ones who realize the composer's concept in pursuit of a continuous state of balance. They select from an array of works by a wide range of composers throughout history so that a performer's career is fulfilled in a balanced way. In other words, their performance skills need to be so flexible that they are able to perform a wide range of musical works. The listeners too need to possess an enormous range of listening skills so that they are able to select and listen to a wide variety of composers and their works performed by a range of performers. Not only do they need to be able to distinguish the active and passive motions in each musical parameter, but they should also be able to select the music that could bring a state of balance in that moment and throughout their lives. Just as performers need to use their flexible performance skills for different composers and different styles, listeners need to develop their dynamic and flexible listening skills so they are able to listen with a versatility that is not limited to any narrow range of musical parameters and styles. This obviously should extend beyond the Western classical tradition.

Likewise, music educators should possess facilities to distinguish the active and passive nature of various musical parameters and be able to use music adequately to help learners to achieve a state of balance within the music session and in their broader lives. Since music educators' actions directly involve learners, they are obliged to use meticulous observations (guan 觀), as described in classic Daoist texts (see Chapter 4). In other words, the musical motions should be observed not only from the teacher's perspective but also from the learner's perspective and the indigenous musicians' perspective. Whether one is composing, performing, listening, teaching, or learning music, the music should be sincere expressions through kind intentions in accordance with human nature that would bring forth harmonious relationships, between humans and nature, among humans, or both.

The second continuum on teacher and learner concerns the role of the person involved. The role determination is dependent upon the setting and the level of expertise in the concerned subject matter. A sub-continuum shows the expert-novice dyad. No one can stay as a teacher or an expert in all circumstances, and no one has to remain as a learner or novice throughout one's life. Flexibility in this continuum means that one should be ready to take up the other role as conditions change. There is a learner in the teacher, and vice versa; likewise, there is a novice in an expert, and vice versa. One should not be fixated on one role. Since the learner and the novice are on the receiving end (*yin*), they should be open to revealing the *yang* element (teacher and expert) within themselves. An opportunity and some guidance may be necessary, so a switching of roles may be facilitated.

The third continuum, on high-energy activities and low-energy activities, is about the energies involved in musical activities. Since music education concerns mainly the activities of the teacher and of the learner, there is one sub-continuum directed to each of their activities. This set of continua suggests that a continuous balance can be achieved by variations in the energy levels between the teacher and the learner. Both parties, the teacher and the learner, hold dynamic exchanges of energies in maintaining a continuous state of balance. To accomplish this, teacher and learner must be flexible and ready to be in high energy or low energy depending on the situation—much like athlete runners who can be ready to run at their top speeds but don't have to run at top speed at all times. They need to rest in preparation for their top performance. Furthermore, when they stroll through shops on the streets, they can put their feet at ease, but still they could run fast if necessary. In both circumstances (top speed and easy stroll), they should be free, flexible, ready, and under control while maintaining a continuous balance as life context changes.

The fourth continuum, familiar musical experience and unfamiliar musical experience, is about the psychological proximity of the musical event involved. The musical event could be exposed, taught, practiced, familiar (structurally or stylistically), local, or traditional versus those that are unexposed, untaught, unpracticed, unfamiliar, foreign, or contemporary. Like the other three continua, this continuum and its sub-continua call for a high degree of dynamic flexibility, so experiences in musical events are not monotonous but filled with interest and variety, with energy exchanges going back and forth. Life with varied musical events perpetuates itself and moves forward in a state of continuous balance, just as how *yin* and *yang* interact and set off forward motions. It implies a need for an open attitude toward musical events that are unexposed, untaught, unpracticed, unfamiliar, foreign, and contemporary.

The music, the personal role, the activity, and the familiarity of the musical event create a broad set of potentials for continuous balance. In every setting, variations in each of the continua have a unique moment that is being synchronized. For example, in kindergarten, a child may be involved in more active dynamic and rhythmic motions on the learner and novice side, in a high-energy learner activity in a mixture of familiar and unfamiliar musical events, or performing a song from a foreign tradition in their own music classroom. This could be a way of achieving a state of continuous balance for this kindergartener. Contrasting this with a retired adult music learner who learns the chord progressions on the guitar (active harmonic motions) as a novice, but has to strum the chords softly and gently (low energy learner activity) on a song that she has been singing and hearing for decades (familiar musical style), there is a completely different set of dynamic interplays in achieving a continuous state of balance. When a music educator takes on the role as music teacher, she is expected to be able to utilize the full range of dynamic exchanges in all of the continua depending on the situation, so that learners can participate and find a state of continuous balance throughout their lives. The teacher should be so flexible that she is ready to go full speed or to stroll at ease, but still under control in all cases.

The act of maintaining a continuous balance is not limited to the four complementary bipolar continua. As pointed out in earlier chapters, music is not an isolated entity or activity. It is important to consider music and music education as part of the organismic world. A state of balance across the four continua is not sufficient, nor a guarantee, for a balanced state. Nevertheless, the maintenance of a continuous balance across the four continua should play a major role for those lives dominated by music and music education.

Balancing across Three Musical Zones

Another way to look at a continuous balance throughout one's life is through an examination of the musical zones postulated in Chapter 6. Acting musically in recognition of changes puts an individual in one of three musical zones at any given time throughout the entire lifespan: zone of musical proactivity, zone of musical passivity, and zone of musical avoidance (Figure 6.2). For those who find a desired state of balance in a life dedicated to music and music education, the zone of musical proactivity is deemed most appropriate throughout most, if not all, of their lives. In this zone, music prospers not only in their life but also as a field. Music and music education get to move forward due to the actions they take. Domination of musical proactivity is likely found in individuals who dedicate to musical pursuits, such as resources, studies, careers, investments, passions, and leisure. There is active energy exchange in the four continua throughout much of their lives. Forward motion is an outcome, as *yin* and *yang* perpetuates endless forward motions.

In the zone of musical passivity, there is little, if any, forward motion. Musical actions are taken just enough to get by without getting into an adversary condition. These actions could sustain survival with minimal music participations, but there is no blossoming of musical growth or heightening of musical potentials that contribute to quality of life. Music and music education are recognized but not among their top priorities in life. Some may feel that they fall into this zone with no choice, because of physical limitations or an inability to find a way to lead a musical life. Others are taking on other priorities or unable to see the importance of music in life.

The zone of musical avoidance is the least desirable in terms of musical prosperity. Prolonged actions in this zone would eventually lead to random chaos. Given the known contributions of music learning in human development, avoiding music is a call for an inhumane and incomplete education, like not allowing a bird to learn to fly or a child to learn to walk. Excluding music participation throughout one's life is a manifestation of an incomplete life or a life underdeveloped.[39] This is particularly evident from a senior citizen's perspective, in which music participation may not occur until after they retire from their careers. They are so glad to have *discovered* music.[40]

Given the characterization of the three musical zones, everyone should be able to find a state of balance in one of them at any given moment. Ideally, all individuals should stay in the zone of musical proactivity for as long as they can. The more they stay in that zone, the more likely that they are active music participants, enthusiasts, and supporters, who contribute to a forward motion in music and music education. Even when life circumstances change, one can still remain in that zone but through a different means by exercising a dynamic flexibility, just like adjusting the body in a different way when cycling through different road conditions and weather elements. This can be demonstrated by an example lifespan: In her earliest years, a girl starts by singing or playing musical toys. Later, in school, she learns the guitar by herself and the clarinet from an instructor. In her teenage years and through university studies, she actively participates in a choir and in an instrumental group. After she is married and works in a law firm, she frequently attends a variety of concerts with great enthusiasm. After giving birth to her twin children, she sings to her children and teaches them songs and musical games. She brings her children to a variety of concerts as her children grow, supports her children's music endeavors, and at the same time continues to enjoy participating in a community musical group. After enjoying a career in the law firm, she retires and learns the mandolin on her own. She participates in a bluegrass band, in which she plays the guitar and the mandolin, in a retirement community. Toward the end of her life, she dedicates a substantial portion of her estate to support musical endeavors for those in need. At every stage of her life, she is able to maintain a balance among all aspects of her activities, with music being an important contributor to her quality of life. By and large, she stays in the zone of musical proactivity throughout. There may be moments when she has to move to the zone of musical passivity, for example, during the time when her children are still young and demand constant care. That is the time when she might have to shift part of her *musical* energy to take care of her family to maintain an overall balance in her life. Nevertheless, she never goes into the zone of musical avoidance. Whenever she can, she sings to her children, which gives her windows of opportunity to be in the zone of musical proactivity.

This example demonstrates that (a) dynamic flexibility is required for different situations to remain in the zone of musical proactivity and for *falling back* and *moving up* across different zones; and that (b) continuous balance throughout a lifespan requires a consideration in aspects of life outside of music. Everyone has a rite of passage involving maturation, family, survival, career, and health conditions. While music may contribute to every life stage, keeping music there despite changing conditions requires a high degree of flexibility.

When living one's entire lifespan in the zone of musical proactivity is not practical, *falling back* to one of the other two zones as a break from musical proactivity may be needed. For example, when a professional singer is hospitalized, moving to the zone of musical passivity may be necessary. Perhaps even falling back to the zone of musical avoidance may be needed temporarily. In another scenario, when a pianist joins the military, in which she has to move from one station to another for a few years at a time, she is not able to find a piano in every station. She may have to fall back to the zone of musical passivity by listening to recorded music rather than making live music or attending a live performance. This act of falling back to the zone of musical passivity is to ensure that her musical live is maintained, that is, not entering an adversary zone. There could be advantages in this musical passivity, which is the opportunity to listen to recordings or live performances that she would not have otherwise, such as exposure to musical genres available at the locale where she is stationed;

and this passivity could turn into another round of proactivity if she develops a curiosity to learn more about a "new" type of music. These examples of *falling* from the zone of musical proactivity to the zone of musical passivity or musical avoidance demands flexibility so that her overall life is in continuous balance. At the same time, she is ready to return to the zone of musical proactivity at any time when circumstances (i.e., *shi* 勢) allow.

By the same token, those who are placed in the zone of musical avoidance or the zone of musical passivity early in their lives[41] should acquire a type of dynamic flexibility, with an open attitude, so they can *move up* to the zone of musical proactivity. This way, music becomes part of the equation for a complete and balanced life. The ability to *fall back* and *move up* across different musical zones requires skills to maintain continuous moments of balance regardless of changing situations. In other words, the ability to observe the changing situation and respond with a dynamic flexibility is critical in bringing a continuous balance in life.

Everyone has a unique path in going through the zones across the lifespan. One may stay in one of the zones for an extended period, while another may move across the zones from one life stage to another. From birth through the formative years, the path may be heavily influenced by the family, the immediate culture, caregivers' beliefs, and educators' actions. In the teenage years and into adulthood, there is an increasing likelihood of making independent decisions on the placement of music in their lives, that is, deciding on a musical zone that offers the best balance in their lives and willfully putting themselves in that zone. Music educators can play a key role here in providing a framework and guidance as these decisions are made during this critical period. Ideally, everyone should stay in the zone of musical proactivity for as long as they can. Regardless of their career choice, they can always be actively participating in music, as music makers, participants, enthusiasts, supporters, and consumers. Preferably, everyone should aim at living a life in the zone of musical proactivity and should never enter the zone of musical avoidance, except in a microscopic sense when one is sleeping, in certain sickness, or preoccupied by other survival needs. In fact, music *is* one of the survival needs.[42] The zone of musical passivity may be appropriate temporarily in various life situations to bring forth a broader balance as they get ready to (re)enter the zone of musical proactivity.

PURSUING A BALANCE

The balance discussed in this chapter is a continuous balance that needs dynamic flexibility in actions as situations change. It is a series of balancing moments, which is extended to include balanced stages in life. The balancing moments are reflected microscopically and can be described as a psychological *state*. The balanced stages in life address longer-term characteristics that can be described as a psychological *trait*. The continuous balance can be musically focused, as reflected in the four complementary bipolar continua and the three musical zones, or it can be broadly defined to include all aspects of life with music being part of it.

It is inevitable that balance must occur in the context of change. To achieve balance, one must be able to observe the constant changing situations and adjust one's actions. The adjustment assumes flexible skills and an open attitude. In music, one should develop keen observations and an understanding of all musical elements and how they are connected to life. This translates into growth and understanding in the nature of music. One should also develop a wide range of musical skills in order to *adjust* one's actions. These skills may involve listening, singing, playing an instrument, and improvising among others. In broader life, one should develop keen observations, understanding, and values in the basic nature of the human spirit, such as sincerity, kindness, benevolence, and continuous cultivation. Musical involvements should always be a reflection of who the person is. One should also develop a wide range of strategies to participate in music to find different ways of participating in music regardless of varying life stages or changing life circumstances. With the skills and strategies in place, one is prepared to be flexible so a continuous balance may be maintained throughout the lifespan. As one's age advances, wisdom may accumulate so a continuous balance is achieved more effectively: becoming more skillful to perform balancing acts while the situation continues to change. This is evident in some senior citizens who are able to maintain a busy but well-balanced schedule so their days are filled with various activities of their choice, including music, and rest.[43]

MUSIC EDUCATORS' OBLIGATION

Music educators are humans with a specific role. While they search for a continuous balance for themselves, they have an added obligation to guide others to pursue the same. To fulfill this role, one is expected to have a high level of musical understanding and skills and a wide range of music participation strategies in order to be exemplary models. In addition, the music educator is obliged to provide a framework for those around her so they can be prepared with the knowledge and skills to be flexible and to be used throughout their lifespan. The music educator should pay close attention to the changing needs of the music learner and of the society, as flexible strategies are desirable. This would involve a wide range of pedagogical skills in various types of music. For example, notation reading for Western classical music, autonomous learning in small groups for popular music, improvisation for jazz, communal music making in *gamelan* music, and so forth; each musical genre has built in a different way of participation. Each person finds her own way to achieve a balance that fits her circumstance of the time. Music educators should guide everyone to search for that balance, be they learners, parents, administrators, community members, and so forth. A dynamic flexibility should be built in to the work of music educators so an open frame of mind for people around them can be used for a lifetime of exploration and adjustments for balance. A deep harmony can be achieved within and among themselves at different life stages and in different situations. Everyone is more likely to maintain a continuous balance regardless of the changing situations and life stages. At the same time, music, music education, and life in general prosper, and the world is likely to be more harmonious and peaceful.[44]

While maintaining a continuous balance is an important accomplishment of musical and life events, it is not an ultimate goal according to the classic Chinese philosophical schools. The following chapter focuses on a supreme ideal of having music in everyone's life—liberation.

CHAPTER 8

Liberation

Liberation connotes a sense of freedom from rule, boundary, limitation, control, or oppression. Most individuals are bounded by many rules and controls so that when one is liberated from a setting, rules of another setting are engaged immediately. For example, when a child is "liberated" from school rules, a set of family rules takes place immediately. When an adult travels from one nation to another for a vacation, she is liberated from the rules of her home country, but the rules of the destination country take over immediately. There is always a reality with a set of rules in any given experience. This type of liberation reflects characteristics governed by an inescapable social system.[1]

This chapter concerns a liberation at the spiritual (*jingshen* 精神) level, which ideally should be transcendental across time and space. Liberation refers to a state of mind characterized as pleasant and worry-free. It is only bounded by ways of nature. Humans are relieved of agonies caused by their determinations. As long as there is a desire or a designated goal for egoistic reasons, liberation is hindered. Liberation allows open potentials that are unknown and nonspecific, just as *dao* cannot be fully known or specific. The state of mind avails one to come into harmony with any circumstances with a great deal of flexibility. Humans are able to go with the flow between the greatness of the sky and the greatness of the earth, making the best use of what they have wherever they are. The space within which liberation works is metaphysical. It is free from any set of rules, except those guided by humanly *dao*, as suggested in classic Confucianism, and heavenly *dao*, as laid out in classic Daoism. The most refined and exquisite expression of this liberation is found in *Laozi* in relation to *dao* (*Laozi* 25; 道大，天大，

地大，人亦大。)²: *Dao* is great as it entails everything, the sky is great as it covers everything, the earth is great as it supports everything, and humans are great too as they can be all they can be. The same expression "great" (*da* 大) is used to describe *dao*, the sky, the earth, and humans. *Dao* is the greatest among the four entities as it embraces the sky and the earth. Humans live in between, and are dependent on, the sky and the earth, but Laozi promotes humans to the same greatness level as *dao*. The greatness in humans is set in relation to the *potentials* offered by *dao*, the sky, and the earth. In other words, humans are liberated and have the potential to be great (*da* 大) within the boundary of everything (i.e., *dao*, the sky, and the earth). Zhuangzi reinforces that between the sky and the earth, there is great beauty and no word is needed (*Zhuangzi* 22.3; 天地有大美而不言). What humans can do is unlimited, and there is great beauty in nature, all around us.³ The qualities of sincerity, kindness, and benevolence are embedded in the beauty of human nature.

Harmony acts as a medium evolved from *dao* (see Chapter 4, Figure 4.4) to maintain a continuous balance of all things. There is balance within the person, between the person and the society, and between the person and nature. Liberation is achieved by *extended practice* in balancing acts in a variety of changing situations, as described in Chapter 7. Much like riding on a unicycle after extended practice, one can do anything while riding on it.⁴ It would not be fair to expect extended practice in riding a unicycle to allow the individual to do anything off the unicycle. The unicycle is meant to be ridden, and one is supposed to be able to do various things while riding with extended practice. Similarly, a clarinetist can express anything after extended practice, as can a pianist, a singer, or any musician. Such examples suggest that liberation is bounded by the *dao* (道 the way)⁵ of the task at hand, and the broader *dao* has everything connected in the organismic world.⁶ Without extended practice in the balancing act, one could hardly experience liberation. From a developmental standpoint, to be good at balancing takes time, therefore liberation is not expected in early stages of life. It takes years if not decades to experience the type of liberation described here.⁷ Regardless of what is forthcoming, there is no fear of problems or new experiences. Due to the changing situation, problems and new experiences are expected. There is strong aspiration to a restraint-free mindset. There is such strong interest in forthcoming events, guided by *dao*, that the unknown experience becomes an impetus to move forward. It involves energy exchanges and back-and-forth motions while the human perceptions, abilities, and attitudes are expanding, perpetuating for more.

Although liberation is discussed on the grounds of classic Chinese wisdoms in this book, some contemporary writers outside China suggest some apparent similarities. Maxine Greene presents a dialectic of freedom in the context of the United States and advocates the arts as a medium to reach the possible and the imaginable.[8] I find Estelle Jorgensen's view on liberation closest to the classic Chinese views:

> Liberation is not something that can ultimately be done for another person or for purely hedonistic reasons. It is achieved through individual *reflection and action*, as one critically *evaluates the situation and acts with others to change it*. Unless one is in the *company of others*, one may not perceive a problem, think to *change a situation*, or feel sufficiently empowered by the affirmation of others to *work for change*. Achieving liberation requires *dialogue, exchange of differing perspectives*, and, through posing questions, expanding one's previously limited understanding; comprehending what can, should, and must *be changed*; and *acting to change it*. [emphases added][9]

In the opening of this quote, Jorgensen points to the fact that liberation is done in coexistence with others but not something that anyone can do for others. It relies on one's self-realization and self-cultivation through reflection, motivation, and action in relation to the changing situation, that is, when dynamic flexibility is developed. It is satisfaction in the inner self. That satisfaction has to occur in coexistence with others who hold different perspectives, bouncing ideas back and forth in dialogue, rooted in change and ends in change, and perpetuating forward motions. This description of liberation parallels the classic Chinese idea of *he* (和 harmony) that contributes to continuous balance. I now turn to an aspect of liberation that is associated with a nature of being humans: music.

MUSICAL LIBERATION

Putting liberation in musical contexts, one is so flexible in dealing with multiple musical roles, skills, genres, cultures, values, meanings, and experiences that barriers for any musical possibilities are dissolved. One could stretch to include any musical possibilities in life without the need to know what the possibilities might be forthcoming. *Dao*, humanly or heavenly, is the guiding principle for all that will come. Harmonious relations and continuous balancing actions are in place to absorb all sorts of changes, leading to prosperity musically and in the broader life.

Music is connected to various aspects of life as presented in the organismic worldview. Music is a key aspect of being human and is rightfully so connected to the broader human experience. Readers should be mindful of other aspects of life as discussions on music and music education continue. Like the other two parts of the trilogy (change and balance), liberation has different layers within and outside the field of music. There could be many ways to represent liberation in music. In this section, the same complementary bipolar continua and musical zones presented earlier in this text, along with an expansion of a prototype of musical experience from my earlier writing, are used to demonstrate three perspectives of musical liberation. While these three perspectives are not the only ways to present a view of musical liberation, they are used as frames of reference based on their alignment with the classic Chinese ideologies, their systematic nature, and their open-endedness. There is room to add more perspectives as new insights arise.

Complementary bipolar continua

At any given moment, an individual involved in music can be described in relation to the musical motions, the teacher-learner role, the energy level of the musical activity, and the familiarity with the musical experience. When someone is *liberated* in musical motions, she would be so flexible in perceiving, producing, or manipulating all sorts of dynamics, rhythms, tempi, pitches, melodies, harmonies, and timbres. These entail music of all traditions, tunings, structures, and concepts, from the Western Classical symphony to Peking opera, to Indonesian gamelan, to Ghanaian drumming, and to Turkish makam. Nothing would come as a surprise, because all variations across the sonic world are conceived as expected unknowns. The perception, production, and manipulation of all sorts in the sonic world are so flexible that the individual develops a high level of versatility in their hearing, vision, sense of touch, and motor skills. They are free to perceive, produce, and manipulate the full range of dynamics, rhythms, tempi, pitches, melodies, harmonies, and timbres with no preset rule, boundary, or limitation. Any way of producing, receiving, and connecting to music is possible, while at the same time she can maintain a continuous balance using a dynamic flexibility that she has developed within her musical experience and in her broader life experience. Despite the changing elements, she is able to maintain a continuous balance. Music from any tradition, in any tuning and any structure, using any concept is under the mastery of her perception, production, and manipulation. There is no constraint in her actions with the music in motion, whether she is composing, performing, or listening. She can learn and operate in any musical system, including the potential of creating a new system. The learning never stops.

She is enthusiastic about the experience, and she looks forward for more. She is *liberated* in musical motions.

When one is *liberated* from the teacher-learner role, the traditional boundary between teacher and learner remains as labels. What they do in reality becomes a mixture of teaching and learning, going back and forth freely. The exchange of energies between the two is constant. Individuals in any of the roles are teaching and learning. One is an expert on something, and the other is an expert on another; one is a novice about something, and the other is a novice about another. This day and age, it is not surprising to find younger learners with expertise in manipulating technological devices while many experienced teachers are novices. In such an incidence, the teacher needs to learn from the learner. In another example, when I taught undergraduate world musics earlier in my career, I had learned from a few Ojibwe native American students about their powwow songs and activities, of which I had no knowledge or experience at the time. These students took over as teachers in teaching the class about something that they had more expertise in than anyone in class.

In both examples, the teacher and the learner need to be flexible physically and psychologically to allow the switching of the roles. Given that no teacher can be an expert in everything, there is always room for teachers to learn. Aside from the traditional teaching roles as a teacher, a lecturer, a facilitator, a mentor, a director, a conductor, a role model, a planner, an evaluator, an adviser, a counselor, and so forth, teachers should always be learning by and among themselves and from the learners. On the learner side, aside from the traditional learning roles as a listener, an observer, a participant, a follower, an imitator, a mentee, an advisee, and so forth, they should take the responsibility to teach or demonstrate to their peers and the less experienced learners. They should also teach their teachers about themselves and their backgrounds. In this exchange of roles, everyone should be free to be an expert-teacher or a novice-learner, depending on the subject and the task at hand. When mutual communication and respect are established, there is sincerity, kindness, and benevolence. They simply work together toward a common goal of being better people, working toward being exemplary persons, *junzi*. Their roles are liberated; they are free to be a teacher or a learner as the situation and context change.

When one is *liberated* from the energy level of a musical activity, there is much flexibility in participating in a variety of musical activities regardless of the demand of energy for that activity. Some activities involve a high energy level in some aspect of their engagements (e.g., moving, dancing, singing, playing instruments, discussing, manipulating), whereas others involve less energy (e.g., sitting, listening). Even within an activity, there could be relatively high- and low-energy involvement, such as playing a loud and fast moving passage (high energy) versus playing a soft and slow moving passage (low energy) on the same musical instrument. If one is well versed in any level of energy involved in a musical activity, there is great flexibility on a range of musical activities, whether it is high- or low-energy involvement. The dynamic flexibility frees the individual from any limitation on the energy required of the activity. For example, a top-notch musician does not have to use all of her virtuosic skills (high energy involvement) every time she performs, but she has the flexibility to do so if circumstances demand such skills. In the contrary, a top-notch performer may sit in the audience quietly (low energy involvement) and be at the receiving end of the energy emitted by other performers. In other words, the energy level involvement is ready at any level and can be used flexibly depending on the situation. There is no pressure or worry about whether she has the appropriate energy ready. She can be ready at just about any time. One should note that by no means being in the audience has to be in a low-energy mode. There are situations in which the audience may be dancing, screaming, and moving, even analyzing the music (high energy, compared to not analyzing). In short, regardless of the individual's role, she can be liberated in her energy level involvement as being called for by the situation. There is no need to intentionally display all the available energy in such forms as skills, speeds, or magnitudes. She can be as energetic as anyone can be in one setting and be on the receiving end using as little energy as possible in a different situation.

When one is *liberated* from familiarity with the musical experience, there is already sufficient exposure to a wide range of musical experience with a well-developed dynamic flexibility in experiencing music that all unfamiliar musical experience would be pleasant and worry-free. One is free to enter any familiar or unfamiliar musical experience and find it meaningful and interesting. There is nothing about music that can make the experience a concern. Whether the musical experience is in a different format, comes from a different culture, requires a different musical role, or is of a different musical genre, there is a dynamic flexibility developed to find meaning, pleasure, and excitement in the musical experience. There is curiosity, impetus, and demand for more, whether the musical event is familiar or unfamiliar.

While the liberation described here pertains to the four complementary bipolar continua, there is room for other ways of organizing a presentation of liberation. Regardless of how it is presented, the underlying principles from the classic Chinese philosophical ideologies remain: observing and acting upon change depends on a web of connected situations in sync; decisions on actions are sincere, kind, and benevolent; dynamic flexibility avails for the capability to deal with any setting stress-free; there should be no egoistic intention to obstruct natural rules; and all subjects and values are treated equally so that nothing stands out as more valuable. *Liberation* requires sensitivity and adaptability to *change* and the ability to maintain a continuous *balance* in constant motion. One should not expect musical liberation right from the beginning or at an early stage in life. It probably takes years if not decades for most people to experience a musical liberation. The following section offers a vintage point from the perspective of musical zones.

Musical zones

In explaining *liberation* in the framework of the three zones of musical actions (musical proactivity, musical passivity, and musical avoidance), it is necessary to place the zone of musical proactivity at the center, because music is inherently a part of human in proactive ways rather than in passivity or avoidance. At birth, the new life per se is a sign of prosperity. Birth is a natural phenomenon on earth (地 *di*, as represented in *kun* with six *yin yao* in the 64 *gua*; see Chapter 2), and it matches the flow of, and depends on, the sky (天 *tian*).[10] It is a premise for sustainability and the basis of continuation and change (*Jicishang, Yizhuan* 《易傳》《繫辭上》: 生生之謂易). Sounds come as a part of a newborn life. In the case of a human, there is the heartbeat, the breathing, the crying, the movements, and the five senses that allow the perception and processing of such. Sounds and movements are organized and coordinated and are synced to other events, such as human emotions and the natural occurrences in the environment. Music is a natural part of the human being. Humans need music. If a natural part of the being is disallowed, ignored, or avoided, life becomes less human, incomplete, and less prosperous. Although classic Confucianism and classic Daoism have different perspectives on music,[11] both philosophical schools recognize the physical, social, and metaphysical effects of music and admit the importance of using music to better oneself. For classic Confucians, music is a reflection of the state of the society and a means for self-cultivation to be an exemplary person (*junzi* 君子). For classic Daoists, music is an intangible phenomenon beyond the sound found on earth or made by humans. Based on the idea that all sounds are part of the synchronized conditions of all matters, the best music comes from heaven, from which meaning is drawn. The greatest music has few intentionally made sounds (*Laozi* 41; 大音希聲), because music is best heard in nature through self-cultivation and philosophical attainment (see Chapter 4).

In other words, no musical liberation is possible if one never experiences the zone of musical proactivity. The more time she spends in the zone of musical proactivity, the more potential for her to be liberated musically. Taken from classic Confucian and classic Daoist views, proactivity infers physical actions, deep reflections, and self-cultivation. The physical action could be interpreted as self-motivated to learn a musical instrument or to sing, to choose a musical activity over many other activities, to seek out more musical opportunities, to share music with others, to advocate for music, or the like. Deep reflections could mean analyzing the music while listening, asking new questions about the music or the musical activity, seeking meaning for the music or the musical activity, establishing rationales to move the music forward, or becoming involved in any type of deep thinking about the music. Self-cultivation could involve seeing a relationship between the music and the self, understanding how the music or the musical activity is connected to self-growth, or pursuing music that supports a sincere, kind, and benevolent identity. Within the zone of musical proactivity, one could be liberated within the sonic world in any direction and at any pace that fits their developmental stage. One may choose from a wide range of musical actions to make her life complete.

In contrast, the zone of musical avoidance makes the pursuit of a complete human impossible. One avoids taking any physical action in music (e.g., not singing or playing an instrument, not choosing a musical activity, and not discussing music with others), avoids thinking in or about music, and fails to relate music to self. Thus, one is bound to live a life of an incomplete human, with music being a missing part. The innate component of music in humans is deliberately taken away.

There is an intermediate zone that appears to be a compromise, but it is still far from helping one to be a complete human. The zone of musical passivity allows for some exposure and awareness of music, but there is no depth or true experience when one is trying to get by with minimal involvement without getting into an adversary condition. Staying in the zone of musical passivity is like staying indoors with the glass windows closed. One can still see the flowers and landscape outside, but there is no breeze, smell, or a birdsong from afar.[12] It is similar to staying on a beachside road without setting foot in the sand for a beach experience, staying ashore without getting into the water for a swimming experience, or looking at a meal without consuming it for a culinary experience. A slightly improved version of these examples could be setting foot on the sand, getting into the water, or taking the meal, but reluctantly with no enjoyment or enthusiasm. These actions are still not taking the full advantage of the beach, the swim, or the cuisine. By the same token, passive engagement in music just to get by does little good. There is no sincerity, kindness, benevolence, reflection, or self-cultivation in such an experience. One may even go so far as to say that a sustained pattern of musical passivity throughout a lifespan is a dishonor to the nature of being human. It is an indication of deliberate efforts to prevent one (including self) from being prosperous. In sum, living a life in the zone of musical avoidance or the zone of musical passivity will not make musical liberation possible. Only substantial amount of time spent in the zone of musical proactivity could make musical liberation possible. This is the zone where the four complementary bipolar continua thrive.

Types of Musical Experience

Extending from the need to stay in the zone of musical proactivity to claim musical liberation, my earlier prototype of musical experience[13] can be expounded from a classic Chinese ideological perspective. Although there was no intention to associate the prototype with classic Chinese ideologies when it was conceived, bringing it to the discussion here testifies to the inclusivity, ubiquity, and strength of the Chinese ideologies, which can be used to explain many systems, ways of thinking, and phenomena.

There are eight types of musical experience in that prototype. Each type of musical experience can fit in with the zone of musical proactivity or the zone of musical passivity. As I stated in 2002, "Each type of experience can be active or passive, depending on one's ability, determination, and social role and setting."[14] However, to achieve musical liberation across these experience types requires the freedom to flow across them in the zone of musical proactivity only. In other words, one might experience music actively or passively, and only the former could lead to a liberating experience.

The eight types of musical experience are re-presented in Table 8.1: Be there and do it; Be there; Do it someplace else; Multimedia; Attend a live concert; Listen to a recording; View a photo, a relevant object, or music notation; and Verbalize (read, write, talk). Each type of experience involves a different set of musical parameters, among which are context, sight, sound, physical action, and mental action. A musically proactive person in the "be there and do it" experience would engage all five senses in the original musical context; receive information most notably through sight and sound; be physically involved in playing an instrument, singing, or dancing; and be mentally involved in creating, analyzing, or evaluating the music. It "involves the reception of all primary parameters . . . and is the fullest of all types of musical experiences, as it involves all relevant senses

Table 8.1. TYPES OF MUSICAL EXPERIENCE AND MUSICAL PARAMETERS

Musical Parameters	Context	Sight	Sound	Physical Action	Mental Action
Types of Experience:					
1. Be there and do it	X	X	X	X	X
2. Be there	X	X	X		X
3. Do it someplace else		Some	X	X	X
4. Multimedia	Some	X	X		X
5. Attend a live concert	Some	Some	X		X
6. Listen to a recording			X		X
7. View a photo, a relevant object, music notation	Some	X			X
8. Verbalize (read, write, talk)	Secondary				X

Note: Adapted from C. Victor Fung, "Experiencing World Musics in Schools: From Fundamental Positions to Strategic Guidelines," in Bennett Reimer, ed., *World Musics and Music Education: Facing the Issues* (Reston, VA: Music Educators National Conference, 2002, p. 197).

and utilizes all relevant human capacities, from playing to thinking and from seeing to hearing."[15] In contrast, the "verbalize (read, write, talk)" experience only allows for a secondary experience of the context and the mental actions of analyzing and evaluating. No sight, sound, or physical action in the music is involved. Most contemporary music teaching and learning settings are designed to experience music from type three through type eight, in which there is no "be there" element. Music making activities are done somewhere else (referring to the classroom, studio, or rehearsal room as opposed to the primary location). Only when music is experienced in the field where the music is created in its intended context, are types one and two in place with the "be there" element.

The eight types of musical experience have embedded in each of them degrees of *yin* and *yang*. One can emit and receive more or less energy in any type of musical experience. Thus, there can be a *yin* or a *yang* way of engagement within each type. Furthermore, there is a relative *yin* and *yang* across all eight types of musical experience. For example, the "be there and do it" and "do it someplace else" experiences are the only ones involving physical actions. None of the other six types of experience includes physical actions. In other words, these two types of musical experience involving physical action are more *yang* than *yin* in relation to the other six types. To the contrary, simply being there, receiving a multimedia presentation, attending a live concert, listening to a recording, or viewing a photo, a relevant object, or music notation, and verbalizing the experience do not call for any physical action; therefore, they are more on the *yin* side relative to the other two experience types. Notice that mental action is expected of all types of experience, which in itself can be more or less involved depending on individual circumstances. One may be aggressively involved in mental action while listening to a recording, yet another may be not so involved mentally while playing the music in a classroom. As stated in the initial publication of the prototype, mental action is "divergent, flexible, and cross-functional, can occur in all types of musical experiences. Any type of musical experience may involve thinking, analyzing, imagining, memorizing, recalling, reflecting, creating, or a combination of these."[16] The different types of musical experience allows for a wide range of energy engagement (*yin* and *yang*) through various musical parameters, creating an enormous range of possibilities in a rather complex permutation across experience types, musical parameters, and energy engagements.

Considering the eight types of musical experience with the array of musical genres and styles available can add to the permutation, which allows any music to be experienced in any of the eight types of experience (see Figure 8.1). The number of musical styles is non-specified here, because it is already insurmountable and is still growing. Any grouping of musical styles is going to leave out something. They include music from all traditions, cultures, genres, geographic regions, and historic periods. New musical styles are continuing to evolve, making the horizontal axis an ever-expanding list of musical styles if one chooses to involve in them. Experience in musical liberation would allow for a landing on any point represented on this

Types of musical experience
1. Be there and do it
2. Be there
3. Do it someplace else
4. Multimedia
5. Attend a live concert
6. Listen to a recording
7. View a photo, a relevant object, music notation
8. Verbalize (read, write, talk)

Musical styles

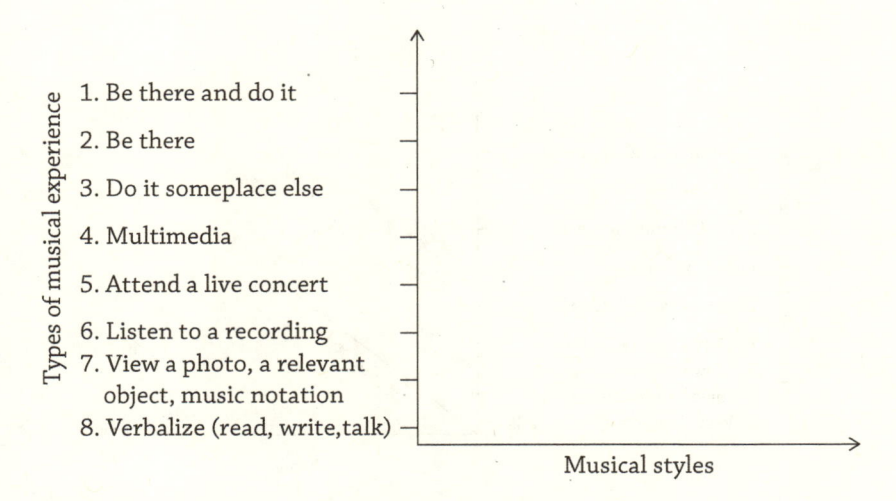

Figure 8.1: Permutation of musical styles and types of musical experience.

two-dimensional chart. If one chooses to become involved in only one narrow type of music, then the landing point would be repeatedly forming a vertical straight line. If one chooses to experience music in only one way, say, listening to recording, then the landing point would form a horizontal line across a range of musical styles. The narrowest musical experience occurs when one keeps experiencing the same type of music in the same way over and over again. Then there is only one landing point on this chart, and every time there is a musical experience, one would land on the same point repeatedly, which is an indication of not being liberated in experiencing music. When one is liberated in experiencing music, all points on this chart should be utilized as a landing point, but of course it takes a long time to accumulate multiple landing points to cover both dimensions of experience type and musical style. When one is sufficiently covered with many points across both axes and is ready to engage in any of these possible musical experiences, one is experiencing a form of musical liberation.

Another implicit dimension of the prototype is the time factor. One may look back in time to record how music is experienced through time. One may also look forward to plan on how to experience music in the future. When the time axis (x) is added (see Figure 8.2), it helps us to conceptualize a prescriptive function and a descriptive function in this frame of reference. For a prescriptive use, the time axis could represent a day, a week, a month, or a year. A period longer than that would be difficult to plan, as changing elements are hard to predict. For a descriptive use, the three-dimensional chart can be used to record one's involvement in music. Then, the chart can be used to record one's involvement in music during a day, all the way up to the entire lifetime. This charting tool should help to understand how

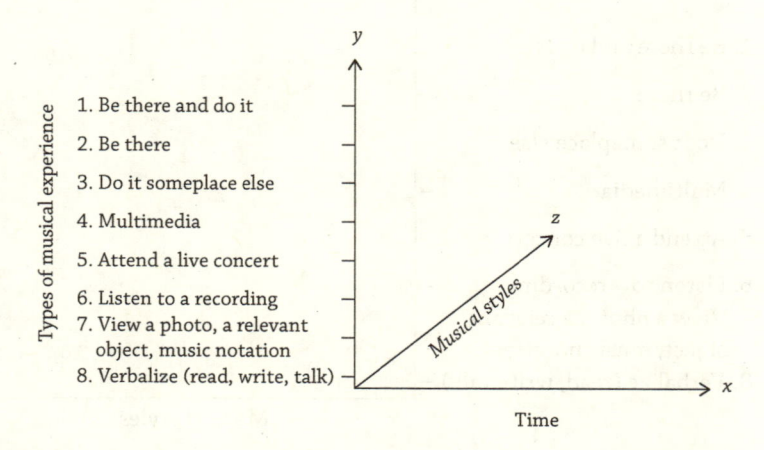

Figure 8.2: Permutation of musical styles, types of musical experience, and time.

musical liberation is taking shape as a result of a cumulative effect to cover all types of experience, all musical parameters (y), and all musical styles (z). It also reflects how different types of musical experience may fulfill one's musical needs at different times throughout life.

When one is actively engaged in all types of musical motions, roles, energy levels, familiarity levels, experiences, and styles as part of life, one is more likely to experience a musical liberation. Most, if not all, existing musical possibilities have become a foundation for a worry-free and enjoyable musical experience. Experience in musical liberation assumes comfort in change and versatility in maintaining continuous balance in music and in life. A forward-moving momentum is built upon curiosity, respect, understanding, and satisfaction. This sets up an ideal condition for one to unleash creativity to its maturity.

CREATIVITY

Creativity is by no means solely attached to liberation. It can be practiced at any time, when dealing with changes or when balancing acts are being developed. However, the experience of liberation and its preconditions (i.e., change and balance) is necessary to bring creativity to its *full maturity*. Imagine any recognized composer; her creativity needs time to develop until her work is recognized. It takes time for her to go through her early compositional exercises, learning pieces, and many experiments before her work is recognized as creative in a mature way. This path of creativity parallels with one that has gone through repeated practices of observing and understanding *change* and of a dynamic flexibility to maintain a continuous *balance* before arriving an experience in *liberation*.

As classic Confucianism and classic Daoism hold contrasting but complementary views on the nature of music, they hold parallel views in their own rights on creativity. Classic Confucians make explicit connections between the inner self and the outer world through *li* (禮) and *yue* (樂) education, whereas classic Daoists take on a metaphorical approach that integrates humans in *dao* (道) where humans are part of the bigger picture in harmony. They are complementary because their perspectives serve different needs, depending on whether the concern is in human relations or in the bigger picture of the universe. When both are considered, it helps us to explore the full potentials as humans and to bring life to a unified whole.

In classic Confucianism, music (described as *yue* 樂) is a reflection of the morale of the people and of the society. The environment, the culture, events, or objects provide inspiration to humans who make musical sounds (see *Yueji*, Liji 1: 凡音之起，由人心生也。人心之動，物使之然也。). Music is used as a tool to educate. The human is at the center of musical activities. Creativity is expressed in terms of "newness" (*xin* 新). According to Confucius, newness is based on prior experience, which suggests an established frame of reference. In the *Analects*, Confucius states that reviewing the known is the foundation of knowing new perspectives (*Analects* 2.11: 溫故而知新).[17] "The known" refers to prior experience and knowledge that provides a frame of reference. Newness makes sense through this frame of reference. Confucius follows that knowing newness is expected of all teachers (*Analects* 2.11: 可以為師矣), which suggests that all teachers should be reviewing the known.

This poses two important implications for musicians and teachers. First, musicians are not creating new music without any frame of reference; teachers are not going to come up with a new teaching strategy without the support of a theory. To some degree, it is similar to Mihaly Csikszentmihalyi's ideas of creativity, in that creativity must be supported by a domain rooted in a cultural system and a field rooted in a social system.[18] The domain and the field in the cultural and social systems are the "known" that become a frame of reference, across which a criteria-selection process evolves. In other words, merely being innovative is not enough. Ideas not agreeable to the community are not acceptable. Another similarity between Confucius' and Csikszentmihalyi's ideas of creativity is that the human plays a key role. For Csikszentmihalyi, the complex family background contributes to the person's creativity; for Confucius, the emphasis is placed on continuous cultivation aiming at an exemplary person and, in the specific passage found in the *Analects* 2.11, with an expectation of a teacher. Second, the teacher is expected to understand new perspectives, and therefore newness should be practiced, or in contemporary terms, creative. When learners have a new idea, the teacher is expected to examine it from an established framework and be able to understand it. When the teacher comes up with a new idea in teaching, she should be sure that the idea is traceable to a frame of reference. All indications suggest that teaching, and being a person in general, should be open to moving forward with new ideas that *make sense*[19] (i.e., with a frame of reference).

Classic Daoism, however, holds a different view on music and on creativity. Classic Daoists' emphasis on metaphysics and philosophical attainment leads to a conclusion that musical sound (described as *lai* 籟)[20] could be made by humans, found in the natural environment on earth, or inaudible. The best music is described as musical sound from the sky or heaven (*tian* 天), that is, the inaudible type. Hence, the term "heavenly music" (*tian lai* 天籟) is used to describe an ontological experience within oneself. It is music that one hears internally, through keen sensitivity in, deep thinking about, and intense reflection on the heavenly *dao*. As this heavenly musical sound (*tian lai* 天籟) could possibly incorporate human-made sounds (*ren lai* 人籟) or natural earthly sounds (*di lai* 地籟), it has superiority over any music that relies on physical sounds. In other words, no sound or any sound can be part of this heavenly music.[21] The best music is an inner experience.

This concept is quite remote from our contemporary notion of music. Today, meditative music is available to accompany meditation. Imagine practicing meditation anywhere in our contemporary environment, preferably away from communities developed by humans, with or without any kind of sound, while being sensitive to events occurring in the environment. This is the closest I can think of to emulate an experience of good music in classic Daoist philosophy. *Laozi* states, "great music has few sounds" (*Laozi* 41: 大音希聲), because great music does not depend on any sound. Great music is found within the individual in connection with the heavenly *dao*. Creativity in this mindset is oriented toward the inner self and is an ongoing process, regardless of what is happening in the physical world. There is little interest in the creative product, but there is a heavy focus on the philosophical attainment of the self. Metaphorically, imagination is the limit, the potentials are immeasurable, and the self is harmonized with the heavenly *dao* where peace and tranquility are found. In this school of thought, creativity is not meant to be observable but resides in one's inner self in connection with *dao*. The self is dissolved into the bigger picture of the universe.

The different views of classic Confucianism and class Daoism provide different strategies to fulfill different needs, much as one needs to rest at night and work during day. No one can work without rest, and no one should be at rest throughout her life without work. This exemplifies the complementarity and dependence of the two perspectives. Musical creativity needs a framework to be plausible (as in classic Confucianism). It also needs to be situated in the broader context of the universe through imagination and reflection (as in classic Daoism). Sometimes, the creation of music needs to include a selection process from an array of physical sounds filtered through human perception, as suggested in classic Confucianism. At other times, one needs to enter a metaphorical world to imagine what is possible between heaven and earth, as suggested in classic Daoism. These two schools seem to suggest opposites, but they may be positioned side by side, going back and forth to perpetuate a unified and balanced experience as a complete human. One might experience liberation in musical creativity somewhere between existing knowledge and the limits of *dao*. In short, musical creativity, or any type of creativity, is the space between the known and *dao*. The following chapter brings closer in creating a way of music education and a way of life as evolved from these classic Chinese wisdoms in an organismic worldview.

PART III

A New Way of Thinking
and Practical Implications

CHAPTER 9

⚬◊⚬

A Way of Music Education as a Way of Life

In the opening chapter of this book, I set off on a journey to take the classic Chinese wisdoms from *Yijing*, classic Confucianism, and classic Daoism to a new level of understanding and interpretation from a contemporary music education perspective. These classic wisdoms were settled, grew, and matured at a juncture between the mid-sixth and the mid-third century BC China before they were modified from their genuine and original ideologies and burst into many branches and modifications; some are recognizable, others are not. Metaphysical principles revealed in these classic ideologies transcend time and space and are still viable in the contemporary world. Many of these principles have become integral to being humans in a megasystem.[1] An examination of these classic wisdoms in a collective whole suggests a restoration and a reaffirmation of some basic human values and their natural positions, which form a basis of music making and music education. This way of thinking in music education is purported to contribute to the growth process in philosophy of music education.

Classic Confucianism and classic Daoism are inspired by *Yijing* and have become two pedestals among Chinese philosophies since the third century BC. This book focuses on the ideologies at the spiritual level,[2] rather than the social systemic or material level.[3] An organismic worldview, dyadic principles, and the elements of change, unchanging principles, easy access, transcendence, synchronicity, situation, and deep harmony are shared across these philosophical schools. While classic Confucianism and classic Daoism take on different directions as they address different perspectives

(153)

in life, their propositions have gone through the test of time notwithstanding modifications, developments, and branching out with influences of all sorts. Despite the evolutions of neo-, religious-, new-, and contemporary- within the purview of Confucianism and Daoism and the development of other schools of philosophy that mix with elements such as local folk rituals, individual thoughts, the import of Buddhism from India, and other developments throughout the last two millennia and more, the classic schools still stand in their own rights to represent genuine and lasting Chinese philosophies.[4] Classic Confucians focus on human relationships and present sincerity, kindness, benevolence, and being an exemplary person (*junzi*) as a sound way of being humans.[5] Classic Daoists focus on a broad universal and natural perspective by acting without egoistic intentions, keen observations from the perspectives of the being observed (including nature, objects, and beings), treating and respecting all things and beings fairly and equally, and being flexible.[6] These philosophical stances collectively become a foundation in conceiving of a trilogy that suggests a new way of thinking in music education: change, balance, and liberation. Changes interacting with acts of balance are constants. Liberation, however, is possible only after change and balance have been practiced for an extended period.

Among all living beings, humans have contributed substantially to the current state of the world, especially since the rise of the Anthropocene. At the same time, humans are cultivated in a changing environment. Humans stand out from among all living beings by way of their socialization, cognition, communication, kindness, morality, reproaching evil, righteousness, ability to connect with nature, sincerity, cordiality, respect, wisdom, adaptability, creativity, and music making. Due to their distinctive qualities, humans form a part of the world who can make many changes with a sense of coherence that other beings cannot, such as mass production of food (as in agriculture and farming); building social and virtual networks; developing sophisticated metropolises and transportation networks; constructing automobiles, airplanes, air shuttles, boats, and submarines; sending satellites to space; manufacturing wearable electronics; developing musical instruments; and making music for the sake of music and for a variety of purposes. The human spirit[7] plays a key role in constructing and reconstructing our social systems and material world. The making and remaking of musical systems and musical materials are among such occurrences.

The organismic worldview across *Yijing*, classic Confucianism, and classic Daoism suggests that neither music nor human is a separate entity. All aspects of the world are connected in some ways, and music and human are two of the most intimately linked entities. Music and human are intertwined since the earliest stage of life. The birth of humans is considered as a prosperous phenomenon and a sign of longevity for the species. Without human life, there would be no music as we understand it. For classic Confucians, humans are the ones who create music based on their sincere expression, kind intent, and sense of beauty. For classic Daoists, humans are the ones who philosophize all sorts of sounds and silence and create a heavenly music internally. Both philosophical schools share a common outlook, in that humans form the basis of all things musical. The human qualities of sincerity, kindness, benevolence, and an exemplary person and the instinctive abilities to observe, reflect, and act according to principles of the natural world are the staple elements of musical experiences and of broader meaningful life experiences. Music and human are among a complex network of connected entities across time and space. Music and the overall way of life are inseparable. Separating them is unnatural and artificial, which goes against the principles of both philosophical schools.

Both philosophical schools also share the proposition that physical musical sound is secondary in musical experiences. Confucius makes it clear that *yue* (樂 music[8]) is not about the sounds made by bells and drums[9] (*Analects* 17.11: 子曰：「禮云禮云，玉帛云乎哉？樂云樂云，鐘鼓云乎哉？」).[10] It is more important to have benevolence (仁 *ren*), as a human spirit, in making music (*Analects* 3.3: 子曰：「人而不仁，如禮何？人而不仁，如樂何？」).[11] Mencius elaborates further by defining the human spirit in greater detail, denouncing the non-humanly aspects of humans: those without compassion, courtesy, and the ability to distinguish between right and wrong and those who do not reproach evil are not humans (*Mencius* 3.6: 由是觀之，無惻隱之心，非人也；無羞惡之心，非人也；無辭讓之心，非人也；無是非之心，非人也。). He continues to state that the development of these necessary human qualities is merely the beginning of benevolence, righteousness, *li* (禮), and wisdom (*Mencius* 3.6: 惻隱之心，仁之端也；羞惡之心，義之端也；辭讓之心，禮之端也；是非之心，智之端也。). These are the basic qualities that drive the forward motion in a *humanly* way of life. As classic Confucians point out, benevolence (*ren* 仁) has no boundaries or social strata across all humans; it is a natural and desirable human quality, implying that it is unnatural to go against it. Qualities postulated in classic Confucianism—sincerity, kindness, benevolence, and being an exemplary person (*junzi*)—and classic Daoism—actions without egoistic intentions, keen observations from the perspectives of the being observed, treatment of all things and beings fairly and equally, and flexibility—collectively capture key elements of the human spirit[12] and its position in nature, suggesting the basis of a prosperous way of life that leads to sincere and natural musical acts.

Despite the different views between the two philosophical schools, they seem to evoke that being a *humanly* human is the basis of living a meaningful life that provides impetus for music making. "Humanly human" refers to the classic Confucians' focus on the humanly *dao* (*ren dao* 人道) and the classic Daoists' focus on the heavenly *dao* (*tian dao* 天道). The former refers to the desirable human qualities and proper relationships and behaviors, which are largely cultivated by humans. The latter refers to human's relationship with the natural world, between heaven (or sky) and earth, which are largely not controlled by humans but sought by humans. Both schools attend to humans who live in the midst of changes with unchanging principles; therefore observing and acting depending on the changing situation are essential. At the same time, humans are part of the change, such as their changing roles, life stages, priorities, and psyches. This explains why the Confucians submit to human-centric role-based actions and the Daoists aspire to a *dao*-centric philosophical attainment as guiding principles. While these are different interpretations of *dao*, they collectively suggest that no one can be a musician, a music educator, or any type of humans unless one is a *humanly* human who live by the humanly *dao* and the heavenly *dao*. One must have a *humanly* life before having a musical life. Putting it in another way, humans are not defined by physical features but by their way of socialization, living with nature, appropriate actions, and reproaching evil, and their cognition, kindness, morality, righteousness, sincerity, cordiality, respect for others, meticulous observations, fairness, equality, flexibility, wisdom, and continuous improvement. Anything humans do should be done in these *humanly* ways. Anyone engages in music should do so in these humanly ways.

IMPORTANCE OF PERSISTENT IMPROVEMENT

The notion of endless and persistent improvement is emphasized in both philosophical schools. Endlessness, inferring longevity, is a sign of prosperity. There is always a new height to be reached regardless of what humans do. The classic Daoists' heavenly *dao* is an endless operation, back and forth between *yin* and *yang*, perpetuating for an onward motion in eternal cycles. One is to seek philosophical understanding of life in the context of the universe, on a path beyond self and into the cyclic events in nature. The underlying meaning is that the way to seek philosophical understanding is to walk the path of life along with *dao*, which never ends. Laozi extends from this idea and confirms the profound nature of *dao*, "there is mysticism within mysticism, it is the source of all subtle mysteries"

(*Laozi* 1: 玄之又玄，眾妙之門。). Once mysticism is understood, there is another deeper level of mysticism in it. The pursuit of understanding *dao* never ends. Persistent improvement is expected. He also states that the ancients who mastered it are unfathomable (*Laozi* 15: 古之善為士者，微妙玄通，深不可識。). To master *dao*, even Laozi sees a level beyond his reach, but he still works hard to pursue it. Musically, this way of thinking prompts a never-ending quest for musical understanding. There is a need to develop sensitivity in the human senses to perceive human-made sounds, earthly natural sounds, and silence. Sounds from all cultures and traditions should be viewed from their native perspective and be treated equally. Then one should reflect and transform these perceptions in creating heavenly musical sounds internally. Throughout one's lifetime there should be a never-ending pursuit for a philosophical understanding of heavenly music. Education should play a key role in walking this path of a lifetime.

The classic Confucians' humanly *dao* leads to an endless pursuit to refine oneself as an exemplary person (*junzi*), who should continue to self-cultivate throughout the entire lifespan and to help others to become an exemplary person. This idea has two built-in notions of endlessness. First, self-cultivation is a lifelong process. The classic Confucian literature suggests a hierarchy of humans from lowest to highest: *xiaoren* (小人 child, uneducated, or villain),[13] *junzi* (君子 exemplary person), and *shengren* (聖人 sage). Neither Confucius nor Mencius admits to having achieved *shengren* themselves. Mencius claims that *shengren* is a "teacher of a hundred generations" (*Mencius* 14.15: 聖人，百世之師也) and granted Confucius that title.[14] However, Confucius declines the title in a conversation with his student and is content to have experienced *junzi*.[15] It is clear that being a *junzi* is a lifelong journey[16] and that is not easy to go beyond *junzi* to be a *shengren*. Mencius even postulates one more level above *shengren*: *shen* (神 god), who is unknowable (*Mencius* 14.25: 大而化之之謂聖，聖而不可知之之謂神。). In the framework of classic Confucianism, there is an unreachable level such that the lifelong journey of *junzi* is endless. Persistent improvement is expected. In terms of the human spirit, promoting from *xiaoren* to *junzi* is already a significant achievement, but maintaining the status of *junzi* for the rest of one's life and to be a better *junzi* continuously demand never-ending efforts.

Second, the expectation of helping others to become *junzi* has a strong tone of endless teaching. Teaching is an act of benevolence and an aspect of life for *junzi*.[17] In classic Confucianism, everyone should become a *junzi*, and every *junzi* should be teaching in some ways. A *junzi* may use any avenue, regardless of context and subject, to teach implicitly, such as living as a model for others, or explicitly, such as taking up the role of being a teacher. The idea is that *junzi* are expected to teach throughout their lives as a way of bringing prosperity to the human spirit.

MUSICAL WAY OF LIFE

In contemporary terms, the phenomenon of music that transcends time and space is more than the physical, tangible sound of music. Music is a way of living that is natural, inherent, and to which humans are predisposed. To make music properly, certain human qualities are expected. To remove music from human life is unnatural,[18] egoistic,[19] and even evil,[20] because it is dehumanizing and eventually brings adversity in life. If music is removed from life, one would not be able to fully discriminate sound materials, perceive sensitive expressions through sound, or think meticulously in the sonic world in combination with silence, all of which are genuinely human.

Wherever one is, there is a culture that includes music to cultivate musical lives, and some are more direct than others. In the concluding chapter of Bennett Reimer's book *A Philosophy of Music Education: Advancing the Vision*, he describes musical ensembles as cultures. To be in an ensemble is to have "a way to live a life."[21] Being in a musical ensemble is more than just the rehearsals and performances; it is a way of living. It is hard to separate the ensemble activities and mindset from the broader life. The way of thinking presented in this book suggests that it is natural for everyone to have a prosperous musical way of life. A musical pathway is enabled at birth. It makes sense to maintain the pathway in the zone of musical proactivity with only occasional fallbacks to the zone of musical passivity and even less so to the zone of musical avoidance. Just as professional athletes do not always use their muscles at peak motions, no one is expected to always stay on the top of the zone of musical proactivity. Moments of falling back to passivity or even avoidance would be necessary to bring about the next proactive move. It is also a way of maintaining a continuous balance in life.

In the zone of musical proactivity, the complementary bipolar continua in musical motions, roles, activities, and events are actively engaged. There is rigorous exchange of energy between the two sides of each continuum, influencing each other, compensating each other, and constantly searching for a balance that supports a forward motion so life continues with a high degree of prosperity. At the same time, other aspects of life are interacting with these continua. Changes in time of the day, day of the month, month of the season, season of the year, and year of life suggest different life events associated with different musical needs. Musical balance throughout the day depends on the individual's life condition, style, and preference in various moments. Musical motions can be active or passive. One can be teaching[22] or learning, in a high- or low-energy activity, and through a familiar or unfamiliar musical event. The demand of various musical balancing acts emerges in similar ways as the days, the months, the seasons, and rituals change throughout the year. Musical situations are different depending on the stage of life; for example, the impact of family and environment in early childhood, the role of school and mass media during the schooling years, music or non-music careers in young adulthood, and the self, family, and socialization in life after retirement—each stage calls for different balancing acts. In this way of thinking, musical experience and music education should not be limited to certain moments, days, months, or years. Everyone can be actively engaged in music at any time.

Throughout these engagements, qualities of *human* and *dao* should permeate the energy exchange. There should be ample opportunities to practice balancing acts throughout the entire lifespan, which would increase opportunities to experience musical liberation. A sense of liberation is felt only after extended practices of the balancing act in numerous changing situations, that is, when *any* change in musical motion, role, activity, or experience becomes a free and satisfying experience. Figure 9.1 presents a visual representation of how the extended practice of change and balance makes liberation reachable. Practices of change and balance initially occur inside a solid-line boundary, which signifies a person's musical world, a musical system, a set of musical materials, or a musical environment. These practices are based on the qualities suggested in the classic Chinese philosophies and in any type of musical changes and musical experiences. In this book, I have suggested four complementary bipolar continua and eight types of musical experiences. The practices are open to other categorizations of musical changes and musical experiences as long as they have a sufficiently comprehensive coverage. The more balancing acts are practiced in the changing environment, the more likely that holes will appear on the boundary (turning the solid line into a broken line, as in Figure 9.1), allowing pathways to experience liberation outside of the boundary.

Taken from the classic Daoists' view to look beyond a lifetime and integrate life into the broader changes in the world across a longer time span, I suggest that the change-balance-liberation trilogy could be applied to describe musical motions and balance across different historical eras. For example, for thousands of years humans had to depend on live performances to experience music, which is, say, the pre-recording era. There was a need to engage more physical and personal-social activities to perform a

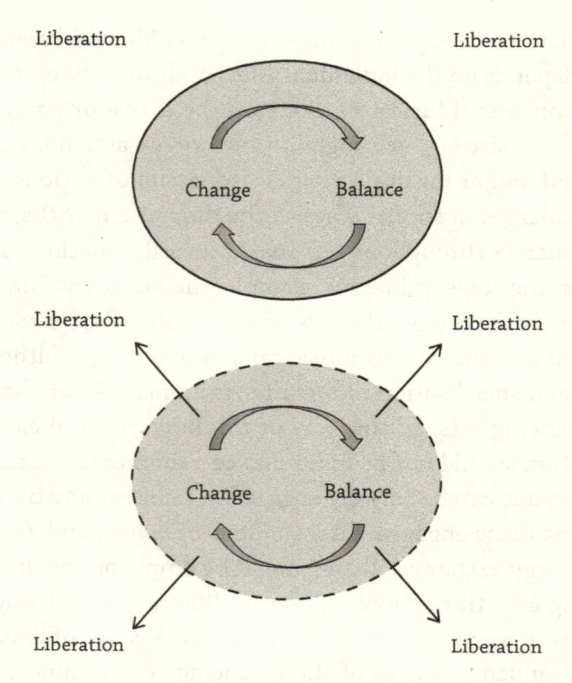

Figure 9.1: Initial practice of change and balance (upper diagram) and extended practice of change and balance (lower diagram), which allows for pathways to liberation outside the boundary.

balanced musical act. The way to maintain a musical balance in the recording era, from analog to digital, demands dramatically different ways of musical living without giving up live performances. When we arrive to the era of the popularization of microcomputers and digital musical instruments, and moving into an era of social media and portable digital music playback devices, yet another round of dynamic flexibility is needed to maintain a musical balance in a wider range of choices. Just like the different musical needs and the call for different balancing acts from moment to moment, day to day, month to month, season to season, and year to year, there is constant change and need for different balancing strategies from era to era; hence, different musical styles are developed to ensure a balanced musical experience for the era. In this sense, liberation is possible for those who are collectively well versed in practicing change and balance in the music of the past and present, developing a pathway into a musical future.

Despite changes in the natural world, in human relationships, or in relationships between human and the natural world, the human spirit is a foundation in the operations of change, balance, and liberation across time and space. The human spirit serves as the fundamental guideline for being humans. It is an unchanging principle. It holds in the third century BC China, and it still holds throughout the contemporary world: the human spirit is a universal axiom of being human. It is a main thread in constructing our social system and material world, including musical systems and musical materials. All people across the world throughout history are members of a team called humans, and the team spirit is the human spirit. We work together to move forward across time and space, toward a more harmonized, peaceful, and prosperous world. It is the same spirit that has been keeping humans making music generation after generation. A musical way of life is a prosperous life.

A WAY OF MUSIC EDUCATION

While music is an internal individual affair, as suggested by classic Daoists, more often than not music is a phenomenon found in two or more individuals due to its humanistic and communicative nature, similar to *ren* (仁 benevolence) as laid out in the classic Confucian texts. To live with meaning, according to classic Confucians, there must be benevolence; to make meaningful music, there must be benevolence. Benevolence carries a mission to set an exemplary model for others, to teach, and to help others to be exemplary persons. In this way of thinking, music and music education are inseparable. The experience of music cannot be detached from some form of teaching and learning, which can be implicit or explicit, a personal event or a group activity, and in the family, a community, or an educational institution. I have defined music education as:

> a complex permutation of activities that is within and outside of the institutions, formally structured and minimally structured, self-guided and guided by others, about learning the music of the past and learning to generate new music, and about learning the music of oneself and learning the music of others.[23]

In other words, anyone in contact with music is learning something about the music, and there is no age, time, or space boundary. A mere musical exposure is sufficient to be considered as a learning experience. Any musical act (e.g., create, play, sing, talk, show, move, read, or write) shared with an individual, self or other, is sufficient to be considered as a teaching experience. In this frame of reference, practicing a musical instrument in solitude is a self-teaching and learning experience. Composing music is an attempt to teach others about the content and meaning of the music. Performing music in a recital is an act of teaching the audience about the content and meaning of music. Attending a musical performance or a lecture on a musical topic is a musical learning experience. The list of possibilities in music education experience is indefinite. All music educational experience is an integral part of a musical experience, and vice versa.

Musicians and music educators are a privileged group of humans who have good reasons to delve into practicing change and balance in the inherently prosperous human phenomenon of music. While they may be the ones who dominate the population experiencing musical liberation, it is not their entitlement. Anyone should be able to achieve musical liberation as long as they practice balancing acts persistently and proactively, that is, to stay in the zone of musical proactivity. Figure 9.2 is an illustration based on Figure 6.2, which shows the zone of musical proactivity, the zone of musical passivity, and the zone of musical avoidance. Using the idea of solid and broken boundaries from Figure 9.1 to represent no liberation and with pathway to liberation, respectively, Figure 9.2 shows that there is no

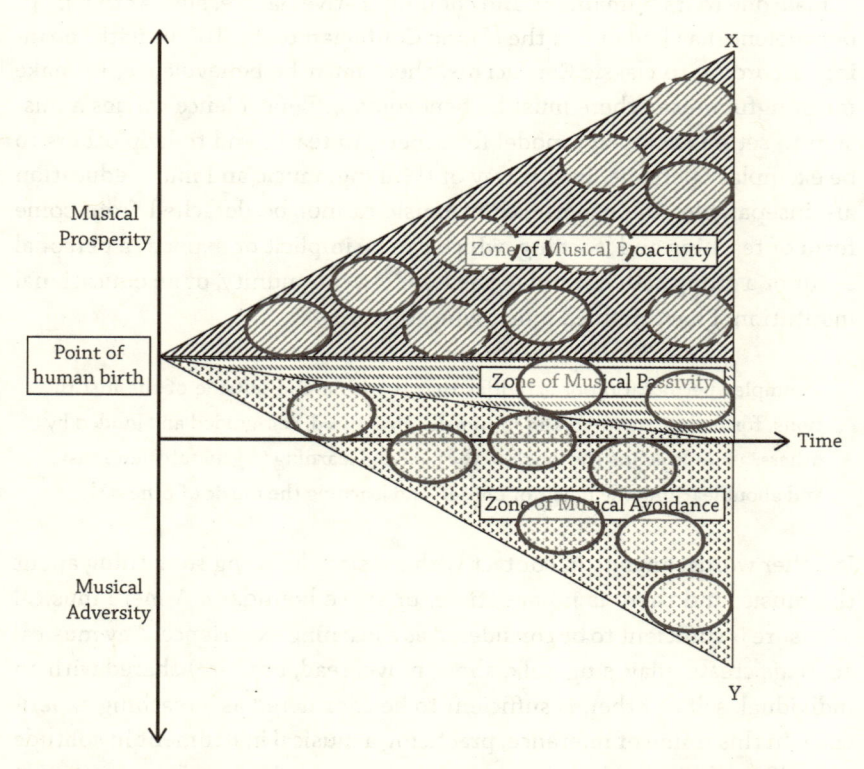

Figure 9.2: Potential for pathways to musical liberation found in the zone of musical proactivity only.

pathway to musical liberation in the zones of musical passivity or musical avoidance. Even in the zone of musical proactivity, pathways to musical liberation are opened only after extended practice of balancing acts across all sorts of musical changes. Staying in the zone of musical proactivity makes musical liberation possible, but it is not a guarantee. It depends on whether the pathways make sense (*tong* 通) in the enabling situation (*shi* 勢).

The way of music education suggested here carries key principles found in the classic Chinese wisdoms. It can be characterized as follows:

1. Music and music education are inseparable and simultaneous. Anyone engaged in music is engaging in music education, and vice versa. Music by nature is educational, but education by nature is not necessarily musical. One is learning about the spirit, the social system, or the material of music when they are in contact with music. The human spirit in music contains a mystical quality that makes music an everlasting phenomenon with great interests. A way of living in music education is a way of living in music, and vice versa.
2. Music education and human life are inseparable. *When* there is life, there is a need for music education. Music education is for the entire lifespan, not for any specific age range or life stage.[24] Each life stage has different music educational needs. In other words, music education should not be tied to educational institutions only, as they tend to serve learners of specific age groups (i.e., the schooling years). There are different music educational needs at various life stages. *Where* there is life, there is a need for music education. As humans are predisposed to music, music education has no boundaries and strata. Everyone should have the opportunity for music education, privileged or underprivileged[25] and near or far.
3. One should observe the situation and context in determining the music educational needs of the moment. Every environment in music education is unique. Every event occurs in synchrony with a multitude of elements, some of which are explainable, others are not. Music learners and teachers should adjust their actions accordingly from moment to moment, and season to season, based on the principles of the humanly *dao* and the heavenly *dao*. A dynamic flexibility is desirable at all times in maintaining a continuous balance.
4. One should acknowledge an organismic worldview in understanding the connections and influences of musical lives between self and others and among others. The acknowledgment per se is a music educational experience.

5. A human spirit is guided by the principles of the humanly *dao* as explained by classic Confucianism and the heavenly *dao* as explained by classic Daoism. These *dao* principles shed light on changing relationships among humans and between human and the natural world. They should be used when interacting with humans, interacting with the environment, and making decisions in continuous balancing acts. Different principles are applied to address different situations with different musical needs.

6. A dynamic flexibility is needed in dealing with any life circumstances, such as a change in social status, a career change, a relocation, or a change in family status. This way one would not fall into an adversary zone by staying in the zone of musical passivity or the zone of musical avoidance for too long. Music could be used to benefit the overall well-being, socially, psychologically, or physically, when one is engaged in it.

7. A dynamic flexibility is needed in dealing with any unique musical circumstances. When exercising this balancing act, some questions to consider are what music to engage, what musical activity to involve, how active the involvement is, and what musical role to play. One may refer to the four complementary bipolar continua—musical motions, teacher-learner role, energy involved in musical activities, and familiarity with musical events—to guide the balancing process. All individuals should have the opportunity to experience all continua and sub-continua as fully and as early as possible. Early balancing exercises in these continua may increase the likelihood of musical liberation later in life, that is, to do anything musical freely and enjoyably in one or more chosen music areas, such as composing, performing, producing, listening, or teaching, and in one or more musical traditions.

8. The longer one stays in the zone of musical proactivity, the more likely one appreciates a state of musical prosperity and experiences a musical liberation. The zone of musical passivity and the zone of musical avoidance should be used as temporary fallbacks only. Neither the zone of musical proactivity nor the experience of musical liberation is reserved for musicians or music educators. They are available for anyone[26] who makes a decision to live in the zone of musical proactivity.

9. All available avenues should be used to experience as many musical styles as possible. These avenues include Be there and do it; Be there; Do it someplace else; Multimedia; Attend a live concert; Listen to a recording; View a photo, a relevant object, or music notation; and Verbalize (read, write, talk).

10. Self-cultivation and self-improvement are expected consistently throughout one's life. There is always something more mystical in anyone's current state of achievement in music and in human spirit.

Notice that the bulk of the characteristics in this way of music education are about continuous balancing acts in the midst of changes. There is only a minuscule hint in liberation. This makes sense because change is only partly maneuverable by individual humans. Humans are not able to understand all connections across all events, as they are synchronized in a mystical way. Many changes are natural occurrences over which humans have little control. In contrast, humans take full responsibility in the balancing act. Regardless of the changes, humans need to actively engage in maintaining a continuous balance that makes sense, so that deep harmony and prosperity may sustain. As liberation is the third and final component of the trilogy, it is possible only after substantial practice of the balancing act in constant change through a great variety of situations. It is rare to experience liberation in the early stages of exercising change and balance. It is more reasonable to expect liberation later in life. It comes when one has sufficient practice in change and balance and when the situation is ripe. Using the bicycle analogy again here, even when a bicyclist has had sufficient practice in a variety of conditions and feels ready to maintain continuous balance in any condition, the situation has to ripen, such as being able to take a vacation, for him to be liberated on his bicycle to go anywhere she wants.

In summary, a way of music education is a humanly way of life. It assumes a constantly changing environment in an organismic world where all elements, musical or nonmusical, are connected and mutually influential. The predisposition of music in humans requires music education practices done in the most humanly way possible. Principles in *Yijing*, classic Confucianism, and classic Daoism collectively offer some of the most humanly ways that are powerful, sustainable, mystical, and widespread. Using these principles, humans take full responsibility in observing each unique situation and acting flexibly to sustain a continuous balance in a satisfying musical life. When balancing acts are practiced extensively, music and life get to move forward with constant improvements. If everyone is pursuing a continuous balance in life with humanly human characters, musical prosperity with deep harmony could be attained. When balancing acts are sufficiently practiced in a wide variety of conditions, the human would be free from worries about any unknown, unnatural, or imbalanced musical possibilities. The human would have the skills to bring a balance back and be able to enjoy the process, just like cycling or surfing across any changing terrains. Liberation in the world of music education allows the human to do anything desired within the parameters of humanly *dao* and heavenly *dao*. Music and the human continue to move forward, perpetuating for more, generation after generation, promoting prosperity with a thriving human spirit in a peaceful milieu. The following chapter presents suggestions on how to put this way of music education into practice.

CHAPTER 10

Toward Practical Implications

In this book I have presented a philosophy of music education in the form of a trilogy—change, balance, and liberation—based on a triad of classic Chinese wisdoms: *Yijing*, classic Confucianism, and classic Daoism. This philosophy suggests a way of thinking in music education as a way of living throughout the entire lifespan. It opens new ways of conceiving and developing music education practices and reinforces the foundation of the source of music—the human spirit and the values bestowed in it. It is intended to contribute to a broader discourse in music education philosophy.

The way of thinking entailed in this philosophy appears to be simple and easy,[1] which is necessary for a way of thinking to be practical, far-reaching, and long-lived. The *yin* and *yang* dyad is a prime example of such simplicity and easiness (- - for *yin* and — for *yang*), yet profound and fertile meanings are embedded in it. It is the basis of an astounding set of complex relationships and operations of all elements in the universe.[2] Similarly, many principles found in classic Confucianism and classic Daoism are not difficult to comprehend. The key is to make conscious efforts to *practice* these principles *persistently*[3] in pursuit of a continuous balance so that they can become an *integral part of life*.[4]

The human is at the center of attention in this philosophy. Humans are the makers of music, internally and physically. Humans define what music is. By nature, humans are predisposed with music, because human activities are prone to be musical due to the sounds and patterns we make, audible or inaudible. Humans are the ones who observe various changes and take initiatives to engage in balancing acts. Humans are the ones who enjoy liberation after extensive exercises of continuous balance in a constantly changing environment. In sum, one has to be a human before she can think, speak, act, and teach musically and before she can enjoy the privileges that music has to offer.

Choosing from among the principles of *Yijing*, classic Confucianism, and classic Daoism is like choosing different foods to fulfill needs in different situations, say, the time, the day, the season, the year, the stage in life, the environment, or the physical condition of the person. A different type of food is necessary so the individual is able to maintain health and satisfaction in life. When all options are good choices, a healthy diet is ensured. Rest assured that the philosophical ideologies presented in this book are all aimed at the well-being and prosperity of the human race.

When applying this way of thinking in music education, a key is to be open to the variety of possibilities offered across any categories of music making or musical experience in any system within the purview of the human spirit. Two such systems are suggested in this book: complementary bipolar continua[5] and a prototype of musical experiences in a wide range of musical styles.[6] In other words, possibilities of change across all continua and sub-continua and all types of musical experiences in a wide range of musical styles should be exposed, addressed, and engaged proactively. Experiences in these changes would become useful resources when performing a balancing act. Through extended practice in these changes and continuous balance, a rich repertoire of musical skills and knowledge is in store in preparation for a liberating musical experience.

Opening up to a variety of possibilities and musical experiences does not equate to a complete displacement of any specific practices. Rather, the notion of deep harmony must be applied so that the strengths of each possibility and each type of musical experience can bring forth a bigger, stronger, harmonized, and more sustainable organic whole: music, human life, and the universe. No one possibility should overshadow the others, and no one type of musical experience is always dominating. All possibilities and experience types should have their fair share of their strengths. In other words, those who advocate for a musical style should recognize the strengths of that style and make those strengths their contributions in the world of music. A musical strength may be found in music notation, improvisation, movement, storytelling, musical structure, ensemble structure, flexible presentation format, participant engagement, and so forth. When all such strengths are gathered in a balanced way, the musical way of living is on a path toward musical liberation.

Another key in this way of practicing music education is to emphasize the *zone of musical proactivity* rather than the zone of musical passivity or the zone of musical avoidance. While most individuals are expected to have experienced all three zones throughout a lifetime, it is important to move as many individuals as possible into the *zone of musical proactivity*, so that more people can enjoy prosperous lives as complete humans. The other two zones (passivity and avoidance) should be used as a temporary refuge only as necessary. The longer one stays in the zone of musical avoidance, the more likely that an adversary effect will take place, socially, psychologically, or physically. In contrast, once in the zone of musical proactivity, support should be provided so that everyone in the zone can stay as long as possible. Everyone should choose actions to support conditions that maintain a continuous balance in that zone.

DEVELOPING HABITUAL WAYS

As in any philosophy of music education, this philosophy is purported to improve professional practice by "refining and improving habitual ways of thinking and acting,"[7] probably not "technically or directly . . . but incrementally and indirectly."[8] As attributes of this philosophy are simple, easy, and practical, I suggest that this philosophy be used as a basis for habitual ways of practicing music education. The following list may serve as points of departure for music educators and anyone who comes into contact with music:

1. Practice human qualities suggested in the classic Chinese philosophies, including but not limited to *cheng* (誠 sincerity), *shan* (善 kindness), *ren* (仁 benevolence), *junzi* (君子 exemplary person), *wuwei* (無為 non-egoistic action), *guan* (觀 observation), *qiwu* (齊物 equality), and *rou* (柔 flexibility), when interacting with others, making decisions, and executing balancing acts, musically or otherwise. These humanly human qualities should be taken seriously and persistently—not superficially, literally, lightly, casually, or occasionally—aiming at continuous self-improvement throughout the lifetime. They should be understood from their respective philosophical roots. When exercising these qualities, one must consider actions and changes with *tong* (通 going through and making sense), the unique *shi* (勢 situation or context), and *he* (和 deep harmony) as continuous balance is maintained in constant changes. Different qualities are necessary in different situations, just as different foods are needed at different times for a prosperous life, and one's sensitivity to the needs of the body is necessary. When these *humanly* human qualities are practiced, music as a human endeavor would continue to prosper, and musical expressions and their associated actions would be sincere, kind, natural, and beautiful.

2. Be mindful of the unique position of the moment in connection with other humans, the surrounding environment, and the universe as balancing acts are performed. The unique and changing role of the moment should be clear (e.g., teacher, learner, ensemble member, conductor, parent, or administrator). Regardless of role, there is a need to constantly reflect on questions such as:
   - Why am I here (e.g., when making music or when switching to a specific role), and what brings me here?
   - How can I do better, so that my life is more prosperous?
   - To what (e.g., the wood of the piano, the ambience of the venue) and to whom (e.g., a composer, fellow music makers, or an audience) am I connecting?
   - How does my state of balance affect others' states of balance? "Others" here include other humans, the surrounding environment, and the universe.
   - How do others' states of balance affect my state of balance?
   - What are my greatest strengths that could contribute to a continuous balance for a broader good?

   Outcomes of such reflections would help to maintain a continuous balance with an understanding of the connection between self and the situation one is in from moment to moment. The "moment" could be extended to the day, the month, the season, the year, or the stage in life.
3. Develop skills to practice experiencing the full range of variations in the four complementary bipolar continua: active musical motions and passive musical motions, teacher and learner roles, high-energy activities and low-energy activities, and familiar musical events and unfamiliar musical events. As musical situations change, skills developed when experiencing these continua may be used to maintain a continuous balance.
4. Include all eight types of musical experiences for a wide range of musical styles throughout life: Be there and do it; Be there; Do it someplace else; Multimedia; Attend a live concert; Listen to a recording; View a photo, a relevant object, or music notation; and Verbalize (read, write, talk). They are not necessarily distributed equally across time, but everyone should be aware of them and have opportunities to exercise them. As musical situations change, proper actions learned from these musical experiences may be used to maintain a continuous balance in any type of musical experience.
5. Stay in the zone of musical proactivity for as long as possible. Explore, create, recreate, spread, transmit, teach, learn, engage, and integrate music in daily activities with enthusiasm. Participation in music should

be sustained with a continuous balance among various energy and familiarity levels. Engage in a wide range of musical techniques, traditions, parameters, and types of musicianship. A pathway to musical liberation is conceivable only when continuous balance is maintained in this zone.
6. Those who are in the zone of musical passivity and the zone of musical avoidance should be set on a journey to move into the zone of musical proactivity, so that a musically liberating experience can be achieved as a complete and satisfying human.

These departure points assume a musical predisposition for everyone at birth. Music educators should practice them for themselves and to offer the same opportunities for music learners to practice in various music educational settings, institutional or community, fully structured or minimally structured, and more. To continue on a path of musical prosperity throughout life depends on how well these suggestions are practiced habitually. Anyone can live a life in musical prosperity. A team of humans in good spirit is necessary to move forward. A deep harmony in all humans promotes balance and peace. Everyone's strength in this diverse team of humans is used to their advantage in moving forward to a better world. Regardless of the changes in time and space, in the individual, in everyday materials, or in the social system, there is always a way to maintain a musical balance if one has sufficient skill, knowledge, flexibility, and desire. Habitual practice and continuous improvement in the balancing act are critical parts of the journey.

EPILOGUE

This book is not meant to be an end but a beginning point of a stream of philosophical dialogues that consider classic Chinese wisdoms as a foundation in the field of music education. As mentioned in the opening chapter of this book, many scholars (including those who operate only in the Chinese language) have dedicated their entire career to study Chinese philosophy. The selected philosophical basis for this book is a small, but a most critical, portion of Chinese philosophy. Chinese ideologies beyond the classics of the pre-Qin period should be explored further, especially those that morph from the classics, incorporate outside influences, or have been widespread within and beyond Asia. There is much richness in Chinese philosophy awaiting further exploration in the field of music education. At the same time, there is still plenty of room to deepen and broaden the study of these classic philosophies from a contemporary music education perspective.

In the practical realm, more details are yet to be worked out. I urge all music educators to contribute to a dialogue to explore this philosophy and put it into their frame of practice. Educators and researchers may, jointly or independently and privately or publicly, share real-life stories about how this philosophy works in specific situations from a microscopic to a lifelong perspective. A collection of these stories may testify to the practicality of this philosophy. Through time, hopefully, everyone may experience a better way of life that champions the human spirit in relation to the ever-changing natural environment, material life, and social system.

While principles revealed in this book are classic and historic, their interpretations and implications for music and music education are new. Beyond music and music education, these principles should be explored in other fields. Replacing the word "music" and its variants with another practical field may still be sound, because principles presented in this book are much broader than music and are connected to the nonmusical aspects of life. Concepts such as musical proactivity, musical passivity, musical avoidance, musical adversity, and musical prosperity could be explored by replacing "musical" with another adjective (e.g., "educational," "financial," "linguistic," "managerial," "mathematical," "medical," "psychological," "scientific," "social," or "technological"). I leave these explorations to experts of these other fields. The human spirit, *dao*, and principles of change are ubiquitous and transcendental and may help to promote prosperity in any field and contribute to better lives.

GLOSSARY

CHAPTER 1

Classic Confucianism (傳統的儒家) Sometimes termed "traditional Confucianism," it emphasizes the original Confucian philosophy posited by Confucius (511–479 BC) and Mencius (372–289 BC). It distinguishes from the later developments of neo-, religious-, new-, or contemporary-Confucianism among other variants of Confucianism. It remains standing as a branch of Confucianism.

Classic Daoism (or classic Taoism) (傳統的道家) Sometimes termed "traditional Daoism," it emphasizes the original Daoist philosophy posited by Laozi (b. ca. 570 BC) and Zhuangzi (369–286 BC). It distinguishes from the later developments of neo-, religious-, new-, or contemporary-Daoism among other variants of Daoism. It remains standing as a branch of Daoism.

***Dao* (or *tao*)** (道) Usually translated as "the way." It has different interpretations in different schools of philosophy. Confucian *dao* emphasizes on the way humans relate to each other, and Daoist *dao* emphasizes the natural way of all matters, including human's relationship with nature. Within the realm of classic Chinese philosophies, there is also heavenly *dao* (*tian dao*), humanly *dao* (*ren dao*), and earthly *dao* (*de dao*), describing various ways of operation in different entities.

Yijing (易經) One of the oldest classics in the world. The book contains simple symbols (*yin* and *yang* that are elements of *gua*) created by Fuxi (伏羲) from about the twenty-ninth to the twenty-eighth century BC, representing various phenomena observed. In the hands of Zhou Wen Wang (周文王, 1152–1056 BC), explanatory sentences were added. Contemporary publications of *Yijing* usually include ten accompanying essays, referred to as *Yizhuan* (易傳), authored by Confucius and his followers. When all three components are included, it is sometimes called *Zhouyi* (周易).

Yue jiao (樂教) Education of *yue* is a Confucian version of music education proposed by Confucius and his followers. It is used to cultivate citizens for political and societal gains. It is tied to the socio-political-cultural system of the time.

CHAPTER 2

Gua (卦) The same word *gua* could be referred to as trigram (with three *yao* 爻) or hexagram (with six *yao*, consisting of two trigrams). All possible combinations of *yin yao* and *yang yao* yield eight trigrams and 64 hexagrams. Each *gua* describes a unique phenomenon that can be interpreted only by those who study it.

Taiji (太極) Literally means the Great Extreme. It is a figure that represents the meaning of, and interactions between, *yin* and *yang*. All phenomena are based on motions created between these extremes.

Yang (陽) In the *yin* and *yang* dyad, *yang* represents the masculine, active, and energy giving side.

Yao (爻) The simple symbol in the form of a straight horizontal line to represent *yin* (broken line) and *yang* (continuous line). Three *yao* together form a trigram (*gua* 卦), and two trigrams together form a hexagram (also known as *gua* 卦).

Yin (陰) In the *yin* and *yang* dyad, *yang* represents the feminine, passive, and energy receiving side.

Yizhuan (易傳) It is the ten accompanying essays, or the ten wings (十翼 *shiyi*), of *Yijing*. It is usually included in contemporary publications of *Yijing*. It is believed to be authored by Confucius and his followers. With these essays, *Yijing* is sometimes called *Zhouyi*.

CHAPTER 3

Cheng (誠) Sincerity based on true knowledge, emotion, intent, and expression.

Junzi (君子) The exemplary person (*junzi*) is one who commits to Confucian principles throughout the entire life span, most notably *ren* (仁). There is constant self-cultivation and self-improvement. While learning never stops, *junzi* carries a mission to teach others, or to model for others, so others can become *junzi*.

Li (禮) Often translated as "ritual," *li* entails rules that govern human behaviors in relation to other humans. It can be construed as culturally appropriate etiquette and codes of conduct. To implement *li* is to act properly in various events, which include the established rituals in the society.

Ren (人) *Ren* (人) means human, person, people, or individuals. This Chinese character is a homophone with the other *ren* (仁) listed below.

Ren (仁) *Ren* (仁), benevolence, is a desirable quality in classic Confucianism. It requires at least two people to enact. It is a quality expected of exemplary persons (*junzi* 君子). This Chinese character is a homophone with the other *ren* (人) listed above.

Ren dao (人道) Proper ways of being humans. It implies that actions derailing from *ren dao* are behaviors of non-humans.

Shan (善) Kindness is an act of choice. It is a necessary choice if benevolence is desired. It also contributes to the Confucian sense of beauty.

Tian dao (天道) A heavenly way governed by natural phenomena. By the time of Confucius, an ethical element may be incorporated.

Yue (樂) Commonly translated as "music," but *yue* includes poetry and dance in the pre-Qin period. It is coupled with *li* (禮) in the Confucian ideal of education during the same timeframe. When the same Chinese character is pronounced as *le*, it means happiness.

CHAPTER 4

Dao (道) It is an unexplainable concept that includes the natural way of all matters, beings, and phenomena. It is understood through philosophical attainment.

De (德) Human behaviors that are aligned with *dao*. It may be translated as "virtue."

Guan (觀) Observe from the perspective of the being observed, so deep and true understanding can be achieved.

Lai (籟) It refers to a wind instrument made of bamboo, but there is a lack of documentation on its shape or size. In *Zhuangzi*, the word is used to describe "music" found in heaven or the sky (*tian lai* 天籟), human (*ren lai* 人籟), and the earth (*de lai* 地籟).

Qiwu (齊物) All beings, objects, and opinions are equally valued. Right can become wrong, and wrong can become right, depending on the situation, context, and perspective. The same holds for true-false and the like.

Rou (柔) Soft and flexible so there is a high level of adaptability in ever changing situations.

Wei (為) Action with human intention and reason. This is a homophone with the other *wei* presented below.

Wei (偽) False. Made up by humans. This is a homophone with the other *wei* presented above.

Wuwei (無為) Take action with no egoistic intent, going along with *dao*.

CHAPTER 5

He (和) It literally means harmony, but the classic Chinese literature infers a "deep" harmony or a "comprehensive" harmony. Different elements are required in this type of harmony. It exerts on the strengths of each element to create a bigger or better whole.

Juntiao (均調) Adjusting something so the elements are blended in for a better whole.

Tianxia (天下) It refers to the world, the universe, or an all-encompassing entity under the sky.

Xiaoren (小人) The opposite of *junzi* (君子), this is used to describe those who are ignorant, undereducated, rude, disrespectful, or the like. It is also used to describe children (i.e., the undereducated) or to self-proclaim as a humble expression.

CHAPTER 6

Bian hua (變化) Change is in constant motion. It relies on humans to act upon and to generate further changes.

Bian tong (變通) An action that accommodates the changing situation so that the changes make sense.

CHAPTER 9

Shen (神) It is the Chinese word for "god." Confucius believes that god is mystical and unknowable. It is a level above *shengren* (聖人).

Shengren (聖人) The term *shengren* (sage) is usually associated with Confucianism. In the classic Chinese literature, no one has self-proclaimed as a *shengren*. Sage is a title granted by others. It is a level above *junzi* (an exemplary person).

NOTES

CHAPTER 1

1. Wayne D. Bowman and Ana Lucía Frega, eds., *The Oxford Handbook of Philosophy in Music Education* (Oxford: Oxford University Press, 2012), 7.
2. Ibid.
3. Wayne D. Bowman and Ana Lucía Frega, "Introduction," in *The Oxford Handbook of Philosophy in Music Education*, ed. Wayne D. Bowman and Ana Lucía Frega (Oxford: Oxford University Press, 2012), 4 and footnote 1.
4. Michael Mark and Patrice Madura, *Contemporary Music Education*, 4th ed. (Boston: Schirmer, Cengage Learning, 2014), 53.
5. See *Jici Shangchuan* in *Yizhuan* 《易傳》《繫辭上傳》:「形而上者謂之道，形而下者謂之器。」.
6. Qian Mu 錢穆, *Lishi yu wenhua lunchong* 歷史與文化論叢 [Essays on history and culture] (Taipei: Tung Da Books 東大圖書有限公司, 1979), 6–17.
7. *Yue jiao* may be literally translated as "music education." However, the meaning of *yue* during the time of Confucius is not the same as our contemporary understanding of "music." Historical documents suggest that *yue* includes integration of dance while singing and playing instruments (*Guyue, Zhongxiaji, Lushichunqiu* 《呂氏春秋》《仲夏紀》《古樂》:昔葛天氏之樂，三人操牛尾投足以歌八闋). During Confucius' time, *yue* may or may not include dance (see *Analects* 《論語》 3.23 and *Yueji, Liji* 《禮記》《樂記》). Furthermore, the notion of *yue jiao* implies Confucius' idea of *liyue jiaohua* (禮樂教化), which is designed to meet the need for social change at the time, not reflecting the contemporary social system at all. Therefore, I leave *yue* (樂) untranslated here.
8. Lao Siguang did not refer to Qian Mu's three levels of culture but posited four types of cultural activities with the first two being similar to Qian's third layer of "spirit": "ideology" and "attitude." Lao's other two types of cultural activities were "system" and "folkway." See Siguang Lao 勞思光, *Zhongguo wenhua yaoyi xinbian* 中國文化要義新編 [Essentials of Chinese culture, new edition] (Hong Kong: The Chinese University Press 中文大學出版社, 1998), 6.
9. Just to provide a snapshot regarding the significance of Fu Pei-Rong's work, a simple search using his Chinese name "傅佩榮" at amazon.cn (i.e., the Chinese version of amazon.com) between May 2013 and September 2017 consistently comes up with well over two hundred publications in Chinese philosophy authored by him for sale. In addition, he has extensive live lecture series throughout China and numerous recorded and broadcast interviews and lectures throughout China.

10. Fu Pei-Rong 傅佩榮, *Lunyu jiedu* 論語解讀 [The *Analects* reader] (Taipei: New Century Publishing Co. 立緒文化事業有限公司, 2012), 3.
11. It is not until the fourth edition of Michael L. Mark's *Music Education: Source Readings from Ancient Greece to Today* (New York: Routledge, 2013), xii–xiv, that a debate between Mozi (ca. 470–391 BC) and Xunzi (ca. 312–230 BC) appears, recognizing two of the many philosophical sources from early China. The previous editions of the source readings were published in 1982, 2002, and 2007 without a trace of thought outside the Western tradition. While there are other non-Greek ancient literary cultures, such as the Egyptans, Mesopotamians, Indians, and Jews, they fall outside my background and experience. Other indigenous non-Greek cultures with less of a literary tradition, and more of an oral tradition, such as those found in Africa, put me even further away from investigating them philosophically. The Chinese tradition, however, is what I was born with and have gone in and out innumerable times physically, philosophically, psychologically, and musically. Writing this book has helped me articulate this way of thinking in a systematized and scholastic way.
12. Leonard Tan provides ex post facto accounts of contemporary phenomena in education and music education from early Chinese philosophical perspectives. See Leonard Tan, "Confucius: Philosopher of Twenty-First-Century Skills," *Educational Philosophy and Theory* 48, no. 12 (2016): 1233–1243, accessed August 2, 2017, http://www.tandfonline.com/doi/full/10.1080/00131857.2016.1182416; and Leonard Tan, "Reimer through Confucian Lenses: Resonances with Classical Chinese Aesthetics," *Philosophy of Music Education Review* 23, no. 2 (2015): 183–201. He also works toward theories of music education as inspired by a selection of ancient Chinese philosophies. See Leonard Tan, "Towards an Ancient Chinese-Inspired Theory of Music Education," *Music Education Research* 18, no. 4 (2016): 399–410, accessed August 2, 2017, http://www.tandfonline.com.ezproxy.lib.usf.edu/doi/full/10.1080/14613808.2015.1122751; Leonard Tan, "Confucian *Creatio in situ*—Philosophical Resource for a Theory of Creativity in Instrumental Music Education," *Music Education Research* 18, no. 1 (2016): 91–108, accessed August 2, 2017, http://www.tandfonline.com.ezproxy.lib.usf.edu/doi/full/10.1080/14613808.2014.993602; and Leonard Tan, "Towards a Transcultural Theory of Democracy for Instrumental Music Education," *Philosophy of Music Education Review* 22, no. 1 (2014): 61–77.
13. Nan Huaijin 南懷瑾, a renowned sinologist, stated that the Confucian culture, the Daoist culture, and all of Chinese culture were all developed since Zhou Wen Wang's *Yijing*. See his *Yijing jishui* 易經集說 [Essays on *Yijing*], in *Nan Huaijin xuanji* 南懷瑾選集 [Collected Works of Nan Huaijin], vol. 4 (Shanghai: Fudan University Press, 2012), 7. He saw that not only Confucianism and Daoism were rooted in *Yijing*, but the entire Chinese culture.
14. See Part I, Chinese Philosophy, edited by Chenyang Li, in Jay L. Garfield and William Edelglass, eds., *The Oxford Handbook of World Philosophy* (Oxford: Oxford University Press, 2011), 7–105. It could generate confusion when none of these prefixes are used when describing the philosophic schools of the later periods.
15. Yan Yuan 颜元 (1635–1704) of the early Qing Dynasty (1644–1911) writes critically about the need to discard neo-Confucianism (represented by Cheng Hao 程顥, Cheng Yi 程頤, and Zhu Xi 朱熹) so one can begin to understand classic Confucianism (represented by Confucius 孔子 and Mencius 孟子) (「必破一分程、朱，始入一分孔、孟。」) in his collected essays. See *Yan Yuan Ji* 颜元集 [Collected essays of Yan Yuan], vol. 2 (Beijing: Zhonghua Book Company 中華書

局, 1987), 774; and Liang Qichao 梁啓超, *Qing dai xueshu gailun* 清代學術概論 [An outline of academic studies in the Qing Dynasty] (Beijing: Zhonghua Book Company 中華書局, 2010), 32.
16. David L. Hall and Roger T. Ames, "Chinese Philosophy," in *Routledge Encyclopedia of Philosophy*, ed. E. Craig (London: Routledge, 1998), accessed August 2, 2017, from https://www.rep.routledge.com/articles/overview/chinese-philosophy/v-1.
17. This idea that picking a strand of hair would affect the entire body (*qian yi fa er dong quan shen* 牽一髮而動全身) is analogous to that of making a minute move would change the situation as a whole. It is rooted in the characteristically Chinese organismic view and reflected in the literary works of Su Shi 蘇軾 (1037–1101) in the Sung Dynasty and Gong Zizhen 龔自珍 (1792–1841) in the Qing Dynasty, who used a strand of hair and the larger body as a metaphor for a tiny element and the entire situation, respectively. Su Shi wrote in his *"Chengdu dabeigeji"* 《成都大悲閣記》：吾頭髮不可勝數，而身之毛孔亦不可勝數，牽一髮而頭為之動，拔一毛而身為之變，然則髮皆吾頭，而毛孔皆吾身也。. See Su Shi 蘇軾, *Su Shi wenji* 蘇軾文集 [Collected works of Su Shi] (Beijing: Zhonghua Shuju 中華書局, 1986), 395. Gong Zizhen wrote in his *"Zi chuncu qiuou you suo ganchu"* 《自春徂秋偶有所感觸》：一髮不可牽，牽之動全身。[One cannot pick a strand of hair or the entire body would move]. See Gong Zizhen, *Gong Zizhen quanji* 龔自珍全集 [Collected works of Gong Zizhen] (Shanghai: Shanghai Peoples Publishing 上海人民出版社, 1975), 485.
18. This idea is also the basis of the meridian system in the human body, which is an important foundation of traditional Chinese medicine. See James D. Adams and Eric J. Lien, *Traditional Chinese Medicine: Scientific Basis for Its Use* (Cambridge, UK: Royal Society of Chemistry Publishing, 2013).
19. This is similar to Carl Gustav Jung's principle of synchronicity. See Carl Gustav Jung, *Synchronicity: An Acausal Connecting Principle* (Princeton, NJ: Princeton University Press, 1960/2011).
20. This is a point recently echoed by Leonard Tan with reference to music education. See Leonard Tan, "Response to Alexandra Kertz-Welzel's '"Two Souls, Alas, Reside within My Breast": Reflections on German and American Music Education regarding the Internationalization of Music Education,' *Philosophy of Music Education Review* 21, no. 1 (Spring 2013): 52–65," *Philosophy of Music Education Review* 23, no. 1 (2015): 113–117.
21. Carl Gustav Jung, *Synchronicity: An Acausal Connecting Principle* (Princeton, NJ: Princeton University Press, 1960/2011), 34.
22. Ibid, 35.
23. Ibid, 73.
24. Thomé H. Fang 方東美, *The Chinese View of Life: The Philosophy of Comprehensive Harmony* (Taipei: Linking Publishing, 1980), 11. Note that Fang is one of the very few Chinese philosophy scholars whose original writing is in English.
25. Ibid.
26. For example, schools of propositions in music education in the United States are found at the philosophical level (e.g., music education as aesthetic education and praxial music education), at the curricular approach level (e.g., based on large ensembles and based on small groups), at the musical stylistic level (e.g., Western classical and contemporary music and world and popular musics), and at the teaching strategic level (e.g., teacher-led and learner-centered).
27. Chenyang Li, *The Confucian Philosophy of Harmony* (New York: Routledge, 2014), 9.
28. Ibid., 23–34.

29. Zong-qi Cai, "In Quest of Harmony: Plato and Confucius on Poetry," *Philosophy East and West* 49, no. 3 (1999): 317–345.
30. Chenyang Li, *The Confucian Philosophy of Harmony* (New York: Routledge, 2014), 23–34.
31. Buddhism was an import from India in the 2nd century AD.
32. Mou Zongsan 牟宗三, *Zhongguo zhexue di tezhi* 中國哲學的特質 [Special qualities of Chinese philosophy] (Taipei: Student Book 學生書局, 1974), 5–6.
33. Qian Mu 錢穆, *Zhongguo wenhuashi daolun* 中國文化史導論 [An introduction to Chinese cultural history] (Taipei: Lantai Publishing House 蘭台出版社, 2001).
34. There is an abundance of examples of Western philosophical domination in the practice of music education in China, with only brief references to fragments of traditional Chinese philosophical ideologies. For example, see Cao Li 曹理, *Putong xuexiao yinyue jiaoyuxue* 普通學校音樂教育學 [General school music education] (Shanghai: Shanghai Education Publishing House 上海教育出版社, 1993), 1–36; Yin Aiqing 尹愛青, *Yinyue kecheng yu jiaoxue lun* 音樂課程與教學論 [Music curriculum and pedagogical theory] (Changchun, China: Northeast Normal University Press 東北師範大學出版社, 2005); Yin Aiqing 尹愛青, *Zhongxue yinyue Jiaoyu shixi xingdong celue* 中學音樂教育實習行動策略 [Secondary school music educational practice action plans] (Changchun, China: Northeast Normal University Press 東北師範大學出版社, 2007); and Xie Jiaxing 謝嘉幸 and Yu Wenwu 郁文武, *Yinyue Jiaoyu Yu Jiaoxuefa* 音樂教育與教學法 [Music education and pedagogy] (Beijing: Higher Education Press 高等教育出版社, 2006).
35. See Xie Jiaxing 謝嘉幸 and Bao Yuanyi 包原銥, "*Zhongguo gudai zhexue sixiang dui dangdai yinyue jiaoyu keneng di qishi*" 中國古代哲學思想對當代音樂教育可能的啟示 [Potential implications of ancient Chinese philosophy on contemporary music education], in *Dangdai yinyue jiaoyu zhexue lungao* 當代音樂教育哲學論稿 [Essays on contemporary philosophy of music education], ed. Ma Da 馬達 and Chen Yaxian 陳雅先 (Shanghai: Shanghai Music Publishing House 上海音樂出版社, 2010), 81–88. Even here, this is only one of fifteen chapters of a book published in China dedicated to the philosophy of music education. The Western domination in music education practices is explicitly stated in another chapter in the same book: Zhu Yujiang 朱玉江, "*Dangdai zhongguo yinyue jiaoyu di zhutixing zhexue fansi*" 當代中國音樂教育的主體性哲學反思 [Reflection on the subjective philosophy of music education in contemporary China], ed. Ma Da 馬達 and Chen Yaxian 陳雅先 (Shanghai: Shanghai Music Publishing House 上海音樂出版社, 2010), 96–113.
36. For example, see John H. Berthrong, *Transformations of the Confucian Way* (Boulder, CO: Westview Press, 1998); Carsun Chang, *The Development of Neo-Confucian Thought*, 2 vols. (New York: Bookman Associates, 1957–1962); Peter K. Bol, *Neo-Confucianism in History* (Cambridge, MA: Harvard University Asia Center, 2008); Chung-ying Cheng, *New Dimensions of Confucian and Neo-Confucian Philosophy* (Albany: State University of New York Press, 1991); Umberto Bresciani, *Reinventing Confucianism: The New Confucian Movement* (Taipei: Taipei Ricci Institute for Chinese Studies, 2001); and John Makeham, ed., *New Confucianism* (New York: Palgrave Macmillan, 2003).
37. See Part I, Chinese Philosophy, edited by Chenyang Li, Chapters 1–4, in Jay L. Garfield and William Edelglass, eds., *The Oxford Handbook of World Philosophy* (Oxford: Oxford University Press, 2011), 13–57.
38. Confucius wrote extensively about *Yijing* in *Yizhuan* 《易傳》, which is a common attachment to *Yijing*. There are also many references to *Yijing* ideologies

in Confucius writings. The ideologies of *Yijing* is clearly a basis for Laozi and Zhuangzi, with extensive references to natural phenomena. Daoists have always treated *Yijing* as one of their earliest and most important records.

39. While most contemporary scholars of early Chinese texts are based on the interpretations and editing of Zhu Xi 朱熹 (1130–1200), some would question his interpretations and editing of the original texts. Fu Pei-Rong 傅佩榮 would go so far as to state that "on the surface Zhu Xi was interpreting [the Confucian texts] but in reality he was using [the Confucian texts] to interpret his own philosophy" (see *Yukai haobianzai: Fu Pei-Rong ping zhuzhu sishu* 予豈好辯哉：傅佩榮評朱注四書 [Do I enjoy debates: Fu Pei-Rong's criticism for Zhu Xi's interpretation of *Sishu*] (Taipei: Linking Books 聯經出版事業股份有限公司, 2013), i. In addition, readers should note that the Neo-Confucianism movement begun in the eleventh century led by a group of social and political elites was strongly influenced by Buddhism and Daoism while maintaining Confucian ideals as the core. Zhu Xi became one of the most important contributing figures in this movement, which permeated throughout China, Japan, and Korea later. The retroactive creation of the New Confucianism movement in 1986, sanctioned by the government in the People's Republic of China, further modified the ideology with "a strong sense of mission to rejuvenate Chinese culture" (Makeham, *New Confucianism*, 30).

40. Philosophy should be open ended (Bowman and Frega, *Oxford Handbook*, 22–23). As this text is an important step to interrogate early Chinese philosophies cohesively in a music educational context, it is possible that future interrogations might focus on their later developments or any of their branches.

41. As quoted in Xiaowen Ye 葉小文, "Nishan Forum: Encounter between Two Sages" 尼山論壇:兩個聖者的相遇, in *Nishan: Listen to Diverse Voices of the World: True Records of the First Nishan Forum on World Civilizations* 尼山：聆聽世界多元聲音——首屆尼山世界文明論壇實錄 (Beijing: China Intercontinental Press 五洲傳播出版社, 2011), 128. Also see Maotian Fang's (方茂田) slightly different version in the same publication, 57. The same quote appears in Chinese version of the document on page 115 and page 49, respectively.

42. See Weiming Tu, *New Horizons in Eastern Humanism: Buddhism, Confucianism, and the Quest for Global Peace* (London: I. B. Tauris, 2011); *Way, Learning, and Politics: Essays on the Confucian Intellectual* (Albany: State University of New York Press, 1993); and *Confucian Thought: Selfhood as Creative Transformation* (Albany: State University of New York Press, 1985).

43. Hsü Fu-kuan 徐復觀, *Zhongguo renxing lunshi—Xianqinpian* 中國人性論史——先秦篇 [The history of the Chinese philosophy of human nature: The Pre-Ch'in period] (Taipei: The Commercial Press, 台灣商務印書館, 1969), 3–13.

44. Bent Nielsen, *A Companion to Yi Jing Numerology and Cosmology: Chinese Studies of Images and Numbers from Han (202 BCE–220 CE) to Song (960–1279 CE)* (New York: RoutledgeCurson, 2003), xv.

45. Ibid.

46. Ibid, xvi.

47. Similar problems are found in translated works of Confucius from the late seventeenth century through the eighteenth century. See Confucius, *The Morals of Confucius, a Chinese Philosopher, Who Flourished above Five Hundred Years before the Coming of Christ. Being One of the Choicest Pieces of Learning Remaining of That Nation*. Printed for Randal Taylor. London, UK: 1691 (1780?). Eighteenth Century Collections Online, the British Library; Confucius, *The Morals of Confucius a Chinese*

Philosopher, who Flourished above Five Hundred Years before the Coming of our Lord and Saviour Jesus Christ. Being One of the Choicest Pieces of Learning Remaining of That Nation. 2nd ed. Printed for T. Horne. London, UK: 1706. Eighteenth Century Collections Online, the British Library. There was also another printing for F. Fayram in 1724.

48. "Education Breeds Confidence. Confidence Breeds Hope. Hope Breeds Peace" (UNESCO, *Rethinking Education: Towards a Global Common Good* [Paris: UNESCO, 2015], 14).

49. *Analects* 14.28: 仁者不憂，知者不惑，勇者不懼。 is selected for the reverse translation, which means "Those with benevolence have no worry. Those with wisdom have no perplexity. Those with bravery have no fear." See footnote 1 in the Chinese version (UNESCO 聯合國教科文組織, *Rethinking Education: Towards a Global Common Good* 反思教育：向"全球共同利益"的理念轉變 [Paris: UNESCO 聯合國教科文組織, 2015], 14).

50. This is similar to Confucius' "unified principle in all of his knowledge" (*yi yi guan zhi* 一以貫之) (*Analects*, 4.15 and 15.3).

51. Kenneth Prewitt, "The Future of International Research," in *Changing Perspectives on International Education*, ed. P. O'Meara, H. D. Mehlinger, and R. M. Newman (Bloomington: Indiana University Press, 2001), 324–336.

52. The *Thirteen Classics* 《十三經》used in this writing include *Shijing* 《詩經》, *Shangshu* 《尚書》, *Yijing* 《易經》 (including *Yizhuan* 《易傳》), *Liji* 《禮記》 (including *Daxue* 《大學》, *Zhongyong* 《中庸》, *Yueji* 《樂記》, and *Xueji* 《學記》), *Chunqiu Zuozhuan* 《春秋佐傳》, *Analects* 《論語》, and *Mencius* 《孟子》.

53. The *Twenty-Two Masters* 《二十二子》used in this writing include *Laozi* 《老子》, *Zhuangzi* 《莊子》, *Liezi* 《列子》, *Xunzi* 《荀子》, *Guanzi* 《管子》, and *Lushichunqiu* 《呂氏春秋》.

54. In addition to the *Thirteen Classics* and *Twenty-Two Masters*, two historical texts are used in this writing: Sima Qian, 司馬遷, *Shiji* 《史記》 [*The Book of History*] (Beijing: Zhonghua Shuju, 2008); and Jin Liangnian 金良年 and Liang Gu 梁谷, eds., *Guoyu* 《國語》 (Shanghai: Shanghai Guji Publishing House 上海古籍出版社, 2008).

55. For details about this justification, see Lao Siguang 勞思光, *Xinbian zhongguo zhexue shi* 新編中國哲學史 [A new history of Chinese philosophy], vol. 1 (Taipei: Sanmin 三民書局, 2010). The "new" in the title is in response to earlier texts on the same topic authored by others, as explained on pp. 1–19. For more about the derailment of Xunzi (313–238 BC) from classic Confucianism, see Fu Pei-Rong 傅佩榮, *Ru dao tianlun fawei* 儒道天論發微 [On heaven in Confucianism and Daoism] (Taipei: Linking Books 聯經出版事業, 2010), 161–178.

56. Mou Zongsan 牟宗三, *Zhongguo zhexue di tezhi* 中國哲學的特質 [Special qualities of Chinese philosophy] (Taipei: Student Book 學生書局, 1974), 5–6.

57. An explicit comment by a Chinese music educator regarding the shift of Xunzi away from Confucius and Mencius is found in Cao Li 曹理, *Putong xuexiao yinyue jiaoyuxue* 普通學校音樂教育學 (General school music education) (Shanghai: Shanghai Education Publishing House 上海教育出版社, 1993), 39.

58. Peter K. Bol, *Neo-Confucianism in History* (Cambridge, MA: Harvard University Asia Center, 2008), 2–3.

CHAPTER 2

1. Zhu Bokun 朱伯崑, *Yixue zhexue shi* 易學哲學史 [History of the philosophy of *Yi*], vol. 1 (Beijing: Huaxia Publications 華夏出版社, 1995), 41–42.

2. *Yijing* 《易經》 and *Yizhuan* 《易傳》 in combination is sometimes referred to as *Zhouyi* 《周易》. In some contemporary publications, *Yijing* includes *Yizhuan* without titling it *Zhouyi*. Due to the Confucian association with *Yizhuan*, I have chosen to make a distinction between *Yijing* and *Yizhuan*, rather than referring to *Zhouyi* as a whole, throughout this text.
3. Zhu Bokun 朱伯崑, *Yixue zhexue shi* 易學哲學史 [History of the philosophy of *Yi*], in four volumes, is a staple for anyone who studies the history and philosophy of *Yijing* (Beijing: Huaxia Publications 華夏出版社, 1995).
4. See Fu Pei-Rong 傅佩榮, *Jiedu Yijing* 解讀易經 [Reading *Yijing*] (Taipei: New Century Publishing Co. 立緒文化事業有限公司, 2005), 4; and *Le tian zhi ming* (樂天知命) (Taipei: Tianxia Wenhua 天下文化, 2011), 15 and 714–715 for supporting *Yijing* being an inspiration for Confucianism; and Chen Guying (陳鼓應), *Daojia yixue jiangou* (Construction of the Daoist *Yijing* 道家易學建構) (Taipei: Commercial Press, 2003), 3–12, for supporting *Yijing* being a Daoist text only.
5. See Fu Pei-Rong 傅佩榮, *Jiedu Yijing* 解讀易經 [Reading *Yijing*] (Taipei: New Century Publishing Co. 立緒文化事業有限公司, 2005), 4.
6. Based on "儒家的倫理觀念，道家和陰陽五行家的天道觀，成了《易傳》解易的指導思想。" in Zhu Bokun 朱伯崑, *Yixue zhexue shi*, vol. 1, 易學哲學史 [History of the philosophy of *Yi*] (Beijing: Huaxia Publications 華夏出版社, 1995), 55.
7. Kong Yingda (孔穎達), the thirty-second descendant of Confucius, authored *Zhouyi zhengyi* 《周易》正義 [Clarifications on *Zhouyi*], as cited in Fu Pei-Rong 傅佩榮, *Jiedu Yijing* (Reading *Yijing* 解讀易經) (Taipei: New Century Publishing Co. 立緒文化事業有限公司, 2005), 3–4. Kong also authored clarifications for other classic texts. For a summary of the most notable interpretations and perspectives of *Yijing* throughout the millennia, see Sun Zhenxing 孫振星, *Baihua Yijing* 白話易經 [*Yijing* in plain language]. (Taipei: Shengguang Publications 星光出版社, 1981), 10–16. For an account of the historical evolution of *Yijing* and *Yizhuan*, see Li Xueqin 李學勤, *Zhouyi suyuan* 周易溯源 [Investigating the origin of *Zhouyi*] (Chengdu, Sichuan, China: Bashu Shushe 巴蜀書社, 2006).
8. Adopted from Fu Pei-Rong 傅佩榮, *Le tian zhi ming* 樂天知命 (Taipei: Tianxia Wenhua 天下文化, 2011), 16.
9. See *Jici Shangchuan, Yizhuan* 《易傳》《繫辭上傳》：「乾以易知，坤以簡能。易則易知，簡則易從。易知則有親，易從則有功。有親則可久，有功則可大。可久則賢人之德，可大則賢人之業。易簡，而天下之理得矣；天下之理得，而成位乎其中矣。」
10. Nan Huaijin 南懷瑾, *Yijing jishui* 易經集說 [Essays on *Yijing*], in *Nan Huaijin xuanji* 南懷瑾選集 [Collected Works of Nan Huaijin], vol. 4 (Shanghai: Fudan University Press, 2012), 10–11.
11. The word *gua* 卦 in Chinese is used to describe both the trigrams and the hexagrams. Here, the 64 *gua* refer to the 64 hexagrams.
12. Zhu Bokun 朱伯崑, *Yixue zhexue shi*, vol. 1, (易學哲學史 History of the philosophy of *Yi*) (Beijing: Huaxia Publications 華夏出版社, 1995), 16–17.
13. Extensive discussions regarding the authorship of the different essays in *Yizhuan* are found in Zhu Bokun 朱伯崑, *Yixue zhexue shi*, vol. 1, (易學哲學史 History of the philosophy of *Yi*) (Beijing: Huaxia Publications 華夏出版社, 1995), 41–54. The view that Confucius and his students were authors of *Yizhuan* has been supported by scholars throughout the millennia, from Sima Qian 司馬遷 (145–86 BC), *Shiji* 《史記》, to Fu Pei-Rong 傅佩榮 (b. 1950), *Jiedu Yijing* 解讀易經 [Reading *Yijing*] (Taipei: New Century Publishing Co. 立緒文化事業有限公司, 2005), 4.

14. For example, in *Wenyan Zhuan, Yizhuan*: "Speech should be trustworthy, action should be prudent, avoid evil to preserve sincerity, be kind but not boost, and use virtue to cultivate others" (《易傳》《文言傳》：「庸言之信，庸行之謹，閑邪存其誠，善世而不伐，德博而化。」). The phrase "Exemplary persons should accumulate virtues as their accomplishments" (君子進德修業) appears two times in *Wenyan Zhuan*. Exemplary persons should also "refine their words to establish their sincerity" (修辭立其誠). "Great people's virtues should be aligned with the functions of heaven and earth" (夫大人者，與天地合其德).
15. For example, in *Jici Shang Zhuan, Yizhuan*: "Coordinated changes of a *yin* and a *yang* is called *dao*. Those who continue with this operation is kindness. Those who complete this process are mature beings" (《易傳》《繫辭上傳》：「一陰一陽之謂道，繼之者善也，成之者性也。」).
16. For example, in the paragraph of *Jici Shang Zhuan, Yizhuan* (《易傳》《繫辭上傳》), there are six pairs of opposing poles: heaven and earth, *qian* and *kun*, low and high, precious and poor, action and still, and hard and soft. The same paragraph ends with *yin* and *yang*, sun and moon, and winter and summer. All are described as normal operations. Many other pairs of opposing poles are found across other paragraphs: male and female, good and bad, loss and gain, day and night, forward and backward, big and small, life and death, and so forth. In the book by Laozi, Chen Guying 陳鼓應 reported at least eighty-five pairs of opposing poles. See his *Daojia yixue jiangou* 道家易學建構 [Construction of the Daoist Yijing] (Taipei: Commercial Press, 2003), 2.
17. The original quote is "占卦容易解卦難." See Fu Pei-Rong, *Bu ke si yi di yi jing zhan bu* (不可思議的易經占卜 *The mysterious I-Ching fortune telling*) (Taipei: Reading Times Publishing 時報文化, 2010), 13.
18. Fu Pei-Rong 傅佩榮, *Le tian zhi ming* 樂天知命 (Taipei: Tianxia Wenhua 天下文化, 2011), 635.
19. Bent Nielsen, *A companion to Yi Jing Numerology and Cosmology: Chinese Studies of Images and Numbers from Han (202 BCE–220 CE) to Song (960–1279 CE)* (New York: RoutledgeCurson, 2003), 227.
20. Zhu Bokun 朱伯崑, *Yixue manbu* 易學漫步 [Strolling in *Yi* studies] (Taipei: Student Book 台灣學生, 1996), 131–138.
21. The formation and meaning of each of the trigram is explained in much more detail in Fu Pei-Rong 傅佩榮, *Le tian zhi ming* 樂天知命 (Taipei: Tianxia Wenhua 天下文化, 2011), 12–25.
22. Construction of *gua* around the *taiji* diagram is found since the Song dynasty (960–1279 AD) and thereafter.
23. For a detailed description of variations of the hexagrams in English, see Bent Nielsen, *A Companion to Yi Jing Numerology and Cosmology: Chinese Studies of Images and Numbers from Han* 漢 *(202 BCE–220 CE) to Song* 宋 *(960–1279 CE)* (New York: RoutledgeCurzon, 2003).
24. It is not too difficult to find evidence of a similar organismic view in contemporary music literature in the West. See Tia DeNora, *Music in Everyday Life* (Cambridge: Cambridge University Press, 2000), 61: "Music is an active ingredient in the organization of self, the shifting of mood, energy level, conduct style, mode of attention and engagement with the world. . . . Music's 'effects' come from the ways in which individuals orient to it, how they interpret it and how they place it within their personal musical maps, within the semiotic web of music and extra-musical associations."

25. See *Jici Shang Zhuan, Yizhuan* 《易傳》《繫辭上傳》：「君子居則觀其象，而玩其辭；動則觀其變，而玩其占。」.
26. Ibid (《易傳》《繫辭上傳》：「樂天知命，故不憂。」).
27. See *Jici Xia Zhuan, Yizhuan* (《易傳》《繫辭下傳》：「吉凶者，貞勝者也。天地之道，貞觀者也。日月之道，貞明者也，天下之動，貞夫一者也。」). The repeated use of *zhen* (貞) here refers to the need to be in a proper position.
28. The Chinese term for "the sun" is *tai yang* 太陽, which literally means the "one big extreme *yang*," or the first and paramount source of energy for all matters. It reflects an extreme end of *yang*.

CHAPTER 3

1. In contemporary context, this statement holds only in philosophy communities, that is, people who study Chinese philosophy. It does not refer to the Chinese general public.
2. See Lao Siguang 勞思光, *Zhongguo wenhua yaoyi xinbian* 中國文化要義新編 [Essentials of Chinese culture, new edition] (Hong Kong: The Chinese University Press 香港中文大學出版社, 1998), 13–14.
3. According to Hsü Fu-kuan, *li* (ritual 禮) evolved from the concept of *yi* (a container used in pre- and early-Zhou religious rituals 彝). See Hsü Fu-kuan 徐復觀, *Zhongguo renxing lunshi—Xianqinpian* 中國人性論史——先秦篇 [The history of the Chinese philosophy of human nature: The Pre-Ch'in period] (Taipei: The Commercial Press, Ltd. 台灣商務印書館, 1969), 36–50.
4. Some would dispute Confucius' direct involvement in writing *Yizhuan*. See Lao Siguang (勞思光), *Xinbian zhongguo zhexue shi* [A new history of Chinese philosophy] 新編中國哲學史), vol. 1 (Taipei: Sanmin 三民書局, 2010), 107–108. Nevertheless, Confucius' direct involvement in writing it is superfluous in the current discussion. It is more important to recognize its alignment with Confucius' ideology. The involvement of Confucius' students in writing it seems to be less debatable.
5. 「一陰一陽之謂道，繼之者善也，成之者性也。」(*Jicishang, Yizhuan* 《易傳》《繫辭上》); see also 「昔者聖人之作《易》也，將以順性命之理，是以立天之道曰陰與陽，立地之道曰柔與剛，立人之道曰仁與義。兼三才而兩之，故《易》六畫而成卦。分陰分陽，迭用柔剛，故《易》六位而成章。」(*Shuiguazhuan, Yizhuan* 《易傳》《說卦傳》).
6. This brief description of Confucius' life is based on Fu Pei-Rong 傅佩榮, *Lunyu jiedu* 論語解讀 [*Analects* reader] (Taipei: New Century Publishing Co. 立緒文化事業有限公司, 2012), 15–16.
7. In brief, *ren* is achieved by being sincere and kind. See *Mencius* (1.5).
8. Fu Pei-Rong 傅佩榮, *Mengzi jiedu* 孟子解讀 [*Mencius* reader] (Taipei: New Century Publishing Co. 立緒文化事業有限公司, 2013), 5.
9. Sima Qian 司馬遷 (ca. 145–86 BC), author of *Shiji* 《史記》 [The book of history], is a renowned historian. Cited in ibid, 4.
10. See Lao Siguang 勞思光, *Xinbian zhongguo zhexue shi* 新編中國哲學史 [A new history of Chinese philosophy], vol. 1 (Taipei: Sanmin 三民書局, 2010), 153.
11. For a discussion on the time and authorship of *Yueji*, see Fang Baozhang 方寶璋 and Zheng Junhui 鄭俊暉, *Zhongguo yinyue wenxianxue* 中國音樂文獻學 [Chinese music bibliography] (Fuzhou, China: Fujian Education Press, 2006), 288–291.
12. Some may attach classic Confucianism with the term "humanism." However, humanism has a totally different connotation in Western philosophy.

"Human-centric" or "humanly" seem to be more appropriate ways to describe classic Confucianism.
13. 子曰：「人能弘道，非道弘人。」 *Analects* (15.29). The translation of "heavenly doctrine" here is derived from one of the trickiest words to translate from Chinese: *dao* (道) in Confucian context. "Achieving one's goal" here is used to connote the *dao* that is influenced by humans. It is critical for readers to distinguish the meaning of *dao* in different philosophical schools. Daoism, for example, has a distinctively different meaning (see Chapter 4).
14. Ibid.
15. 物格而後知至，知至而後意誠，意誠而後心正，心正而後身脩，身脩而後家齊，家齊而後國治，國治而後天下平。 *Great Learning* (3, also see 2). Note that "family (家)," "nation (國)," and "world (天下)" should be understood in the context of the Warring States period, when the family includes the entire clan, not just the immediate family, the nation refers to the feudal boundary, and the world is the divided nation. Other continents were not known.
16. On an application of this concentric circle of human influences in music education, see Charlene Tan and Leonard Tan, "A Shared Vision of Human Excellence: Confucian Spirituality and Arts Education," *Pastoral Care in Education* 34, no. 3 (2016): 156–166.
17. 齊景公問政於孔子。孔子對曰：「君君，臣臣，父父，子子。」公曰：「善哉！信如君不君，臣不臣，父不父，子不子，雖有粟，吾得而食諸？」 *Analects* (12.11).
18. 父子有親，君臣有義，夫婦有別，長幼有序，朋友有信。 *Mencius* (5.4).
19. 是君臣、父子、兄弟終去仁義，懷利以相接；然而不亡者，未之有也。...為人臣者懷仁義以事其君，為人子者懷仁義以事其父，為人弟者懷仁義以事其兄，是君臣、父子、兄弟去利，懷仁義以相接也。 *Mencius* (12.4).
20. 仁之於父子也，義之於君臣也，禮之於賓主也，智之於賢者也，聖人之於天道也，命也，有性焉，君子不謂命也。 *Mencius* (14.24).
21. This is similar to how some close-but-unrelated friends, colleagues, schoolmates, and others call each other "brothers" or "sisters" today. They care for each other like one of their own.
22. 子夏曰：「商聞之矣：『死生有命，富貴在天。君子敬而無失，與人恭而有禮。四海之內，皆兄弟也。』君子何患乎無兄弟也？」 *Analects* (12.5).
23. 孟子曰：「居下位而不獲於上，民不可得而治也。獲於上有道，不信於友，弗獲於上矣。信於友有道，事親弗悅，弗信於友矣。悅親有道，反身不誠，不悅於親矣。誠身有道，不明乎善，不誠其身矣。是故誠者，天之道也；思誠者，人之道也。...」 *Mencius* (7.12).
24. Ibid. Also see *Zhongyong* (20.5) (Sincerity is a heavenly way of operation. To allow sincerity to work is the humanly *dao* 誠者，天之道也；誠之者，人之道也。).
25. *Wenyan, Yizhuan* (《易傳》《文言》).
26. Ibid.
27. See *Analects* 17.9 for a more extensive description of the functions of studying poetry.
28. 子曰：「興於詩，立於禮，成於樂。」 *Analects* (8.8).
29. The view on kindness is a major point of departure between classic Confucianism and Neo-Confucianism. While Mencius (372–289 BC) emphasized kindness, Xunzi (313–238 BC) proposed a view on evil, which is described as human nature to be rectified by human efforts in producing kindness (*Xunzi* 《荀子》 17.23; 人之性惡，其善者偽也。). Over a thousand years later, Zhu Xi 朱熹 (1130–1200) interprets kindness (*shan* 善) as an inherent quality in humans. See Fu Pei-Rong

傅佩榮, *Yukai haobianzai: Fu Pei-Rong ping zhuzhu sishu* 予豈好辯哉：傅佩榮評朱注四書 [How can it be argued: Fu Pei-Rong's criticism for Zhu Xi's interpretation of *Sishu*] (Taipei: Linking Books 聯經出版事業股份有限公司, 2013), ii–iii.

30. 子曰：「君子成人之美，不成人之惡。小人反是。」(*Analects*, 12.16). See Fu Pei-Rong's interpretation in Fu Pei-Rong 傅佩榮, *Lunyu jiedu* 論語解讀 [The *Analects* reader] (Taipei: New Century Publishing Co. 立緒文化事業有限公司, 2012), 306.

31. 告子曰：「性猶湍水也，決諸東方則東流，決諸西方則西流。人性之無分於善不善也，猶水之無分於東西也。」孟子曰：「水信無分於東西。無分於上下乎？人性之善也，猶水之就下也。人無有不善，水無有不下。今夫水，搏而躍之，可使過顙；激而行之，可使在山。是豈水之性哉？其勢則然也。人之可使為不善，其性亦猶是也。」*Mencius* (11.2).

32. Ibid.

33. 魯欲使樂正子為政。孟子曰：「吾聞之，喜而不寐。」公孫丑曰：「樂正子強乎？」曰：「否。」「有知慮乎？」曰：「否。」「多聞識乎？」曰：「否。」「然則奚為喜而不寐？」曰：「其為人也好善。」「好善足乎？」曰：「好善優於天下，而況魯國乎？夫苟好善，則四海之內，皆將輕千里而來告之以善。夫苟不好善，則人將曰：『訑訑，予既已知之矣。』訑訑之聲音顏色，距人於千里之外。士止於千里之外，則讒諂面諛之人至矣。與讒諂面諛之人居，國欲治，可得乎？」*Mencius* (12.13).

34. See Wei-ming Tu, *Way, Learning, and Politics: Essays on the Confucian Intellectual* (Albany: State University of New York Press, 1993).

35. Elaborated descriptions of the dyadic ideals of *li* and *yue* are found in *Yueji* 《樂記》. However, some of these descriptions are infused with post-Mencius Confucian thoughts.

36. Classic Confucians tend to emphasize on the humanly *dao* rather than the heavenly *dao*. See Mencius' reference to the humanly *dao* in *Mencius* 7.12 when he describes the self-reflection of sincerity (note 21 above).

37. For a contemporary interpretation of *junzi* based on the *Analects*, see Liu Linrui 劉林睿, "*Lunyu zhong de junzi xingxiang*" 《論語》中的"君子"形象 [Image of *junzi* in the *Analects*], in *Chuantong ruxue de lishi xingcha* 傳統儒學的歷史省察 [Reflections and observations of traditional Confucianism], ed. Li Zonggui (李宗桂) and Zhang Zaoqun (張造群) (Guangzhou, China: Flower City Publishing House 廣東花城出版社, 2012), 57–66. Furthermore, most explicit are the *Analects* passages (2.14, 4.11, 4.16, 7.37, 12.16, 12.19, 13.23, 13.25, 13.26, 14.6, 14.23, 15.2, 15.21, 15.34, and 16.8) that contrast between *junzi* (君子) and *xiaoren* (小人). The latter has multiple meanings, but it most prominently refers to the uneducated and the ill-developed in humanity standards or villains. Other meanings of *xiaoren* are (a) people in the general public (see *Analects* 17.14); (b) self-reference as a humble gesture, especially in front of someone in a higher status educationally, socially, politically, and otherwise; and (c) children or younger people. However, in classic Confucian philosophical discussions, *xiaoren* are those with low humanity standards, such as those who are dishonest, disrespectful, untrustworthy, greedy, short-sighted, display a lack of meaning and purpose, and so forth.

38. Confucius said, "*junzi* has three *daos* [not to be confused with the *dao* in Daoism] that I have not yet accomplished: *ren* and without worries, wisdom and without temptations, and courage without fear" (*Analects* 14.28; 子曰：「君子道者三，我無能焉：仁者不憂，知者不惑，勇者不懼。」; see also *Analects* 9.29).

39. For a more extensive description of courage based on Confucius' ideology, see Wu Linkun 吳林坤, *Kongzi lun yong de sange cengci* 孔子論勇的三個層次 [Confucius'

three levels of courage], in *Chuantong ruxue de lishi xingcha* 傳統儒學的歷史省察 [Reflections and observations of traditional Confucianism], ed. Li Zonggui 李宗桂 and Zhang Zaoqun 張造群 (Guangzhou, China: Flower City Publishing House 廣東花城出版社, 2012), 73–81.

40. Non-Chinese readers must be cautious here in reading *"ren,"* which is the same Romanization of two different Chinese words "人" (human) and "仁" (benevolence).

41. For example, see *Mencius* 3.6 (*ren . . . yi . . . li . . . zhi* 仁 . . . 義 . . . 禮 . . . 智) and 3.7 (*ren . . . zhi . . . li . . . yi* 仁 . . . 智 . . . 禮 . . . 義).

42. Mencius said, "without compassion is not human, without shame on evil is not human, without civility is not human, and without a sense of right and wrong is not human" (*Mencius* 3.6; 孟子曰：「...無惻隱之心，非人也；無羞惡之心，非人也；無辭讓之心，非人也；無是非之心，非人也。...」).

43. Also see *Mencius* 11.6.

44. 孟子曰：「君子所以異於人者，以其存心也。君子以仁存心，以禮存心。仁者愛人，有禮者敬人。愛人者人恆愛之，敬人者人恆敬之。有人於此，其待我以橫逆，則君子必自反也：我必不仁也，必無禮也，此物奚宜至哉？其自反而仁矣，自反而有禮矣，其橫逆由是也，君子必自反也：我必不忠。自反而忠矣，其橫逆由是也，君子曰：『此亦妄人也已矣。如此則與禽獸奚擇哉？於禽獸又何難焉？』是故君子有終身之憂，無一朝之患也。*Mencius* (8.28).

45. *Analects* 13.9; Confucius visited the nation of Wei, Ran You served as his guide. Confucius said, "there are so many common people here." Ran You asked, "when there are so many common people, what should we do with them?" Confucius responded, "enrich their lives." Ran You continued, "when their lives are already enriched, what should we do with them?" Confucius answered, "teach them." 子適衞，冉有僕。子曰：「庶矣哉！」冉有曰：「既庶矣。又何加焉？」曰：「富之。」曰：「既富矣，又何加焉？」曰：「教之。」. The conversation stopped, because "teaching" is a never-ending task.

46. 昔者子貢、問於孔子曰：「夫子聖矣乎？」孔子曰：「聖則吾不能，我學不厭而教不倦也。」子貢曰：「學不厭，智也；教不倦，仁也。仁且智，夫子既聖矣！」*Mencius* (3.2).

47. 孟子曰：「君子之所以教者五：有如時雨化之者，有成德者，有達財者，有答問者，有私淑艾者。此五者，君子之所以教也。」*Mencius* (13.40).

48. This explanation is a paraphrase from the introduction to *Yueji* 《樂記》in Wang Mengou 王夢鷗, ed., *Liji jinzhujinyi* 禮記今註今譯 [*Liji* modern annotation and translation], 2nd ed. (Taipei: The Commercial Press, Ltd., 2009), 655.

49. Confucius does not seem to care about letting others know that he is sad or that he cries. It is a normal human emotion as it arises in some life situations. The sadness described here could be related to his work as a funeral director. See also *Analects* 7.9, where his student described his reduced appetite when he ate with someone with a deceased family member (子食於有喪者之側，未嘗飽也。).

50. *Analects* 17.11; 子曰：「禮云禮云，玉帛云乎哉？樂云樂云，鐘鼓云乎哉？」

51. Another account of Confucius hearing the same type of music indicates that he could not taste the meat he ate for a very long time (literally, three months) afterwards. He commented that he could not have imagined that music could be so perfect (*Analects* 7.14; 子在齊聞《韶》，三月不知肉味，曰：「不圖為樂之至於斯也。」).

52. Throughout the ideologies of classic Confucianism, music is a reflection of the characteristics of the regime from which it comes. The earliest prominent documentation

of such a relationship between music and the society is found in the historical account of Li Zha's (李札, 576–484 BC) visit to Lu (魯) in 544 BC and being invited to comment on music from various states (*Xianggong Year 29, Chunqiu ZuoZhuan* 《春秋左傳》《襄公二十九年》). Li Zha was Confucius' teacher.

53. *Mencius* 2.1; 曰：「獨樂樂，與人樂樂，孰樂？」曰：「不若與人。」曰：「與少樂樂，與眾樂樂，孰樂？」曰：「不若與眾。」.
54. *Mencius* 1.2 and 2.1.
55. This should not be confused with Confucianism as a religion, which was being transformed in the Western Han period (206 BC–AD 24), not during the time of Confucius (551–479 BC) or Mencius (372–289 BC). See Feng Dawen 馮達文, *Zhongguo gudian zhexue lueshu* 中國古典哲學略述 [Brief description of classical Chinese philosophy] (Guangzhou, China: Guangdong Peoples Publishing House 廣東人民出版社, 2009), 163–165. Although classic Confucianism may function *like* a religion, it is a philosophy, not a religion. See Lao Siguang 勞思光, *Zhongguo wenhua yaoyi xinbian* 中國文化要義新編 [Essentials of Chinese culture, new edition] (Hong Kong: The Chinese University Press 香港中文大學出版社, 1998), 192–194.
56. This continuum is not an interpretation of *yin* and *yang*, because interaction between the two sides does not necessarily exist.
57. When Yan Yuan (顏淵) (521–481 BC), a student of Confucius, asked about how to lead a nation, Confucius mentioned using the music from honorable states in the past, but rejected the music from ignoble states (*Analects* 15.11).

CHAPTER 4

1. The years of Laozi remain largely a mystery, as much as Laozi as a person. His life dates have been reported in great disparities: 604–531 BC, 600–470 BC, 571–471 BC, or leaving the years out altogether to state only the centuries (sixth–fifth century BC). After consulting multiple sources, I have become inclined to agree with Hu Shi 胡適 (1891–1962) in that Laozi was born ca. 570 BC and lived until he was around ninety. See Hu Shi 胡適, *Zhongguo zhexueshi dagang* 中國哲學史大綱 [Outline of the history of Chinese philosophy] (Taipei: The Commercial Press, Ltd. 台灣商務印書館, 2008), 44–45.
2. The meeting of Laozi and Confucius is recorded in *Shiji* 《史記》 [The Book of History] by Sima Qian 司馬遷 (ca. 145–86 BC). The passage from *Laozi Hanfei, Liezhuan 3* (《列傳三》《老子韓非》) is also cited and explained in Fu Pei-Rong 傅佩榮, *Laozi jiedu* 老子解讀 [*Laozi* reader] (Taipei: New Century Publishing Co. 立緒文化事業有限公司, 2012), 4. However, as in some other historic incidences with vulnerable documentations, some would question its authenticity. See Lao Siguang 勞思光, *Xinbian zhongguo zhexue shi* 新編中國哲學史 [A new history of Chinese philosophy], vol. 1 (Taipei: Sanmin 三民書局, 2010), 204–207.
3. *Laozi Hanfei, Liezhuan 3, Shiji* [*The Book of History*] 《史記》《列傳三》《老子韓非》 by Sima Qian 司馬遷 (ca. 145–86 BC) (老子修道德，其學以自隱無名為務。居周久之，見周之衰，乃遂去。至關，關令尹喜曰：「子將隱矣，彊為我著書。」於是老子乃著書上下篇，言道德之意五千餘言而去，莫知其所終。). See Sima Qian 司馬遷, *Shiji* 《史記》 [*The Book of History*], vol. 3 (Beijing: Zhonghua Shuju, 2008), 1318.
4. Although Sima Qian is an authoritative historian, his accounts are being questioned by some. See Lao Siguang 勞思光, *Xinbian zhongguo zhexue shi* 新編中國哲學史 [A new history of Chinese philosophy], vol. 1 (Taipei: Sanmin 三民書局, 2010), 203–209.

5. For a detailed analysis of how *Yijing* is connected to *Laozi*, see Chen Guying 陳鼓應, *Daojia yixue jiangou* 道家易學建構 [Construction of the Daoist *Yijing*] (Taipei: Commercial Press, 2003).
6. Xue Ming-Sheng 薛明生, *Xian Qin liang Han Dao jia siwei yu shjian* 先秦兩漢道家思維與實踐 [Thoughts and practices of pre-Qin and two-Han Daoism] (Taipei: Wen Chin 文津出版社, 2007).
7. Fu Pei-Rong used this illustration multiple times in his classes at National Taiwan University in Spring 2013.
8. Alan Chan, "Laozi," *The Stanford Encyclopedia of Philosophy* (Spring 2014 Edition), ed. Edward N. Zalta, accessed August 2, 2017, http://plato.stanford.edu/archives/spr2014/entries/laozi/.
9. For discussions on the uncertainties of Laozi as a person, see Fu Pei-Rong 傅佩榮, *Laozi jiedu* 老子解讀 [*Laozi reader*] (Taipei: New Century Publishing Co. 立緒文化事業有限公司, 2012), 3–5; and Lao Siguang 勞思光, *Xinbian zhongguo zhexue shi* 新編中國哲學史 [A new history of Chinese philosophy], vol. 1 (Taipei: Sanmin 三民書局, 2010), 203–205.
10. See Lao Siguang 勞思光, *Xinbian zhongguo zhexue shi* 新編中國哲學史 [A new history of Chinese philosophy], vol. 1 (Taipei: Sanmin 三民書局, 2010), 245. Here I take it that Zhuangzi's completion of Daoism described by Lao Siguang refers to "classic Daoism" in the same spirit of this current book.
11. "If *dao* can be stated, it's not the everlasting *dao*. If a name can be used, it's not an everlasting name" (道可道，非常道。名可名，非常名。) in *Laozi* (1). The labeling of *dao* was done reluctantly. *Laozi* states, "I don't know its name, I reluctantly label it as *dao*" (吾不知其名，強字之曰道) (*Laozi*, 25; for an explanation about why this version, rather than the one in *Twenty-Two Masters* 《二十二子》, is used here, see Chen Guying 陳鼓應, ed., *Laozi jinzhujinyijipingjia* 老子今註今譯及評價 [*Laozi* modern annotation, translation, and criticism], 2nd ed. (Taipei: The Commercial Press, 2013), pp. 144–145, fn 6.).
12. Here I am referring to *Yijing*, *Laozi*, and *Zhuangzi*. There are, of course, other Daoist texts, but they are not as widely known as classic Daoist texts.
13. This is based on my studies of the original texts and their interpretations and discussions by the great masters and scholars listed in Chapter 1 (p. 17) of this text.
14. Fu Pei-Rong 傅佩榮, *Laozi jiedu* 老子解讀 [*Laozi* Reader] (Taipei: New Century Publishing Co. 立緒文化事業有限公司, 2012), 88.
15. The Chinese word *tian* (天) has been an all-time interest among sinologists. It is a noun that has been commonly referred to as heaven, sky, or god. The translations used in this text switch between heaven and sky depending on the context or the syntactical emphasis. The choices are based entirely on interpreting classic Daoism as a philosophy, *not* a religion that becomes one of the branches later. For an in-depth inquiry on the meaning of *tian* from 1324 BC to AD 25 China, see Fu Pei-Jung's (傅佩榮, presented as Fu Pei-Rong throughout this book) dissertation, "The Concept of T'ien in Ancient China: With Special Emphasis on Confucianism" (PhD diss., Yale University, 1984), in which a fivefold meaning of *tian* is presented: a physical *tian* (i.e., "sky"), a ruling *tian*, a fatalistic *tian*, a naturalistic *tian*, and an ethical *tian*.
16. *Laozi* 25; 有物混成，先天地生。寂兮寥兮，獨立不改，周行而不殆，可以為天下母。吾不知其名，強字之曰道，強為之名曰大。大曰逝，逝曰遠，遠曰反。... 人法地，地法天，天法道，道法自然。
17. There are multiple interpretations of this passage. The one presented here is based on Fu Pei-Rong's. See Fu Pei-Rong 傅佩榮, *Laozi jiedu* 老子解讀 [*Laozi* reader] (Taipei: New Century Publishing Co. 立緒文化事業有限公司, 2012), 137.

18. Edward Slingerland, *Effortless Action: Wu-wei as Conceptual Metaphor and Spiritual Ideal in Early China* (New York: Oxford University Press, 2003).
19. For an excellent example of how *wuwei* relates to *dao* based on a Zhuangzi's view in action in a musical context, see Leonard Tan, "Towards an Ancient Chinese-Inspired Theory of Music Education," *Music Education Research* 18, no. 4 (2016): 399–410, accessed August 2, 2017. http://www.tandfonline.com.ezproxy.lib.usf.edu/doi/full/10.1080/14613808.2015.1122751; especially pp. 405–408.
20. Readers should be alert when reading the pinyin (or Romanization) only. Many Chinese words share the same pinyin but they are indeed completely different words. In this case, the pinyin *wei* is used in the two Chinese words here with completely different meanings: 為 and 偽.
21. Fu Pei-Rong 傅佩榮, *Kong Meng Lao Zhuang jinghua CD ban* 孔孟老莊精華CD版 [Kong Meng Lao Zhuan essential CD edition] (Taipei: Xiangfei Yinyue Gong Zuo Shi 象飛音樂工作室, 2008), Laozi, CDs 7–9; also see Fu Pei-Rong 傅佩榮, *Zhuangzi jiedu* 莊子解讀 [*Zhuangzi* reader] (Taipei: New Century Publishing Co. 立緒文化事業有限公司, 2012), 120, 262.
22. *Zhuangzi* 2.17; 昔者莊周夢為胡蝶，栩栩然胡蝶也。自喻適志與！不知周也。俄然覺，則蘧蘧然周也。不知周之夢為胡蝶與？胡蝶之夢為周與？周與胡蝶則必有分矣。此之謂物化。
23. Fu Pei-Rong 傅佩榮, *Zhuangzi jiedu* 莊子解讀 [*Zhuangzi* reader] (Taipei: New Century Publishing Co. 立緒文化事業有限公司, 2012), 53.
24. Zhuangzi's description (*Zhuangzi* 17.5) has referred to *dao*, self, matters, heaven and earth, grain of rice, hair, mountain, and two rulers with opposing views, Yao (堯) and Jie (桀).
25. I elaborate on the concept of harmony in some of the following chapters, especially in Chapters 5 and 7.
26. More about the differences and compatibility between classic Confucianism and classic Daoism are presented in the following chapter.
27. *Laozi* 15; 孰能濁以靜之徐清？孰能安以動之徐生？保此道者不欲盈。夫唯不盈，故能蔽而新成。
28. See *Zhuangzi*, 2.1 and 2.2. The interpretation of *tian lai*, *ren lai*, and *de lai* are based on Fu Pei-Rong 傅佩榮, *Zhuangzi jiedu* 莊子解讀 [*Zhuangzi* reader] (Taipei: New Century Publishing Co. 立緒文化事業有限公司, 2012), 28–31.
29. This annotation of Wang Bi (王弼) (AD 226–249) is found in *Laozi* 41 as recorded in *Twenty-Two Masters* 《二十二子》: 聽之不聞名曰希，不可得聞之音也。有聲則有分，有分則不宮而商矣。分則不能統眾，故有聲者非大音也。

CHAPTER 5

1. See Jay L. Garfield and William Edelglass, eds., *The Oxford Handbook of World Philosophy* (Oxford: Oxford University Press, 2011).
2. The significance of the Chinese in the contemporary global context is obvious. It is a culture, a philosophical current, an economic and political powerhouse, and a most populous nation. The Chinese is one of the oldest, continuous, and most widespread heritages. Chinese immigrants and Chinese restaurants are found everywhere, from small towns to major metropolitan areas in most nations. Its importance and influences are inevitable.
3. Throughout this text, classic Confucianism and classic Daoism are described as philosophical schools, but *Yijing* is not a stand-alone philosophical school. When all three sources are grouped together, they are described as ideologies, philosophical sources, or thoughts.

4. See Chapter 3, note 36.
5. Chenyang Li, *The Confucian Philosophy of Harmony* (New York: Routledge, 2014), 21.
6. Li Zonggui 李宗桂, *An Introduction to Chinese Culture* 中國文化導論 (Guangzhou, China: Guangdong Peoples Publishing House 廣東人民出版社, 2002), 166–177.
7. Buddhism may be the third significant philosophical lineage in Chinese communities. However, due to its foreign and religious origin and its importation to China after the Qin period (221–207 BC), it is beyond the scope of this text.
8. For example, living in Hong Kong in the 1970s and 1980s, I have observed many Cantonese Chinese families refraining from meat consumption on Chinese New Year day, but such abstinence is not observed throughout the rest of the year.
9. See *Great Learning* (1, 2) and *Laozi* (54).
10. Mencius, 14.25; 可欲之謂善，有諸己之謂信。充實之謂美，充實而有光輝之謂大，大而化之之謂聖，聖而不可知之之謂神。(Kindness is desirable. Achieving kindness is sincerity. Achieving sincerity is beauty. Perfecting kindness so brightness is shining upon others is great. Shining upon others so others are moved is a sage. Being a sage at such a high level that no one can understand is godly.).
11. Chenyang Li, *The Confucian Philosophy of Harmony* (New York: Routledge, 2014), 34.
12. *Zhuangzi* 13.1; 均調天下，與人和者也。
13. *Zhongyong* 1; 喜怒哀樂之未發，謂之中；發而皆中節，謂之和。
14. Chenyang Li, *The Confucian Philosophy of Harmony* (New York: Routledge, 2014), 9.
15. Ibid.
16. Ibid.
17. The concept of *yin* and *yang* is also a foundation for a new breed of philosophy, *yin yang wu xing* (陰陽五行), evolved during the Spring and Autumn and Warring States periods. It mixes *yin* and *yang* with the idea of *wuxing* (五行), which is documented in *Hongfan* and *Ganshi, Shangshu* (《尚書》《甘誓》與《洪範》), a book of history and philosophy edited by various individuals, including Confucius, since the Spring and Autumn period (772–476 BC) but includes recorded events that are much earlier. *Wuxing* describes the five basic elements that create all substances: water, fire, wood, metal, and clay (五行：一曰水，二曰火，三曰木，四曰金，五曰土。). They were used in conjunction with *yin* and *yang* in explaining the formation of all matters and phenomena. To maintain consistency in the current inquiry in the classic thoughts in *Yijing* and of Confucius, Mencius, Laozi, and Zhuangzi, I deliberately remove myself from the idea of *wuxing* and stick to *yin* and *yang* only.
18. Stanislaus Fung and Mark Jackson, "Dualism and Polarism: Structures of Architectural and Landscape Architectural Discourse in China and the West," *Interstices* 4 (1996): 1–22.
19. Ruma Banerjee, "The Yin-Yang of Cobalamin Biochemistry," *Chemistry & Biology* 4, no. 3 (1997): 175–186.
20. Tony Fang and Guy Olivier Faure, "Chinese Communication Characteristics: A *yin yang* Perspective," *International Journal of Intercultural Relations* 35, no. 3 (2011): 320–333.
21. Akira Kageyama and Tetsuya Sato, "'Yin-yang Grid': An Overset Grid in Spherical Geometry," *Geochemistry Geophysics Geosystems* 5, no. 9 (2004): 1–15.
22. Zheng Dong, Yan Lavrovsky, Manjeri A. Venkatachalam, and Arun K. Roy, "Heme Oxygenase-1 in Tissue Pathology: The Yin and Yang," *The American Journal of Pathology* 156, no. 5 (2000): 1485–1488.

23. Shinobu Kitayama and Hazel Rose Markus, "*Yin* and *Yang* of the Japanese Self: The Cultural Psychology of Personality Coherence," in *The Coherence of Personality: Social-Cognitive Bases of Consistency, Variability, and Organization*, ed. Daniel Cervone and Yuichi Shoda (New York: Guilford Press, 1999), 242–302.
24. Zhao Xiaosheng 趙曉生, *Taiji zuoqu xitong* 太極作曲系統 [Taiji system of music composition] (Guangzhou, China: Kexue Puji Chubanshe 科學普及出版社, 1990). Another one is found in Fang Xiaomin 房曉敏, *Wuxing zuoqu fa* 五行作曲法 [Five elements composition method] (Hunan, China: Hunan Wenyi Chubanshe 湖南文藝出版社, 2010).
25. For example, see Miao Lingna 苗凌娜, "*Yin yang wuxing yu yinyue yangsheng* 陰陽五行與音樂養生 [Yin yang five elements and music for wellness]," *Zhongguo Zhongyiyao Zixun* 中國中醫藥資訊 *Journal of Traditional Chinese Medicine Information* 2, no. 31 (2010): 45.
26. A hint of *yin* and *yang* as applied in music education philosophy can be found in Leonard Tan, "Reimer through Confucian Lenses: Resonances with Classical Chinese Aesthetics," *Philosophy of Music Education Review* 23, no. 2 (2015): 183–201. In this article he uses *yin* and *yang* to reconcile some of the apparent contradictions in Bennett Reimer's writings. Furthermore, a few writers have presented notions that may resemble *yin* and *yang* on the surface, but they are fundamentally different from the principles of *yin* and *yang*. Examples of these include Jorgensen's *this-with-that* approach (Estelle R. Jorgensen, *Transforming Music Education* [Bloomington: Indiana University Press, 2003]); Schipper's continua for music education in a global perspective (Huib Schippers, *Facing the Music: Shaping Music Education from a Global Perspective* [New York: Oxford University Press, 2010]); and Turino's participatory and presentational music making (Thomas Turino, *Music as Social Life: The Politics of Participation* [Chicago: University of Chicago Press, 2008]).
27. Although Confucius is recognized as one of the greatest master teachers, evidence suggests that he learned from his students also. See *Analects* 3.8 where Confucius admits that his student, Zixia 子夏, has enlightened him.
28. This is supported by a well-known Confucian axiom found in *Xueji, Liji*: "Teaching and learning support each other and lead to growth" (*Xueji*; 教學相長). *Xueji* is believed to be authored by Yuezhengke 樂正克 or Yuezhengzi 樂正子 (ca. 300–200 BC), who was a student of Mencius and identified as the head of one of eight branches of Confucianism during the late Warring States period. See Liu Zhen 劉震, *Xueji shiyi* 學記釋義 [Explaining *Xueji*] (Jinan, China: Shandong Education Publishing House 濟南: 山東教育出版社, 1984). Yuezhengke is cited in five chapters in *Mencius*. He is most notable as someone who loves kindness (see *Mencius* 12.13).
29. Elapsed time or a decline in memory as a natural part of aging could cause one to forget an experience. For example, if one has learned music reading as a child, she might forget how to read music as a senior citizen if such a skill is not practiced for the decades in between.
30. It would have been more accurate if the *taiji* figure can be represented in three-dimensional space. Since no such figure is available in the arrangement shown in Figure 5.9, the tennis ball is my next best option, given its interwoven pattern of two elements, connoting *yin* and *yang*.

CHAPTER 6

1. Among Heraclitus' most well-known ideas include "Everything flows, nothing stands still"; "one cannot step into the same river twice"; and "The only constant is change." All are quoted in Plato's *Cratylus*. These ideas suggest that the flow of

time makes each moment unique. One cannot change the past or go back. In the case of the river analogy, as time elapses, the river is different, and the person seeing it or stepping into it is different also.
2. In classic Doaist terms, *dao* is the only unchanging entity.
3. Many animals, for example, can perceive certain changes and signals that humans cannot. And some change can be detected by sophisticated instruments (e.g., a microscope, a sonogram, or a sonar) but not directly by humans.
4. For example, changes in weather patterns throughout the year are one of such notable changes. They can be gradual or dramatic. Humans depend on it for such basic survival needs as food sources, mobility, and shelter.
5. Considerable parallels can be seen in John Blacking's view. He stated, "The laws of nature require that an organism, to survive, should constantly adapt to its changing environment, . . . and music obeys these laws, in that it has to be remade at every performance and it is felt anew inside each individual body" (John Blacking, "Some Problems of Theory and Method in the Study of Musical Change," *Yearbook of the International Folk Music Council* 9 [1977]: 5). At the same time, he recognized the "*non*-change and the repetition of carefully rehearsed passages of music" as "most interesting and characteristically human features" (Ibid., 7).
6. The sun and the moon follow a cyclic principle to brighten the sky forever, the back and forth of seasons make eternity viable, and the sage who walk persistently with *dao* is able to cultivate all humans under the sky (日月得天而能久照，四時變化而能久成，聖人久於其道而天下化成). See *Tuanchuan, Heng, Yizhuan* 《易傳》《恆》《象傳》. The ideas of "forever brightening" (久照), "viability of eternity" (久成), and "persistence in walking with *dao*" (久於其道) all have the notion of eternity embedded in the changes. The changes of time, the seasons, and humans are part of the makeup of the eternity (久), which is also translated as "forever" and "persistence" here.
7. For example, one might seek shelter if a heavy storm is anticipated due to changing weather patterns.
8. To put this in simple terms, for example, it is up to the human to decide to stay inside or go outside under a severe thunder weather condition. Staying inside is likely to remain dry and comfortable, whereas going out is a definite prediction of getting wet and an increased risk of being strike by lightning. Given that the coming of the weather is a change that humans cannot control, humans can change their own prospects by their own decisions and actions, that is, staying dry or getting wet, and being comfortable or risk being strike by lightning.
9. The idea of pushing parallels the figurative representation of the *taiji* diagram, in which *yin* and *yang* are pushing each other to create motion and change (see Figures 2.1, 5.5, 5.6, and 5.7).
10. To extend from *xiang* (象) and *li* (理), every phenomenon has numbers (*shu* 數) attached also. See Chapter 2 in this book. However, numbers are not the focus in this discussion.
11. Urie Bronfenbrenner, *The Ecology of Human Development: Experiments by Nature and Design* (Cambridge, MA: Harvard University Press, 1979), 22.
12. Ibid., 21.
13. Ibid., 25.
14. Ibid., 25.
15. Ibid., 26.
16. Ibid., 26.
17. Ibid., 26.

18. To give a real-life example, a technician who fixed telephones in phone booths and coin-operated pay phones was living reasonably well in the 1970s and 1980s. In the advent of the popularization of cell phones since the 1990s, the telecommunications industry has changed dramatically, and the technician's business went downhill. He complains that he lives poor in the 2010s as he chooses not to make changes in himself to be in sync with the changes in the world.
19. Lucy Green, *Music, Informal Learning, and the School: A New Classroom Pedagogy*. (Hampshire, UK: Ashgate Publishing Limited, 2008).
20. This is similar to an idea described in *Xueji* 《學記》, included in *Liji* 《禮記》: Teaching and learning promote growth on both sides (*jiaoxue xiangzhang* 教學相長). According to Guo Moruo 郭沫若 (1892–1978), *Xueji* is believed to be authored by Yuezhengke 樂正克 (ca. 300–200 BC), who was a student of Mencius. See Guo Moruo 郭沫若, *Shi pipanshu* 十批判書 [Ten criticisms] (Beijing: People's Publishing House 人民出版社, 1982), 141. The idea is that learning makes one aware of insufficiencies, teaching makes one aware of difficulties, knowing insufficiencies leads to self-reflection, knowing difficulties leads to self-strengthening. In other words, learning makes a better teacher, and teaching makes a better learner; both activities complement each other for growth to occur (*Xueji, Liji* 3: 故學然後知不足，教然後知困。知不足，然後能自反也；知困，然後能自強也，故曰：教學相長也。). This passage was used to substantiate a historical document of a monarchic advise to Wuding (武丁) of the Shang (商) Dynasty, who ruled 1250–1192 BC (see *The Book of History*, or *Yueming Xia, Shangshu, Shangshu* 《尚書》《商書》《說命下》): *xiao xue ban* (斅學半), which means that teaching and learning should be half and half. The Chinese characters may also be interpreted as to be enlightened by others (斅) and learning (學) should be half and half. *Xiao* (斅) is a character not in use in contemporary Chinese.
21. Avoiding music for a short period could lead to a nostalgic feeling for music, which takes the person involved back to participating in music and appreciate it more.
22. Relativity of low-high energy level is directly associated with the indexical quality of *yin* and *yang*. Determination of the *yin-yang* position or high-low energy depends on the relative situation.
23. While any activity can be musical (e.g., working, dinning, bathing, sleeping), music is not always a part of everyday activities in most cultures. As John Blacking puts it, "'musical' activities overlap non-'musical' activities, but they are not wholly interchangeable" (Blacking, "Some Problems of Theory and Method in the Study of Musical Change," *Yearbook of the International Folk Music Council* 9 [1977]: 2).
24. Confucius clearly points out that it is necessary to have music in a complete human (see *Analects*, 8.8: 成於樂). Highly developed musical structures and activities are also among the few phenomena that are unique to humans. Music, whether it is a noun or a verb, is part of being human.
25. Support for music being an essential part of education and of human life in general is found pervasively throughout classic texts and contemporary research in multiple cultures, not just the Chinese. For example, see Music Educators National Conference, *Becoming Human through Music: The Wesleyan Symposium on the Perspectives of Social Anthropology in the Teaching and Learning of Music* (Middletown, CT: Wesleyan University; Reston, VA: Music Educators National Conference, 1984); Michael L. Mark, ed., *Music Education: Source Readings from Ancient Greece to Today*, 4th ed. (New York: Routledge, 2013); and National Commission on Music Education, *Growing Up Complete: The Imperative for Music Education* (Reston, VA: Music Educators National Conference, 1991).

26. For example, a parent decides whether to expose a newborn to a specific type of music or not to expose to music at all, be it singing or playing from a recording.
27. This is similar to the choices humans have when heavy thunderstorm is predicted. Humans can make a potentially life-changing decision by staying inside, dry, and doing something productive (i.e., a prosperity); waiting for the storm to stop inside while doing nothing (i.e., doing the minimum to maintain status without getting into an adversary condition); or going outside, getting wet, and risk striking by lightning (i.e., an adversity).
28. From a scientific research perspective, researchers are striving to explain as much variance (including cause and effect) as possible, but they could hardly explain it with 100 percent certainty. They try to eliminate as much error as possible, but there is always room for error.
29. On a sociocultural level, humans made music with a culture as the foundation, which is more remote from the *control* of the individual making the music. The individual and the culture could enter into a negotiation or relate to each other in a symbiotic way. Bennett Reimer states, "Music and culture exist in symbiosis, each dependent on, receiving reinforcement from, influencing change within, the other" (Reimer, *A Philosophy of Music Education*, 3rd ed. [Upper Saddle River, NJ: Prentice Hall, 2003], 176).
30. This is evident in the global warming trend attributed to a human lifestyle that leads to an increase in carbon dioxide, methane, and nitrous oxide. See NASA Global Climate Change webpage, updated on July 25, 2017: http://climate.nasa.gov/causes/.
31. The short story is recorded in *Shuiyuan* 《說苑》 17. It is also collected in *Zhisi, Kongzi Jiayu* 《孔子家語》《致思》：孔子曰：「季孫之賜我粟千鍾也，而交益親；自南宮敬叔之乘我車也，而道加行。故道雖貴，必有時而後重，有勢而後行，微夫二子之貺財，則丘之道，殆將廢矣。」. See Yang Chunqiu 羊春秋, ed. (annotated), *Xinyi Kongzi Jiayu* 《新譯孔子家語》 (Taipei: Sanmin 三民書局, 2008), 77, 83–84.
32. Carl Gustav Jung, *Synchronicity: An Acausal Connecting Principle* (Princeton, NJ: Princeton University Press, 1960/2011), 25.
33. Ibid, 103.
34. Carl Gustav Jung, *Synchronicity: An Acausal Connecting Principle* (Princeton, NJ: Princeton University Press, 1960/2011).
35. Ibid.
36. Ibid, 25.
37. An external event is a key component but not the totality of the given, because there could be other elements involved, such as religious beliefs, which may not be clearly defined as a maneuverable or a given.
38. Carl Gustav Jung, *Synchronicity: An Acausal Connecting Principle* (Princeton, NJ: Princeton University Press, 1960/2011), 115.

CHAPTER 7

1. From an ecological perspective, the existence of humans has changed the course of development in the natural world. For example, industrialization and urbanization have drastically modified how the natural environment would have evolved.
2. The metaphor of "moving carpet" is also found in Jacky Dakin's *Learn to Dance on a Moving Carpet: How to Create a Balanced and Meaningful Life* (Samford Valley, Australia: Australian Academic Press Group, 2015).
3. Musically, this idea of realizing the full potential of an individual regardless of the significance of the potential is in line with Edwin Gordon's underlying philosophy

of his music aptitude tests. He explicitly states in the manual of one of his landmark tests, *Musical Aptitude Profile*, that the music aptitude test "should never be used to deprive any student from fully realizing his or her music potential . . . students with low music aptitude should not be discouraged from participating in special music activities." Rather, "low-scoring students . . . can make the most of whatever music aptitude they have." Furthermore, "extra-musical factors" and "individual musical differences" should be considered too when planning for participation in musical activities. See Edwin E. Gordon, *Manual: Musical Aptitude Profile* (Chicago: GIA Publications, Inc., 1995), 55–56.

4. See Fu Pei-Rong 傅佩榮, *Le tian zhi ming* 樂天知命. (Taipei: Tianxia Wenhua 天下文化, 2011), 556.
5. The Chinese word for "shade" is *yin* (陰), the same *yin* as in *yin-yang*.
6. See Fu Pei-Rong 傅佩榮, *Le tian zhi ming* 樂天知命 (Taipei: Tianxia Wenhua 天下文化, 2011), 556.
7. Ibid.
8. Many scholars consider *Zhongyong* 《中庸》, collected in *Liji* 《禮記》, as a culmination of classic Confucian thoughts, cultivated in the pre-Qin period (i.e., prior to 221 BC). Although there is uncertainty around the authorship or the time of completion, there is confidence that it is a key text based on Confucius' teaching. See Fu Pei-Rong 傅佩榮, *Daxue Zhongyong jiedu* 《大學》《中庸》解讀 [*Daxue* and *Zhongyong* reader] (Taipei: New Century Publishing Co. 立緒文化事業有限公司, 2012), 74–77.
9. The earliest categorization of musical instruments in China, found in the Zhou Dynasty (1122–255 BC), is based on materials available in the natural environment: metal (金 *jin*), stone (石 *shi*), silk (絲 *si*), bamboo (竹 *zhu*), gourd (匏 *pao*), clay (土 *tu*), skin (革 *ge*), and wood (木 *mu*).
10. Uniformly described in *Laozi* (41) and *Lecheng, Xianshilan, Lushichunqiu* 《呂氏春秋》《先識覽》《樂成》: 大音希聲 (*da yin xi sheng* or great music [has] few sounds).
11. 「調和之事，必以甘酸苦辛鹹，先後多少，其齊甚微，皆有自起。」This quotation comes from Yin Yi's explanation to Emperor Tang (湯) (ca. 1670–1587 BC) of the Shang (商) Dynasty (1766–1122 BC) regarding culinary art found in a historical document with a mixture of philosophical schools, *Benwei, Xiaohanglan, Lushichunqiu* 《呂氏春秋》《孝行覽》《本味》. *Lushichunqiu* was completed around 239 BC under the scholastic leadership of Lu Buwei (呂不韋, 292–235 BC), who served as a prime minister in the State of Qin (秦) during the Warring States period.
12. Yanzi served as a prime minister for Qi Jinggong (齊景公), who ruled the State of Qi 547–490 BC. He once disagreed that Qi Jinggong should hire Confucius, who was age thirty-five. Nevertheless, Yanzi was regarded highly by Confucius (see *Analects* 5.16). Yanzi's culinary art metaphor is found in the first Chinese historical text by year (December, *Zhao Gong* yr. 20 [i.e., 522 BC], *Chunqiu Zuozhuan* 《春秋左傳》《昭公二十年》十二月), authored by a pioneer historian Zuo Qiuming (左丘明 556–451 BC):「. . . 和如羹焉，水火醯醢鹽梅以烹魚肉，燀之以薪，宰夫和之，齊之以味，濟其不及，以洩其過，. . .」.
13. The word "羹" (*geng*) is translated as "thick soup" here. It is a type of soup with a thicker texture than a regular soup, which would be written as "湯" (*tang*) in Chinese.
14. Note that fire and water are opposing elements, yet they are used simultaneously (and harmoniously) to cook.

15. Although Yanzi uses water as an example, he implies that it would apply to any ingredient. No ingredient could be used to remedy the same ingredient. It is also interesting to note that Yin Yi (伊尹) refers to water as the foundation of deliciousness (*Benwei, Xiaohanglan, Lushichunqiu* 《呂氏春秋》《孝行覽》《本味》：「凡味之本，水最為始。」). In classic Daoism, water is considered as the most powerful, yet flexible, substance (see *Laozi* 78: 天下莫柔弱於水，而攻堅強者莫之能勝，其無以易之。).

16. This idea, coincidentally, is similar to the one suggested by the Greek philosopher Heraclitus (535–475 BC), with a focus on concord, discord, opposition, and harmony: "Opposition brings concord. Out of discord comes the fairest harmony" (Philip Wheelwright, *Heraclitus* [Princeton, NJ: Princeton University Press, 1959], fragment 98, 90).

17. Some writers in the West also include dance as music. See Christopher Small, *Musicking: The Meanings of Performing and Listening* (Hanover, NH: Wesleyan University Press, 1998), 9.

18. This is clearly documented in *Yueji, Liji* and supported by other classic texts of the time (see Chengyang Li, *The Confucian Philosophy of Harmony* [New York: Routledge, 2014], 39–44). However, the authorship of *Yueji* is heavily contested, and a portion of ideologies presented in *Yueji* is debatable on whether it is Confucian. Regardless, the integration of dance and social elements in *yue* is unquestionable. See Ji Liankang 吉聯抗, *Yueji* 《樂記》 (Beijing: People's Music Publishing House 人民音樂出版社, 1958), 1; and Fang Baozhang 方寶璋 and Zheng Junhui 鄭俊暉, *Zhongguo yinyue wenxianxue* 中國音樂文獻學 [Chinese music bibliography] (Fuzhou, China: Fujian Education Press, 2006), 288–291.

19. See *Yueji, Liji* 《禮記》《樂記》: 感於物而動，故形於聲。聲相應，故生變；變成方，謂之音；比音而樂之，及干戚羽旄，謂之樂。是故知聲而不知音者，禽獸是也；知音而不知樂者，眾庶是也。唯君子為能知樂。. Also see C. Victor Fung, "Music and Culture: A Chinese Perspective," *Philosophy of Music Education Review* 2, no. 1 (1994), 47–52.

20. Chengyang Li, *The Confucian Philosophy of Harmony* (New York: Routledge, 2014), 47.

21. Ibid.

22. Ibid.

23. Ibid, 48.

24. This documentation comes from a historical text, *Zhouyu C, Guoyu* 《國語》《周語下》. The authorship of *Guoyu* has been heavily debated for over a millennium. It is possible that there was more than one author. If there were multiple authors, they might have been writing at different times or in different locations. Regardless of who the author is, there is general consensus that *Guoyu* was written during the early years of the Warring States period (475–221 BC) by those familiar with the history and events of the feudal nations. The collection of twenty-one chapters describes events, dialogues, and principles of ruling from around 990 BC to 453 BC, going across from the Zhou Dynasty through the Spring and Autumn period. The earliest found version *Guoyu* is annotated by a renowned historian, Wei Sho (韋昭) (204–273) of Wu (吳). See Jin Liangnian 金良年 and Liang Gu 梁谷, eds., *Guoyu* 《國語》 (Shanghai: Shanghai Guji Publishing House 上海古籍出版社, 2008).

25. This quote comes from 522 BC, that is, Zhou Jingwang year 23 (周景王二十三年).

26. See *Analects* 1.12: 「禮之用，和為貴。」 "When using *li*, it is best to aim at a harmonizing outcome."

27. Chengyang Li, *The Confucian Philosophy of Harmony* (New York: Routledge, 1994), 48.
28. Chengyang Li used a similar translation: "[good] governance is like music; music is about harmony; and harmony is about balancing (*ping*)," ibid., 48.
29. Chengyang Li, *The Confucian Philosophy of Harmony*, 48.
30. Chenyang Li uses the word "authenticity." I use the word "sincerity" to be consistent with the idea of *cheng* (誠) throughout this text. The opposite of *cheng* is *wei* (偽), which is a quality denied for *yue*.
31. Chenyang Li uses the word "virtue." I use the word "kindness" to be consistent with the idea of *shan* (善) throughout this text.
32. Based on the definition of *yue*, then, sung poems, songs, dance, and their associated social activities are part of it.
33. These ideas come from *Yueji, Liji*: 「詩言其志也，歌詠其聲也，舞動其容也。三者本於心，然後樂氣從之。是故情深而文明，氣盛而化神。和順積中而英華發外，唯樂不可以為偽。」.
34. *Yueji, Liji*: 「窮本知變，樂之情也；著誠去偽，禮之經也。」. The idea of maintaining sincerity and discarding falsehood corroborates with Confucius' proposition in *Wenyan, Yizhuan*: 「閑邪存其誠」.
35. Fu Pei-Rong 傅佩榮, *Lunyu jiedu* 論語解讀 [*Analects* reader] (Taipei: New Century Publishing Co. 立緒文化事業有限公司, 2012), 69: 盡善是就德之效應.
36. *Analects* 7.14: 子在齊聞韶，三月不知肉味。曰：「不圖為樂之至於斯也！」
37. 「至矣哉，直而不倨，曲而不屈，邇而不偪，遠而不攜，遷而不淫，復而不厭，哀而不愁，樂而不荒，用而不匱，廣而不宣，施而不費，取而不貪，處而不底，行而不流，五聲和，八風平，節有度，守有序，盛德之所同也。」
38. Chengyang Li, *The Confucian Philosophy of Harmony* (New York: Routledge, 2014), 23–38.
39. Numerous sources from antiquity to contemporary, and from the East to the West, support the necessity of music in humans. For example, Michael L. Mark, *Music Education: Source Readings from Ancient Greece to Today*, 4th ed. (New York: Routledge, 2013); Music Educators National Conference, *Becoming Human through Music: The Wesleyan Symposium on the Perspectives of Social Anthropology in the Teaching and Learning of Music* (Reston, VA: Music Educators National Conference, 1984); and National Commission on Music Education, *Growing Up Complete: The Imperative for Music Education* (Reston, VA: Music Educators National Conference, 1991).
40. See Chapter 7 in C. Victor Fung and Lisa J. Lehmberg, *Music for Life: Music Participation and Quality of life of Senior Ccitizens* (New York: Oxford University Press, 2016).
41. Although individuals begin their lives with an edge on musical prosperity simply by the natural relationship between humans and music, the choice to enter one of the three musical zones is controlled by others around them, most notably the parents, other family members, a guardian, or caregivers. Therefore, everyone is *placed* in one of the musical zones at the earliest stages of their lives. However, it does not mean that they have to stay in that zone forever. Entrance and moving across different musical zones rely on the amount of dynamic flexibility they develop as they mature and gain independence.
42. Evidence of music being a survival need can be found in senior citizens who face severe adversity. See C. Victor Fung and Lisa J. Lehmberg, *Music for Life: Music Participation and Quality of Life of Senior Citizens* (New York: Oxford University Press, 2016), 105 and 113–114.

43. See C. Victor Fung and Lisa J. Lehmberg, *Music for Life: Music Participation and Quality of Life of Senior Citizens* (New York: Oxford University Press, 2016), 208.
44. In Chinese semantics, harmony (*he* 和) and balance (*ping* 平) are combined to make peace (*heping* 和平).

CHAPTER 8

1. The three layers of culture are material (*wuzhi* 物質), social (*shehui* 社會), and spiritual (*jingshen* 精神). The social layer is not the focus in this discussion, and neither is the material layer. See Qian Mu 錢穆, *Lishi yu wenhua lunchong* 歷史與文化論叢 [Essays on history and culture] (Taipei: Tung Da Books 東大圖書有限公司, 1979), 6–17.
2. Extensive discussions are found in the literature regarding two versions of this quote: the one I accept here ends with "... 人亦大," and the other version found in the *Twenty-Two Masters* 《二十二子》 ends with "... 王亦大." There is overwhelming evidence to support the version I use here. For an extensive justification, see Chen Guying 陳鼓應, ed., *Laozi jinzhujinyijipingjia* 老子今註今譯及評價 [*Laozi* modern annotation, translation, and criticism], 2nd ed. (Taipei: The Commercial Press, Ltd., 2013), 145–147, fn 10.
3. The idea of being free between the sky and the earth reminds me of the English idiom "the sky is the limit." However, in this idiom there is no mentioning of the earth being the foundation and *dao* being the superseding principle.
4. This can be seen in some circus shows in the United States and some acrobatic shows in China.
5. *Dao* henceforth refers to both the Confucian *dao* and the Daoist *dao* unless stated otherwise. The former focuses on human relations, and the latter focuses on natural principles.
6. To extend from this explanation, let me use the clarinetist example to illustrate further. When I state that the clarinetist can express anything, I am assuming that to express is the natural way, as a form of *dao*, of being a clarinetist. It is normally not the *dao* of a clarinetist (using the clarinet) to, say, cook, clean, fight, or ride. Therefore, the "anything" in the statement is only good within the bounds of the *dao* of being a clarinetist, excluding all things that are outside these bounds, among which I boldly name cooking, cleaning, fighting, or riding. By naming these activities as outside the bounds of being a clarinetist, I face the risk of excluding such possibilities of using the instrument, because no humans can specify what exactly the *dao* for being a clarinetist is. At the same time, I am confident to state that the *dao* of being a clarinetist is connected to aspects of life without which there can be no clarinetist, such as health (enough to play the instrument), sincerity (enough to learn the instrument and to express through it), parents (from whom the clarinetist was born), or grenadilla (African blackwood traditionally used to make the clarinet among other woodwind instruments).
7. Confucius reflects that he could do as he wished without bending any rules at age seventy years (*Analects* 2.4; 七十而從心所欲不踰矩。). In the contemporary Western culture, similarities are found in Cohen's and Weiss and Bass's models of life-stages. In Cohen's (2000, 2005) model, liberation occurs around one's late fifties to early seventies, when one is able to speak the mind and act according to one's need. As retirement usually occurs during this stage, individuals are free to use their time to explore new experiences. Similarly, Weiss and Bass (2002) suggest that after retirement, "within fairly wide limits, [retirees may] live their lives as they please" (p. 3) before the stage of decline occurs. See Gene

D. Cohen, *The Creative Age: Awakening Human Potential in the Second Half of Life* (New York: HarperCollins Publishers, 2000); Gene D. Cohen, *The Mature Mind: The Positive Power of the Aging Brain* (New York: Basic Books, 2005); and Robert S. Weiss and Scott A. Bass, "Introduction," in *Challenges of the Third Age: Meaning and Purpose in Later Life*, ed. Robert S. Weiss and Scott A. Bass (New York: Oxford University Press, 2002), 3–12.
8. Maxine Greene, *The Dialectic of Freedom* (New York: Teachers College Press, 1988).
9. Estelle R. Jorgensen, *Transforming Music Education* (Bloomington: Indiana University Press, 2003), 37.
10. See *Tuanchuan, Kun, Yizhuan* 《易傳》《坤》《象傳》;「至哉坤元，萬物資生，乃順承天。」. This is in accord with *Laozi* 25 where it states, "Human depends on the earth, the earth depends on heaven (the sky), heaven (the sky) depends on *dao*, and *dao* depends on its natural way of operation" (人法地，地法天，天法道，道法自然。).
11. Classic Confucians manifest music in terms of *yue* (樂, see Chapter 3), and classic Daoists manifest music in terms of *lai* (籟, see Chapter 4).
12. A similar analogy is used elsewhere regarding quality of life and music participation. See C. Victor Fung and Lisa J. Lehmberg, *Music for Life: Music Participation and Quality of Life of Senior Citizens* (New York: Oxford University Press, 2016), 103.
13. C. Victor Fung, "Experiencing World Musics in Schools: From Fundamental Positions to Strategic Guidelines," in *World Musics and Music Education: Facing the Issue*, ed. Bennett Reimer (Reston, VA: MENC Association for Music Education, 2002), 187–204.
14. Ibid., 194.
15. Ibid., 197.
16. Ibid., 197.
17. The exact same words (溫故而知新) also appear in *Zhongyong* 《中庸》: 27.
18. Mihaly Csikszentmihalyi and Rustin Wolfe, "New Conceptions and Research Approaches to Creativity: Implications of a Systems Perspective for Creativity in Education," in *The Systems Model of Creativity: The Collected Works of Mihaly Csikszentmihalyi*, ed. Mihaly Csikszentmihalyi (Dordrecht, Netherlands: Springer Science + Business Media, 2014), 161–184.
19. This idea parallels the making sense or going through, *tong* (通), in change. See Chapter 6.
20. *Lai* (籟) is the name of an ancient musical instrument. It is a vertical pipe with three holes on the side or a series of pipes with different lengths. It is also used to refer to sound coming from wind blowing across hollow pipes or spaces (e.g., a cave or a hallway). Here, the word is used to infer musical sound in general.
21. A detail explanation of the relationship among human-made musical sound (人籟), earthly musical sound (地籟), and heavenly musical sound (天籟) is found in a fictitious teacher-learner dialogue (*Zhuangzi* 2.1 and 2.2: 南郭子綦隱几而坐，仰天而噓，嗒焉似喪其耦。顏成子游立侍乎前，曰：「何居乎？形固可使如槁木，而心固可使如死灰乎？今之隱几者，非昔之隱几者也？」子綦曰：「偃，不亦善乎，而問之也！今者吾喪我，女知之乎？女聞人籟而未聞地籟，女聞地籟而未聞天籟夫！」子游曰：「敢問其方。」子綦曰：「夫大塊噫氣，其名為風。是唯無作，作則萬竅怒呺。而獨不聞之翏翏乎？山林之畏佳，大木百圍之竅穴，似鼻，似口，似耳，似枅，似圈，似臼，似洼者，似污者。激者，謞者，叱者，吸者，叫者，譹者，宎者，咬者。前者唱于而隨者唱喁。泠風則小和，飄風則大和，厲風濟則眾竅為虛。而獨不見之調調、之刁刁乎？」子游曰：「地籟則眾竅是已，人籟則比竹是已。敢問天籟。」

子綦曰：「夫吹萬不同，而使其自已也。咸其自取，怒者其誰邪！」). Also see Chung-yuan Chang, *Creativity and Taoism: A Study of Chinese Philosophy, Art, and Poetry* (London: The Julian Press, Inc., 2011), 135–139.

CHAPTER 9

1. The megasystem refers to a system of the human race, superimposing Bronfenbrenner's micro-, meso-, exo-, and macro-systems. It contains a shared human spirit across nations, time, and space. See Chapter 6.
2. Spiritual here refers to the human spirit, not spiritual in a religious sense.
3. This is based on the three layers of culture postulated by Qian Mu (錢穆): material (物質 *wuzhi*), social (社會 *shehui*), and spirit (精神 *jingshen*) (see Chapter 1, 5–6). Material and social system have already been changed since the third century BC, but the human spirit persists. This is why these ancient Chinese philosophical sources are still viable in the contemporary world.
4. I emphasize the early and mature classic Confucianism and classic Daoism throughout this book as being philosophies rather than religions because of the formation and spread of religious Confucianism and religious Daoism after the third century BC. Similarly, the focus on the classics in this book sets apart the ideologies of neo-Confucianism, new-Confucianism, neo-Daoism, and new-Daoism.
5. Sincerity, kindness, benevolence, and *junzi* (exemplary person) are the four primary principles selected for discussion in this text, but they are not the only principles postulated by classic Confucians. Other principles tend to support quality and orderly human relationships (a key to *li* 禮) and relate to, or extend from, these four primary principles. For example, the principle of filial piety (*xiao* 孝) is a component of benevolence (see *Analects* 1.2, 1.6, 1.11, 2.6, and 2.7; *Mencius* 7.28) and *li* (禮) (see *Analects* 2.5) and is expected of *junzi* (see *Analects* 1.2, *Mencius* 9.1 and 9.4). Other renditions also include appropriate actions (*yi* 義), being proper (*zheng* 正), and learning (*xue* 學). They tend to be closely synonymous to the ideas presented in this book. See Peimin Ni, "Classical Confucianism I: Confucius," in *The Oxford Handbook of World Philosophy*, ed. Jay L. Garfield and William Edelglass (Oxford: Oxford University Press, 2011), 26–36; and Manyul Im, "Classical Confucianism II: Mencius and Zunzi," in *The Oxford Handbook of World Philosophy*, ed. Jay L. Garfield and William Edelglass (Oxford: Oxford University Press, 2011), 37–42.
6. No obstruction, observation, equality, and softness/flexibility are the four primary principles selected for discussion in this text. There are other ways to present classic Daoist principles, but they are highly similar to these four. See Xiaogan Liu, "Daoism: Laozi and Zhuangzi," in *The Oxford Handbook of World Philosophy*, ed. Jay L. Garfield and William Edelglass (Oxford: Oxford University Press, 2011), 47–57.
7. "Human spirit" refers to a shared spirit across all humans, much like a team spirit shared across members of a sports team. When teaming up with all humans with a goal to move forward, the team of humans share the human spirit.
8. "Music" is not the exact translation of *yue*, but it is the closest.
9. Bells and drums imply the system and materials used in music. They suggest the physical aspect of music.
10. This quote from *Analects*, as in many other Confucius' passages, includes *li* (禮) and *yue* (樂) side by side to demonstrate their properties. In this case, *li* is similar to *yue* in that both should downplay the aspect of physical materials.
11. As a parallel to *yue*, *li* (禮) needs benevolence (*ren* 仁) to make its practice meaningful.

12. Some may argue that the qualities of classic Daoism are centered on *dao* rather than humans. I present them as human-centered here in reference to the ultimate philosophizing of the *dao* done by humans.
13. The term *xiaoren* is also used as a humbling gesture when referring to oneself.
14. *Mencius* 3.2 contains explanations by Mencius and three students of Confucius why Confucius is entitled to be a *shengren*. He also admits that he aspires to be like Confucius: 曰：「惡！是何言也？昔者子貢、問於孔子曰：『夫子聖矣乎？』孔子曰：『聖則吾不能，我學不厭而教不倦也。』子貢曰：『學不厭，智也；教不倦，仁也。仁且智，夫子既聖矣！』夫聖，孔子不居，是何言也？」...曰：「不同道。非其君不事，非其民不使；治則進，亂則退，伯夷也。何事非君，何使非民；治亦進，亂亦進，伊尹也。可以仕則仕，可以止則止，可以久則久，可以速則速，孔子也。皆古聖人也，吾未能有行焉；乃所願，則學孔子也。」...曰：「宰我、子貢、有若智足以知聖人。汙，不至阿其所好。宰我曰：『以予觀於夫子，賢於堯舜遠矣。』子貢曰：『見其禮而知其政，聞其樂而知其德。由百世之後，等百世之王，莫之能違也。自生民以來，未有夫子也。』有若曰：『豈惟民哉？麒麟之於走獸，鳳凰之於飛鳥，太山之於丘垤，河海之於行潦，類也。聖人之於民，亦類也。出於其類，拔乎其萃，自生民以來，未有盛於孔子也。』」
15. *Analects* 7.26; 子曰：「聖人，吾不得而見之矣；得見君子者，斯可矣。」.
16. For Confucius, he went from being committed to be a *junzi* at age fifteen, being established in the society at age thirty, being able to refuse temptation at age forty, being able to comprehend the meaning of life in a larger universal context at age fifty, being satisfied and accepting at age sixty, and being able to do as wished without breaking rules at age seventy. These age markers show that he goes from learning, through socialization, to increased understanding and wisdom, to being satisfied and free. There is a trace of change and balance in the earlier stages and liberation during his final years. He lived for seventy-two years. His journey with the age markers are found in *Analects* 2.4; 子曰：「吾十有五而志於學，三十而立，四十而不惑，五十而知天命，六十而(耳)順，七十而從心所欲，不踰矩。」.
17. See *Analects* 13.9, 15.39; *Mencius* 3.2, 13.20, 13.40.
18. Humans' attachment to music is a natural phenomenon like water's natural property to flow downward. It is possible for water to go upward, but it is not the natural property of water, and an unnatural (human) action must be involved.
19. In classic Daoist terms, *wuwei* is taking no egoistic actions.
20. In classic Confucian terms, one must reject evil to maintain genuine human qualities such as sincerity, kindness, and benevolence that live within music.
21. Bennett Reimer, *A Philosophy of Music Education: Advancing the Vision*, 3rd ed. (Upper Saddle River, NJ: Prentice Hall), 283.
22. Teaching is broadly defined as showing or interacting with another person or people so others gain knowledge or skill, consciously or subconsciously.
23. C. Victor Fung, "Education," in *SAGE Encyclopedia of Music and Culture*, ed. J. Sturman and J. G. Golson (Thousand Oaks, CA: SAGE Publications, Inc., forthcoming).
24. For a perspective of music education based on a study of senior citizens' music participation, see C. Victor Fung and Lisa J. Lehmberg, *Music for Life: Music Participation and Quality of Life of Senior Citizens* (New York: Oxford University Press, 2016).
25. Privileged or underprivileged is a broad description for rich or poor, healthy or weak, majority or minority, high social status or low social status, high ability or low ability, and so forth.
26. Before one is able to decide for herself, it is up to the caregiver's decision.

CHAPTER 10

1. One of the meanings of *yi* (易) in *Yijing* is simple and easy. See Chapter 2, 23.
2. Based on the ideas of *ying* and *yang*, some areas have evolved into highly systematic practices with worldwide recognition, such as traditional Chinese medicine (including acupuncture and herbal intervention) and Tai Chi (as in the martial art and well-being exercises), both of which are rooted in the same simple concept of *yin* and *yang* found in *Yijing*.
3. Persistence is emphasized here to indicate that the practice is not casual, selective, or occasional. In other words, everyone must be mindful about this way of thinking; through persistent practice they become habitual, as a part of life.
4. There are many parallels between broader life principles and principles in learning musical instruments. Concepts of some musical techniques are simple and easy, such as learning to use the fourth finger on the left hand in playing the violin, but it takes a while to practice on it to make it a natural part of the playing. Another example is found in sustaining a long tone with crescendo and decrescendo on any wind instrument without altering the pitch. Conceptually it is simple and easy to understand, but it takes conscious efforts to practice for a long time to make it an integral part of playing music. Such examples can be found in many other music learning scenarios. Similarly, many concepts and human qualities suggested in the classic Chinese philosophies are simple and easy, but they need conscious efforts to practice persistently to make them integral parts of life.
5. See Chapter 5.
6. See Chapter 8 and C. Victor Fung, "Experiencing World Musics in Schools: From Fundamental Positions to Strategic Guidelines," in *World Musics and Music Education: Facing the Issue*, ed. Bennett Reimer (Reston, VA: MENC Association for Music Education, 2002), 187–204.
7. Wayne D. Bowman and Ana Lucía Frega, eds., *The Oxford Handbook of Philosophy in Music Education* (Oxford: Oxford University Press, 2012), 7.
8. Ibid.

BIBLIOGRAPHY

Adams, James D., and Eric J. Lien. *Traditional Chinese Medicine: Scientific Basis for Its Use*. Cambridge, UK: Royal Society of Chemistry Publishing, 2013.
Banerjee, Ruma. "The Yin-Yang of Cobalamin Biochemistry." *Chemistry and Biology* 4, no. 3 (1997): 175–186.
Barker, Andrew, ed. *Greek Musical Writings: Volume 1, The Musician and His Art*. Cambridge, UK: Cambridge University Press, 1989.
Berthrong, John H. *Transformations of the Confucian Way*. Boulder, CO: Westview Press, 1998.
Blacking, John. "Some Problems of Theory and Method in the Study of Musical Change." *Yearbook of the International Folk Music Council* 9 (1977): 1–26.
Bol, Peter K. *Neo-Confucianism in History*. Cambridge, MA: Harvard University Asia Center, 2008.
Bowman, Wayne D., and Ana Lucía Frega, eds. *The Oxford Handbook of Philosophy in Music Education*. Oxford: Oxford University Press, 2012.
Bresciani, Umberto. *Reinventing Confucianism: The New Confucian Movement*. Taipei: Taipei Ricci Institute for Chinese Studies, 2001.
Bronfenbrenner, Urie. *The Ecology of Human Development: Experiments by Nature and Design*. Cambridge, MA: Harvard University Press, 1979.
Cai, Zong-qi. "In Quest of Harmony: Plato and Confucius on Poetry." *Philosophy East and West* 49, no. 3 (1999): 317–345.
Cao, Li 曹理. *Putong xuexiao yinyue jiaoyuxue* 普通學校音樂教育學 [General school music education]. Shanghai: Shanghai Education Publishing House 上海教育出版社, 1993.
Chan, Alan. "Laozi." *The Stanford Encyclopedia of Philosophy* (Spring 2014 Edition), edited by Edward N. Zalta. Accessed August 2, 2017. http://plato.stanford.edu/archives/spr2014/entries/laozi/
Chang, Carsun. *The Development of Neo-Confucian Thought*. 2 vols. New York: Bookman Associates, 1957–1962.
Chang, Chung-yuan. *Creativity and Taoism: A Study of Chinese Philosophy, Art, and Poetry*. London: The Julian Press, 2011.
Chen, Guying 陳鼓應. *Daojia yixue jiangou* 道家易學建構 [Construction of the Daoist Yijing]. Taipei: Commercial Press, 2003.
Chen, Guying 陳鼓應, ed. *Laozi jinzhujinyijipingjia* 老子今註今譯及評價 [*Laozi* modern annotation, translation, and criticism]. 2nd ed. Taipei: The Commercial Press, 2013.
Cheng, Chung-ying. *New Dimensions of Confucian and Neo-Confucian Philosophy*. Albany: State University of New York Press, 1991.

Cohen, Gene D. *The Creative Age: Awakening Human Potential in the Second Half of Life*. New York: HarperCollins Publishers, 2000.

Cohen, Gene D. *The Mature Mind: The Positive Power of the Aging Brain*. New York: Basic Books, 2005.

Csikszentmihalyi, Mihaly. *The Systems Model of Creativity: The Collected Works of Mihaly Csikszentmihalyi*. Dordrecht, Netherlands: Springer Science + Business Media, 2014.

Dakin, Jacky. *Learn to Dance on a Moving Carpet: How to Create a Balanced and Meaningful Life*. Samford Valley, Australia: Australian Academic Press Group, 2015.

DeNora, Tia. *Music in Everyday Life*. Cambridge: Cambridge University Press, 2000.

Dong, Zheng, Yan Lavrovsky, Manjeri A. Venkatachalam, and Arun K. Roy. "Heme Oxygenase-1 in Tissue Pathology: The Yin and Yang." *The American Journal of Pathology* 156, no. 5 (2000): 1485–1488.

Fang, Baozhang 方寶璋, and Junhui Zheng 鄭俊暉. *Zhongguo yinyue wenxianxue* 中國音樂文獻學 [Chinese music bibliography]. Fuzhou, China: Fujian Education Press, 2006.

Fang, Maotian 方茂田. "Speech by the Secretary-General of the China National Commission for UNESCO Fang Maotian" 中國聯合國教科文組織全國委員會秘書長方茂田致辭. In *Nishan: Listen to Diverse Voices of the World: True Records of the First Nishan Forum on World Civilizations* 尼山：聆聽世界多元聲音——首屆尼山世界文明論壇實錄, 56–57. Beijing: China Intercontinental Press 五洲傳播出版社, 2011.

Fang, Thomé H. 方東美. *The Chinese View of Life: The Philosophy of Comprehensive Harmony*. Taipei: Linking Publishing, 1980.

Fang, Tony, and Guy Olivier Faure. "Chinese Communication Characteristics: A *yin yang* Perspective." *International Journal of Intercultural Relations* 35, no. 3 (2011): 320–333.

Fang Xiaomin 房曉敏, *Wuxing zuoqu fa* 五行作曲法 [Five elements composition method]. Hunan, China: Hunan Wenyi Chubanshe 湖南文藝出版社, 2010.

Fautley, Martin. *Assessment in Music Education*. Oxford: Oxford University Press, 2010.

Feng, Dawen 馮達文. *Zhongguo gudian zhexue lueshu* 中國古典哲學略述 [Brief description of classical Chinese philosophy]. Guangzhou, China: Guangdong Peoples Publishing House 廣東人民出版社, 2009.

Fu, Pei-Jung (a.k.a. Pei-Rong) 傅佩榮. "The Concept of *T'ien* in Ancient China: With Special Emphasis on Confucianism." PhD diss., Yale University, 1984.

Fu, Pei-Rong 傅佩榮. *Bu ke si yi di yi jing zhan bu* 不可思議的易經占卜 [The mysterious I-Ching fortune telling]. Taipei: Reading Times Publishing 時報文化, 2010.

Fu, Pei-Rong 傅佩榮. *Daxue Zhongyong jiedu* 《大學》《中庸》解讀 [*Daxue* and *Zhongyong* reader]. Taipei: New Century Publishing Co. 立緒文化事業有限公司, 2012.

Fu, Pei-Rong 傅佩榮. *Jiedu "Yijing"* 解讀《易經》 [Reading *Yijing*]. Taipei: New Century Publishing Co. 立緒文化事業有限公司, 2005.

Fu, Pei-Rong 傅佩榮. *Kong Meng Lao Zhuang jinghua CD ban* 孔孟老莊精華CD版 [Kong Meng Lao Zhuan essential CD edition]. Taipei: Xiangfei Yinyue Gong Zuo Shi 象飛音樂工作室, 2008.

Fu, Pei-Rong 傅佩榮. *Laozi jiedu* 《老子》解讀 [*Laozi* reader]. Taipei: New Century Publishing Co. 立緒文化事業有限公司, 2012.

Fu, Pei-Rong 傅佩榮. *Le tian zhi ming* 樂天知命. Taipei: Tianxia Wenhua 天下文化, 2011.

Fu, Pei-Rong 傅佩榮. *Lunyu jiedu* 《論語》解讀 [The *Analects* reader]. Taipei: New Century Publishing Co. 立緒文化事業有限公司, 2012.

Fu, Pei-Rong 傅佩榮. *Mengzi jiedu* 《孟子》解讀 [*Mencius* reader]. Taipei: New Century Publishing Co. 立緒文化事業有限公司, 2013.

Fu, Pei-Rong 傅佩榮. *Ru dao tianlun fawei* 儒道天論發微 [On heaven in Confucianism and Daoism]. Taipei: Linking Books 聯經出版事業, 2010.

Fu, Pei-Rong 傅佩榮. *Yukai haobianzai: Fu Pei-Rong ping zhuzhu sishu* 予豈好辯哉：傅佩榮評朱注四書 [Do I enjoy debates: Pei-Rong Fu's criticism for Xi Zhu's interpretation of *Sishu*]. Taipei: Linking Books 聯經出版事業股份有限公司, 2013.

Fu, Pei-Rong 傅佩榮. *Zhuangzi jiedu* 《莊子》解讀 [*Zhuangzi* reader]. Taipei: New Century Publishing Co. 立緒文化事業有限公司, 2012.

Fung, C. Victor. "Education." In *SAGE Encyclopedia of Music and Culture*, edited by Janet Sturman and J. G. Golson. Thousand Oaks, CA: SAGE Publications, forthcoming.

Fung, C. Victor. "Experiencing World Musics in Schools: From Fundamental Positions to Strategic Guidelines." In *World Musics and Music Education: Facing the Issue*, edited by Bennett Reimer, 187–204. Reston, VA: MENC Association for Music Education, 2002.

Fung, C. Victor. "Music and Culture: A Chinese Perspective." *Philosophy of Music Education Review* 2, no. 1 (1994): 47–52.

Fung, C. Victor, and Lisa J. Lehmberg. *Music for Life: Music Participation and Quality of Life of Senior Citizens*. New York: Oxford University Press, 2016.

Fung, Stanislaus, and Mark Jackson. "Dualism and Polarism: Structures of Architectural and Landscape Architectural Discourse in China and the West." *Interstices* 4 (1996): 1–22.

Garfield, Jay L., and William Edelglass, eds. *The Oxford Handbook of World Philosophy*. Oxford: Oxford University Press, 2011.

Gong, Zizhen 龔自珍. *Gong Zizhen quanji* 龔自珍全集 [Collected works of Zizhen Gong]. Shanghai: Shanghai Peoples Publishing 上海人民出版社, 1975.

Gordon, Edwin E. "Aptitude and Audiation: A Healthy Duet." *Medical Problems of Performing Artists* 3, no. 1 (1988): 34–35.

Gordon, Edwin E. *Manual: Musical Aptitude Profile*. Chicago: GIA Publications, Inc., 1995.

Greene, Maxine. *The Dialectic of Freedom*. New York: Teachers College Press, 1988.

Guo, Moruo 郭沫若. *Shi pipan shu* 十批判書 [Ten criticisms]. Beijing: People's Publishing House 人民出版社, 1982.

Hall, David L., and Roger T. Ames. "Chinese Philosophy." In *Routledge Encyclopedia of Philosophy*, edited by E. Craig. London: Routledge, 1998. Accessed August 2, 2017. https://www.rep.routledge.com/articles/overview/chinese-philosophy/v-1.

Hsü, Fu-kuan 徐復觀. *Zhongguo renxing lunshi—Xianqinpian* 中國人性論史——先秦篇 [The history of the Chinese philosophy of human nature: The Pre-Ch'in period]. Taipei: The Commercial Press 台灣商務印書館, 1969.

Hu, Shi 胡適. *Zhongguo zhexueshi dagang* 中國哲學史大綱 [Outline of the history of Chinese philosophy]. Taipei: The Commercial Press 台灣商務印書館, 2008.

Ji, Liankang 吉聯抗. *Yueji* 《樂記》. Beijing: People's Music Publishing House 人民音樂出版社, 1958.

Jin, Liangnian 金良年, and Gu Liang 梁谷, eds. *Guoyu* 《國語》. Shanghai: Shanghai Guji Publishing House 上海古籍出版社, 2008.

Jorgensen, Estelle R. *Transforming Music Education*. Bloomington: Indiana University Press, 2003.

Jung, Carl Gustav. *Synchronicity: An Acausal Connecting Principle.* Princeton, NJ: Princeton University Press, 1960/2011.

Kageyama, Akira, and Tetsuya Sato. "'Yin-yang Grid': An Overset Grid in Spherical Geometry." *Geochemistry Geophysics Geosystems* 5, no. 9 (2004): 1–15.

Kitayama, Shinobu, and Hazel Rose Markus. "*Yin* and *Yang* of the Japanese Self: The Cultural Psychology of Personality Coherence." In *The Coherence of personality: Social-Cognitive Bases of Consistency, Variability, and Organization,* edited by Daniel Cervone and Yuichi Shoda, 242–302. New York: Guilford Press, 1999.

Lao, Siguang 勞思光. *Xinbian zhongguo zhexue shi* 新編中國哲學史 [A new history of Chinese philosophy], Vol. 1. Taipei: Sanmin 三民書局, 2010.

Lao, Siguang 勞思光. *Zhongguo wenhua yaoyi xinbian* 中國文化要義新編 [Essentials of Chinese culture, new edition]. Hong Kong: The Chinese University Press 中文大學出版社, 1998.

Li, Chenyang. *The Confucian Philosophy of Harmony.* New York: Routledge, 2014.

Li, Chenyang, ed. "Chinese Philosophy." In *The Oxford Handbook of World Philosophy,* edited by Jay L. Garfield and William Edelglass, 13–57. Oxford: Oxford University Press, 2011.

Li, Xueqin 李學勤. *Zhouyi suyuan* 周易溯源 [Investigating the origin of *Zhouyi*]. Chengdu, Sichuan, China: Bashu Shushe 巴蜀書社, 2006.

Li, Zonggui 李宗桂. *An Introduction to Chinese Culture* 中國文化導論. Guangzhou, China: Guangdong Peoples Publishing House 廣東人民出版社, 2002.

Liang, Qichao 梁啓超. *Qing dai xueshu gailun* 清代學術概論 [An outline of academic studies in the Qing Dynasty]. Beijing: Zhonghua Book Company 中華書局, 2010.

Liu, Ching-chih 劉靖之. "*Xiao Youmei di yinyue sixiang yu shijian*" 簫友梅的音樂思想與實踐 [Musical thoughts and practices of Youmei Xiao]. In *History of New Music in China: The Development of Chinese Music* 中國新音樂史論集, edited by Ching-chih Liu 劉靖之 and Ganbo Wu 吳贛伯, 203–234. Hong Kong: University of Hong Kong, 1994.

Liu, Linrui 劉林睿. "*Lunyu zhong de junzi xingxiang*" 《論語》中的"君子"形象 [Image of *junzi* in the *Analects*]. In *Chuantong ruxue de lishi xingcha* 傳統儒學的歷史省察 [Reflections and observations of traditional Confucianism], edited by Zonggui Li 李宗桂 and Zaoqun Zhang 張造群, 57–66, Guangzhou, China: Flower City Publishing House 廣東花城出版社, 2012.

Liu, Zhen 劉震. *Xueji shiyi* 學記釋義 [Explaining *Xueji*]. Jinan, China: Shandong Education Publishing House 濟南: 山東教育出版社, 1984.

Makeham, John, ed. *New Confucianism.* New York: Palgrave Macmillan, 2003.

Mark, Michael L., ed. *Music Education: Source Readings from Ancient Greece to Today.* New York: Routledge, 2013.

Mark, Michael L., and Patrice Madura. *Contemporary Music Education.* 4th ed. Boston: Schirmer, Cengage Learning, 2014.

Miao Lingna 苗凌娜. "*Yin yang wuxing yu yinyue yangsheng* 陰陽五行與音樂養生 [Yin yang five elements and music for wellness]." *Zhongguo Zhongyiyao Zixun* 中國中醫藥資訊 *Journal of Traditional Chinese Medicine Information* 2, no. 31 (2010): 45.

Mills, Janet, and John Paynter, eds. *Thinking and Making: Selections from the Writings of John Paynter on Music Education.* Oxford: Oxford University Press, 2008.

Mou, Zongsan 牟宗三. *Zhongguo zhexue di tezhi* 中國哲學的特質 [Special qualities of Chinese philosophy]. Taipei: Student Book 學生書局, 1974.

Music Educators National Conference. *Becoming Human through Music: The Wesleyan Symposium on the Perspectives of Social Anthropology in the Teaching and Learning of Music.* Middletown, CT: Wesleyan University; Reston, VA: Music Educators National Conference, 1984.

Nan, Huaijin 南懷瑾. "*'Yijing' jishui*" 《易經》集說 [Essays on *Yijing*]. In *Nan Huaijin xuanji* 南懷瑾選集 [Collected Works of Huaijin Nan], Vol. 4, 3–227. Shanghai: Fudan University Press, 2012.

National Commission on Music Education. *Growing Up Complete: The Imperative for Music Education.* Reston, VA: Music Educators National Conference, 1991.

Nielsen, Bent. *A Companion to Yi Jing Numerology and Cosmology: Chinese Studies of Images and Numbers from Han (202 BCE–220 CE) to Song (960–1279 CE).* New York: RoutledgeCurson, 2003.

Prewitt, Kenneth. "The Future of International Research." In *Changing Perspectives on International Education*, edited by P. O'Meara, H. D. Mehlinger, and R. M. Newman, 324–336. Bloomington: Indiana University Press, 2001.

Qian, Mu 錢穆. *Lishi yu wenhua lunchong* 歷史與文化論叢 [Essays on history and culture]. Taipei: Tung Da Books 東大圖書有限公司, 1979.

Qian, Mu 錢穆. *Zhongguo wenhuashi daolun* 中國文化史導論 [An introduction to Chinese cultural history]. Taipei: Lantai Publishing House 蘭台出版社, 2001.

Reimer, Bennett. *A Philosophy of Music Education.* 3rd ed. Upper Saddle River, NJ: Prentice Hall, 2003.

Schippers, Huib. *Facing the Music: Shaping Music Education from a Global Perspective.* New York: Oxford University Press, 2010.

Sima, Qian 司馬遷. *Shiji* 《史記》 [The book of history]. Beijing: Zhonghua Shuju, 2008.

Slingerland, Edward. *Effortless Action: Wu-wei as Conceptual Metaphor and Spiritual Ideal in Early China.* New York: Oxford University Press, 2003.

Small, Christopher. *Musicking: The Meanings of Performing and Listening.* Hanover, NH: Wesleyan University Press, 1998.

Su, Shi 蘇軾. *Su Shi wenji* 蘇軾文集 [Collected works of Shi Su]. Beijing: Zhonghua Shuju 中華書局, 1986.

Sun, Zhenxing 孫振星. *Baihua Yijing* 白話易經 [*Yijing* in plain language]. Taipei: Shengguang Publications 星光出版社, 1981.

Suzuki, Shinichi. *Nurtured by Love: A New Approach to Talent Education.* Miami: Warner Bros, 1968.

Tan, Charlene, and Leonard Tan. "A Shared Vision of Human Excellence: Confucian Spirituality and Arts Education." *Pastoral Care in Education* 34, no. 3 (2016): 156–166.

Tan, Leonard. "Confucian *Creatio in situ*—Philosophical Resource for a Theory of Creativity in Instrumental Music Education." *Music Education Research* 18, no. 1 (2016): 91–108. Accessed August 2, 2017. http://www.tandfonline.com.ezproxy.lib.usf.edu/doi/full/10.1080/14613808.2014.993602.

Tan, Leonard. "Confucius: Philosopher of Twenty-First-Century Skills." *Educational Philosophy and Theory* 48, no. 12 (2016): 1233–1243. Accessed August 2, 2017. http://www.tandfonline.com/doi/full/10.1080/00131857.2016.1182416.

Tan, Leonard. "Reimer through Confucian Lenses: Resonances with Classical Chinese Aesthetics." *Philosophy of Music Education Review* 23, no. 2 (2015): 183–201.

Tan, Leonard. "Response to Alexandra Kertz-Welzel's '"Two Souls, Alas, Reside within My Breast": Reflections on German and American Music Education regarding the Internationalization of Music Education.' *Philosophy of Music Education Review* 21, no.1 (Spring 2013): 52–65." *Philosophy of Music Education Review*, 23, no. 1 (2015): 113–117.

Tan, Leonard. "Towards a Transcultural Theory of Democracy for Instrumental Music Education." *Philosophy of Music Education Review* 22, no. 1 (2014): 61–77.

Tan, Leonard. "Towards an Ancient Chinese-Inspired Theory of Music Education." *Music Education Research* 18, no. 4 (2016): 399–410. Accessed August 2, 2017. http://www.tandfonline.com.ezproxy.lib.usf.edu/doi/full/10.1080/14613808.2015.1122751.

Thirteen Classics with Commentaries 《十三經注疏》. Beijing: Zhonghua Shuju, 2009.

Tu, Weiming. *Confucian Thought: Selfhood as Creative Transformation*. Albany: State University of New York Press, 1985.

Tu, Weiming. *New Horizons in Eastern Humanism: Buddhism, Confucianism and the Quest for Global Peace*. London: I. B. Tauris, 2011.

Tu, Weiming. *Way, Learning, and Politics: Essays on the Confucian Intellectual*. Albany: State University of New York Press, 1993.

Turino, Thomas. *Music as Social Life: The Politics of Participation*. Chicago: University of Chicago Press, 2008.

Twenty-Two Masters 《二十二子》. Shanghai: Shanghai Guji Press, 1986.

UNESCO 聯合國教科文組織. *Rethinking Education: Towards a Global Common Good* 反思教育：向"全球共同利益"的理念轉變. Paris: UNESCO聯合國教科文組織, 2015.

Von Bertalanffy, Karl Ludwig. *General System Theory*. New York: George Braziller, 1969.

Wang, Mengou 王夢鷗, ed. *Liji jinzhujinyi* 禮記今註今譯 [*Liji* modern annotation and translation]. 2nd ed. Taipei: The Commercial Press, Ltd., 2009.

Weiss, Robert S., and Scott A. Bass. "Introduction." In *Challenges of the Third Age: Meaning and Purpose in Later Life*, edited by Robert S. Weiss and Scott A. Bass, 3–12. New York: Oxford University Press, 2002.

Wheelwright, Philip. *Heraclitus*. Princeton, NJ: Princeton University Press, 1959.

Wu, Linkun 吳林坤. "*Kongzi lun yong de sange cengci*" 孔子論勇的三個層次 [Confucius' three levels of courage]. In *Chuantong ruxue de lishi xingcha* 傳統儒學的歷史省察 [Reflections and observations of traditional Confucianism], edited by Zonggui Li 李宗桂 and Zaoqun Zhang 張造群, 73–81. Guangzhou, China: Flower City Publishing House 廣東花城出版社, 2012.

Xie, Jiaxing 謝嘉幸, and Yuanyi Bao 包原鉉. "*Zhongguo gudai zhexue sixiang dui dangdai yinyue jiaoyu keneng di qishi*" 中國古代哲學思想對當代音樂教育可能的啟示 [Potential implications of ancient Chinese philosophy on contemporary music education]. In *Dangdai yinyue jiaoyu zhexue lungao* 當代音樂教育哲學論稿 [Essays on contemporary philosophy of music education], edited by Da Ma 馬達 and Yaxian Chen 陳雅先, 81–88. Shanghai: Shanghai Music Publishing House 上海音樂出版社, 2010.

Xie, Jiaxing 謝嘉幸, and Wenwu Yu 郁文武. *Yinyue Jiaoyu Yu Jiaoxuefa* 音樂教育與教學法 [Music education and pedagogy]. Beijing: Higher Education Press 高等教育出版社, 2006.

Xue, Ming-Sheng 薛明生. *Xian Qin liang Han Dao jia siwei yu shjian* 先秦兩漢道家思維與實踐 [Thoughts and practices of pre-Qin and two-Han Daoism]. Taipei: Wen Chin 文津出版社, 2007.

Yan Yuan Ji 颜元集 [Collected essays of Yan Yuan]. Vol. 2. Beijing: Zhonghua Book Company 中華書局, 1987.

Yang, Chunqiu 羊春秋, ed. (annotated). *Xinyi Kongzi Jiayu* 新譯孔子家語. Taipei: Sanmin 三民書局, 2008.

Ye, Xiaowen 葉小文. "Nishan Forum: Encounter between Two Sages" 尼山論壇:兩個聖者的相遇. In *Nishan: Listen to Diverse Voices of the World: True Records of the First Nishan Forum on World Civilizations* 尼山：聆聽世界多元聲音——首屆尼山世界文明論壇實錄, 127–128. Beijing: China Intercontinental Press 五洲傳播出版社, 2011.

Yin, Aiqing 尹愛青. *Yinyue kecheng yu jiaoxue lun* 音樂課程與教學論 [Music curriculum and pedagogical theory]. Changchun, China: Northeast Normal University Press 東北師範大學出版社, 2005.

Yin, Aiqing 尹愛青. *Zhongxue yinyue Jiaoyu shixi xingdong celue* 中學音樂教育實習行動策略 [Secondary school music educational practice action plans]. Changchun, China: Northeast Normal University Press 東北師範大學出版社, 2007.

Zhao, Xiaosheng 趙曉生. *Taiji zuoqu xitong* 太極作曲系統 [Taiji system of music composition]. Guangzhou, China: Kexue Puji Chubanshe 科學普及出版社, 1990.

Zhu, Bokun 朱伯崑. *Yixue manbu* 易學漫步 [Strolling in Yi studies]. Taipei: Student Book 台灣學生, 1996.

Zhu, Bokun 朱伯崑. *Yixue zhexue shi* 易學哲學史 [History of the philosophy of Yi], Vol. 1. Beijing: Huaxia Publications 華夏出版社, 1995.

Zhu, Yujiang 朱玉江. "*Dangdai zhongguo yinyue jiaoyu di zhutixing zhexue fansi*" 當代中國音樂教育的主體性哲學反思 [Reflection on the subjective philosophy of music education in contemporary China], edited by Da Ma 馬達 and Yaxian Chen 陳雅先, 96–113. Shanghai: Shanghai Music Publishing House 上海音樂出版社, 2010.

INDEX

Page numbers followed by *f* or *t* indicate figures or tables, respectively. Numbers followed by n indicate notes.

acculturation, 6, 104, 179n7
action in response to change: avoidance, 100, 100*f*, 104–105; disposition of, 108–110; example outcomes, 103–108, 109*t*; passivity, 100, 100*f*, 105–106; proactivity, 100, 100*f*, 106–108; zones of, 110–112, 111*f*
action, non-egoistic (*wuwei*), 64–67, 66*f*, 169, 177, 192n19, 205n19
active musical motions, 85–86, 86*f*, 126–128, 170
adversity, 96, 99, 105, 106, 110, 111–113, 111*f*, 117, 158, 162*f*, 198n27, 201n42
aging, 195n29
Alfvén, Hannes, 14
Ames, Roger T., 9
Analects (Lunyu), 38–40, 44, 45, 47, 49, 51–53, 78, 79, 123, 125, 148, 155, 179n7, 184n49, 184n50, 188n13, 188n17, 188n21, 188n27, 189n29, 189n36, 189n37, 190n44, 190n48, 190n49, 190n50, 191n56, 195n27, 197n24, 199n12, 200n26, 201n36, 202n7, 204n5, 204n10, 205n15, 205n16; translations, 16–17
Applications outside of music, 84, 173–174
art, culinary, 122–123
avoidance, 100, 100*f*, 104–105; example outcomes, 103–108, 109*t*; zone of musical avoidance, 110–112, 111*f*, 130–132, 141–142, 158, 171

bagua (eight trigrams), 22, 24–29, 27*f*; contemporary, 26–27, 27*f*; variations, 29–30
balance, 117–134, 159–160, 164, 171; continuous, 126–132; across musical zones, 129–132; practices of, 159–160, 160*f*; pursuit of, 132–133; relative perspective on, 118–119
beauty, 41–43, 52, 82, 124–126, 136, 155, 194n10
bells, 155, 204n9
benevolence (*ren*), 38, 43–46, 46*f*, 155, 161, 169, 176, 187n7, 190n39, 204n5, 204n11; in classic Chinese philosophical works, 78; practice of, 47–48, 50*f*, 51–54; as way of living, 50*f*, 51–54
Berthrong, John H., 182n36
bian (change), 95–97
bian hua, 96, 177
bian tong, 177
Blacking, John, 196n5, 197n23
Bol, Peter K., 18–19, 182n36
Bowman, Wayne D., 3
Bresciani, Umberto, 182n36
Bronfenbrenner, Urie, 98–99
Buddhism, 11, 18, 59, 154, 182n31, 183n39, 194n7
buwei, 65–66, 66*f*

Cao Li, 182n34
Chang, Carsun, 182n36

(215)

change, 35, 37, 95–116, 159–160, 174; *bian*, 95; example outcomes in response to, 103–108, 109*t*; options regarding, 99–112, 100*f*; practices of, 159, 160*f*; zones of action in response to, 110–112, 111*f*
changing needs, 115–116
Chen Guying, 185n4, 186n16, 192n5, 202n2
Chen Tuan, 26
cheng (sincerity), 41–42, 44*f*, 169, 176, 201n30; as way of *junzi* living, 50*f*, 51–52
Cheng, Chung-ying, 182n36
Cheng Yi, 16
Chinese civilization, 12
Chinese medicine, traditional, 206n2
Chinese New Year day, 194n8
Chinese philosophy: cautionary note, 18–20; classic, 3–73, 14*f*; scholarship in, 15–18
Chunqiu Zuozhuan, 13, 125, 191n52, 199n12
classic Chinese philosophy, 3–73; scholarship in, 15–18; timeline of, 13, 14*f*
classic Confucianism, 9, 121, 141, 147–150, 153–158, 167, 175, 180n15, 187–188n12, 188n28, 190–191n51, 191n54, 193n3, 203n11, 204n3, 204n5, 205n20; complementarity with classic Daoism and *Yijing*, 78–82; foundations, 21–22, 36–57; fundamental premise, 39; human-centric ideology of, 39–41; scholarship in, 17–18
classic Daoism, 9, 119–122, 147–150, 153–156, 167; complementarity with classic Confucianism and *Yijing*, 78–82; foundations of, 21–22, 58–73; Jung on, 10; scholarship in, 17–18
climate change, 198n30
community, 43, 54, 55, 80, 85, 104, 118, 119, 121, 123, 131, 134, 148, 161, 171
complementarity, 35, 37, 84, 149; between classic Confucianism and classic Daoism, 78–82
complementary bipolar continua, 85–94; 86*f*, 91*f*, 93*f*, 103–108, 109*t*, 168; balance across, 126–129; musical liberation in, 138–141; skills to practice experiencing, 170
comprehensive harmony, 10–11
concomitance, 84
Confucianism, 13, 59, 80; background, 36–37; cautionary note, 18–20; classic, 9, 17–18, 21–22, 36–57, 78–82, 121, 141, 147–150, 153–158, 167, 175, 180n15, 187–188n12, 188n28, 190–191n51, 191n54, 193n3, 203n11, 204n3, 204n5, 205n20; complementarity with classic Confucianism and *Yijing*, 78–82; foundations, 25, 36–57; as mainstream, 11; Neo-Confucianism, 18–19, 180n15, 183n39, 188n28; New Confucianism, 19, 183n39; primary principles, 204n5; as religion, 191n54; scholarship in, 17–18; traditional, 175
Confucius (*Kongzi*), 13, 24, 36–38, 157, 175, 183n47, 189n37, 190n50, 191n54, 202n7; on change, 96; on creativity, 148; as funeral director, 190n48; journey with age markers, 205n16; on *junzi*, 47–49; on leadership, 191n56; meeting with Laozi, 191n2; motto for education, 49, 57; on music, 125, 155, 197n24; on music of Shao, 125; as music teacher, 195n27; quote translation, 16–17; on *ren*, 44–45; as *shengren*, 205n14; on *shi*, 113; on sincerity, 41; singing behaviors, 51; "unified principle in all of his knowledge" (*yi yi guan zhi* 一以貫之), 184n50; visit to Wei, 190n44; *Yizhuan (Ten Wings)*, 21–22, 24–25, 30, 40, 120, 176, 182n38, 185n2, 185n13, 187n4
connectedness, 35, 37
consistency, 35
contemporary global context, 193n2
continuous balance, 126–132
continuum, 84, 90–92, 91*f*–93*f*
cooking, 122, 199n14, 200n15
creative tension, 126
creativity, 73, 112, 147–150, 154
Csikszentmihalyi, Mihaly, 148
culinary art, 122–123

culture: layers of, 5–6, 202n1, 204n3; material *(wuzhi)*, 5; social *(shehui)*, 5; spiritual *(jingshen)*, 5–6, 204n2; types of, 179n8

Dakin, Jacky, 198n2
dance, 123, 124, 176, 179n7, 200nn17–18, 201n32
dao (or *tao*), 5, 59, 61–64, 62f–65f, 156–157, 174–176, 186n15, 188n13, 192n10, 196n2, 202n5; of change, 96; as circular continuum, 90–92, 91f; in classic Chinese philosophical works, 78–79; of *junzi*, 47; music education with, 72–73; persistence in walking with, 196n6; relation to *wuwei*, 192n19; *ren dao* (humanly), 79, 137, 155, 157, 164, 176, 189n35; *tian dao* (heavenly), 79, 137, 156, 164
dao-centric ideology, 61–64, 156
Daodejing, 59
Daoism, 13, 80, 183n38; background, 58–59; cautionary note, 19; classic, 9, 17–22, 58–73, 78–82, 119–122, 147–150, 153–156, 167, 175, 192n10, 192n12, 192n15, 193n3, 196n2, 200n15, 203n11, 204n3, 204n6, 205n12, 205n19; complementarity with classic Confucianism and *Yijing*, 78–82; foundations, 25, 58–73; primary principles, 204n6; scholarship, 17–18
Daxue (Great Learning), 38–40, 48, 78, 188n15
de (virtue), 59, 62–63, 176; complete cycle of, 63, 65f; *xuan de*, 63
de lai (earth music), 70–72
deep harmony *(he)*, 11, 61, 62f–65f, 63, 82–83, 119–126, 169, 171, 177
DeNora, Tia, 186n24
dependency, 35, 37
drums, 155, 204n9
dynamic flexibility, 126–132, 134, 137, 138, 140, 147, 160, 163, 164, 201n41

early Chinese philosophy, 15–18
earth music *(de lai)*, 70–72
ecological perspective, 97–99, 198n1
education. *See also* music education; *liyue jiaohua* (*li* and *yue* in education and acculturation), 6, 179n7; mottos for, 49, 57; music as essential to, 197n25
ego: *wuwei* (non-egoistic action), 64–67, 66f, 169, 177, 192n19, 205n19
energy transmission, 84; high- and low-energy musical activities, 87–88, 88f, 128–129, 139–140, 159, 170; liberation from energy levels, 139–140
equality *(qiwu)*, 68–69, 72–73, 169, 177
eternity: viability of, 196n6
exemplary person *(junzi)*, 40, 46–54, 122–123, 155, 169, 176, 189nn36–37, 204n5; as lifelong teacher, 157–158; teaching mission, 55–56; way of life, 50f, 51–52
exosystem, 98–99

familiarity, 129; familiar and unfamiliar musical events, 88–89, 90f, 128–129; liberation from, 140
Fang Baozhang, 187n11, 200n18
Fang, Maotian, 14, 183n41
Fang, Thomé H., 10, 17, 181n24
Fang Xiaomin, 195n24
Feng Dawen, 17, 191n54
Feng Yu-lan, 17
fire, 199n14
flexibility: dynamic, 126–132, 164; *rou*, 69–70, 73, 169, 177
forever brightening, 196n6
forward moving, 84
Frega, Ana Lucia, 3
Fú Pei-Jung, 192n15
Fu Pei-Rong, 6, 17, 25, 59, 66, 125, 179n9, 183n39, 184n55, 185n4, 185n13, 186n17, 186n21, 189n29, 191n2, 192n7, 192n15, 192n17, 199n8
Fung, C. Victor, 144t, 200n19, 201n42, 202n43, 203n12, 203n13, 205n23, 205n24, 206n6
Fuxi, 22, 26, 175

Gaozi, 42–43
geng (thick soup), 199n13
global appeal, 98
global context, contemporary, 193n2
global perspective, 195n26
global warming, 198n30
Gongsunchou, 43

Gong Zizhen, 181n17
Gordon, Edwin, 198n3
Great Learning (Daxue), 38–40, 48, 78, 188n15
Greene, Maxine, 137
gua (hexagrams), 22, 25, 175, 185n11; *kun gua*, 27f, 28, 35; *qian gua*, 27f, 28, 35
guan (observation), 67–68, 72, 169, 177
Guanju, 52, 125
Guanzi, 13
Guo Moruo, 197n20
Guoyu, 13, 124, 200n24

habit and habitual ways, 3, 8, 46, 114, 169–171, 206n1
Hall, David L., 9
Han Dynasty, 19, 39, 59
Han Kangbo, 22
harmony, 10–11; adjusting for, 122; culinary art metaphor, 122–123; deep *(he)*, 11, 61, 62f–65f, 63, 82–83, 119–126, 171, 177; intellectual, 11; social, 11
he (deep harmony), 11, 61, 62f–65f, 63, 82–83, 119–126, 169, 171, 177
heavenly *dao (tian dao)*, 79, 137, 156, 164
heavenly music *(tian lai)*, 70–72, 148–149
heping (peace), 124, 202n44
Heraclitus, 95, 195n1, 200n16
high- and low-energy musical activities, 87–88, 88f, 128–129, 139–140, 159, 170
Hsü Fu-kuan, 15, 17
hua (cultivation), 96
Huaxia culture, 36–37
human-centered philosophy, 167–168, 205n12
humanism, 187n12
humanly *dao (ren dao)*, 79, 137, 155, 157, 164, 176, 189n35
human music *(ren lai)*, 70–72, 148–149
humans: options for, 99–112, 100f; *ren* (human), 176, 190n39
human spirit, 6, 80, 99, 133, 154, 155, 157, 158, 160, 161, 163–168, 174, 204n7
hundun, 91
Hu Shi, 191n1

ignorance, 99–100, 102–103; example outcomes, 103–108, 109t; musical, 113
improvement: persistent, 156–158; self-improvement, 48–49, 165
indexical, 84
industrialization, 198n1
intellectual harmony, 11

Jao Tsung-I, 17
Japanese theater, 103
Ji Liankang, 200n18
jingshen (spiritual culture), 5, 135
Jin Liangnian, 200n24
Jorgensen, Estelle, 137
judgment, 84
jun, 83
Jung, Carl Gustav, 10, 114, 115, 181n19
juntiao (adjustment), 122, 177
junzi (the exemplary person), 40, 46–54, 122–123, 155, 169, 176, 189nn36–37, 204n5; as lifelong teacher, 157–158; teaching mission, 55–56; way of life, 50f, 51–52

kindness *(shan)*, 42–43, 44f, 169, 176, 188n28, 201n31; in music, 125; as way of *junzi* living, 50f, 51–52
Kong Yingda, 22, 185n7
kun gua, 27f, 28, 35

lai (music or sound), 70–71, 177, 203n11, 203n20; *de lai* (earth music), 70–72; *ren lai* (human music), 70–72, 148–149; *tian lai* (heavenly music), 70–72, 148–149
Lao Siguang, 17, 179n8, 187n4, 191n4, 192n10
Laozi, 13, 24, 58–61, 63, 66–67, 70, 71, 91f, 136, 156–157, 175, 183n38; life dates, 191n1; meeting with Confucius, 191n2; as person, 192n9; on *shi*, 113
Laozi (or *Daodejing*), 59–61, 63, 66, 67, 70, 71, 78, 81, 82, 91, 113, 121, 135, 141, 149, 157, 186n16, 192n5, 192n11, 192n16, 193n27, 193n29, 194n9, 199n10, 200n15, 203n10
le, 51
learners: teacher-learner roles, 34, 87, 87f, 128–129, 139, 170
Legalism, 59

Legge, James, 16
Lehmberg, Lisa J., 201n42, 205n24
li (philosophy, principle, or theory), 23–24, 98
li (ritual), 51, 155, 176, 187n3, 204n5, 204nn10–11
Liang Gu, 200n24
liberation, 135–150, 159–160, 160f, 166
Li, Chengyang, 201n30, 201nn28–29
Li, Chenyang, 83, 123
Liezi, 13
lifelong, 46, 49, 50, 53, 157, 173
lifespan, 69, 98, 99, 129–133, 143, 157, 159, 163, 167
lifestyle. *See* way of life
Liji (*Book of Rituals*), 13, 38, 40, 47, 197n20, 200n19
linguistics, 15–16
listening, 143–147, 144t, 145f
literary traditions, 180n11
Liu Linrui, 189n36
Liu Xiang, 113
live music, 143–147, 144t, 145f, 146–147, 146f
Li Xueqin, 185n7
liyue jiaohua (*li* and *yue* in education and acculturation), 6, 179n7
Li Zha, 191n52
Li Zonggui, 17
low-energy musical activities, 87–88, 88f, 128–129, 139–140, 159, 170
Lu, state of, 43, 191n52
Lu Buwei, 199n11
Lunyu (*Analects*), 38–40, 44, 45, 47, 49, 51–53, 78, 79, 123, 125, 148, 155, 179n7, 184n49, 184n50, 188n13, 188n17, 188n21, 188n27, 189n29, 189n36, 189n37, 190n44, 190n48, 190n49, 190n50, 191n56, 195n27, 197n24, 199n12, 200n26, 201n36, 202n7, 204n5, 204n10, 205n15, 205n16; translations, 16–17
Lushichunqiu, 13, 179n7, 199n10, 199n11, 200n15

macrosystem, 98–99
Madura, Patrice, 4–5
Makeham, John, 182n36
Mark, Michael L., 4–5, 201n39
material culture (*wuzhi*), 5

materialization (*wuhua*), 67
materials (*qi*), 5
megasystem, 97–99, 204n1
Mencius, 13, 37–45, 47–56, 79, 80, 113, 155, 157, 175, 180n15, 184n57, 191n54
Mencius (*Mengzi*), 38, 40, 42, 45–49, 53, 56, 78, 113, 155, 157, 187n7, 188n18, 188n19, 188n20, 188n22, 188n28, 189n30, 189n32, 189n35, 190n40, 190n41, 190n42, 190n43, 190n45, 190n46, 190n52, 190n53, 194n10, 195n28, 204n5, 205n14, 205n17
meridian system, 181n18
mesosystem, 98–99
metaphysics (*xing er shang*), 5
microsystem, 98–99
Ming Dynasty, 91
motto for education, 49, 57
Mou Zongsan, 11, 17
moving carpet metaphor, 118, 198n2
Mozi, 180n11
multimedia, 143–147, 144t, 145f, 146f
music, 31–33, 51–54, 129, 163; aspects of, 107, 108t; in classic Confucianism, 147–148; in classic Daoism, 148–149; Confucius on, 197n24; dance as, 200n17; definition of, 167; developing habitual ways, 169; discovery of, 130; earthly (*de lai*), 70–72; as essential part of education, 197n25; facets of, 107, 108t; heavenly (*tian lai*), 70–72, 148–149; human (*ren lai*), 70–72, 148–149; human attachment to, 205n18; *lai* (music or sound), 70–71, 177, 203n11, 203n20; live, 143–147, 144t, 145f, 146–147, 146f; making, 123–124, 155; meaningful, 53; as necessary, 201n39; participation in, 170–171, 203n12, 205n24; as phenomenon, 22; predisposition of, 158, 163, 165, 167, 171; as reflection of society, 190–191n51; of Shao, 125; sharing, 53; as state of mind, 70–72; as survival need, 201n42; of Wu, 125; *yue*, 51, 123–126, 155, 176, 179n7, 200n18, 201n30, 203n11, 204n8, 204n10
musical activity, 129, 197n23; high- and low-energy activities, 87–88, 88f, 128–129, 139–140, 159, 170; liberation from energy levels in, 139–140

musical avoidance: zone of, 110–112, 111f, 130–132, 141–142, 158, 171
musical experience(s): avenues for, 164; familiar and unfamiliar events, 88–89, 90f, 128–129, 170; secondary, 143–147, 144t, 145f, 146f; types of, 143–147, 144t, 145f, 146f, 168, 170
musical ignorance, 113
musical instruments, 199n9, 206n4
musical liberation, 137–147; in complementary bipolar continua, 138–141; in musical zones, 141–143; in types of musical experience, 143–147; pathways to, 162–168, 162f, 171
musical motions: active and passive, 85–86, 86f, 126–128, 159, 170; liberation in, 138–139
musical parameters, 107, 108t
musical passivity: zone of, 110–112, 111f, 118–119, 130–132, 141–143, 158, 171
musical proactivity: zone of, 110–112, 111f, 118–119, 129–132, 141–142, 158–159, 162–164, 162f, 168–171
musical sounds, 203n21
musical styles, 145–147, 145f, 146f, 164, 168
musical techniques, 107, 108t
musical traditions, 107, 108t
musical way of life, 158–161
musical zones, 110–112; balance across, 129–132; liberation in, 141–143
music aptitude tests, 199n3
music education, 33–35, 54–57, 72–73, 77–94; complementary bipolar continua in, 85–94, 86f, 91f, 93f, 103–108, 109t, 126–129; definition of, 161; example outcomes in response to change, 103–108, 109t; explicit, 55–57; implicit, 56–57; key principles of, 163–165; across the lifespan, 129–133, 157, 159, 163, 167; as natural, 3–4; as phenomenon, 22–23; philosophy of, 4–5; process of, 34–35; schools of propositions, 181n26; as way of life, 161–166; Western domination of, 182nn34–35; *yin* and *yang* in, 84–85; *yue jiao* (education of *yue*), 6, 54–55, 175, 179n7

music educator: Confucius as, 195n27; lifelong teachers, 157–158; obligation of, 133–134; teacher-learner roles, 34, 87, 87f, 128–129, 139, 170
musician-educators, 54–57
musicians, 54–57
musicianship, 107, 108t
music notations, 143–147, 144t, 145f, 146f
mysticism, 78, 82, 126, 156, 157, 163, 165

Nan Huaijin, 17, 23, 180n13
nature, 8, 10, 22–25, 27, 30, 59, 61, 79, 80, 121, 122, 135, 136, 141, 154–156, 196n5
needs: changing, 115–116; music as survival need, 201n42
negation, 65
Neo-Confucianism, 18–19, 180n15, 183n39, 188n28
New Confucianism, 19, 183n39
Nielsen, Bent, 16, 186n23
noh tradition, 103
non-judgmental, 84
numerology, 25

observation (*guan*), 67–68, 72, 169, 177
organismic worldview, 21–35, 59, 97–99, 154–155, 163, 181n17, 186n24; change in, 31–33; significance of, 30–31

parents, 198n26
passivity, 100, 100f, 105–106; example outcomes, 103–108, 109t; passive musical motions, 85–86, 86f, 126–128, 170; zone of musical passivity, 110–112, 111f, 118–119, 130–132, 141–143, 158, 171
peace (*heping*), 124, 202n44
People's Republic of China (PRC), 183n39
persistence: persistent improvement, 156–158; in walking with *dao*, 196n6
philosophy, 3; classic Chinese, 3–73, 14f; human-centered, 167–168; *li* (philosophy, principle, or theory), 22–23, 51, 98, 155; music education, 4–5; as open-ended, 183n40

physical matters *(xing er xia)*, 5
Plato, 11
practice, 167; extended, 168; habitual, 169–171; professional, 169–171
Prewitt, Kenneth, 17
privilege, 205n25
proactivity, 100, 100f, 106–108; example outcomes, 103–108, 109t; zone of musical proactivity, 110–112, 111f, 118–119, 129–132, 141–142, 158–159, 162–164, 162f, 168–171
professional practice, 169–171
prosperity, 37, 96, 97, 100, 101, 106, 108, 110–114, 111f, 119, 121, 125, 137, 141, 156, 158, 162f, 164–166, 168, 171, 198n27, 201n41
psychometric, 90, 92

qi (materials), 5
qi (vital energies), 61
qian gua, 27f, 28, 35
Qian Mu, 5, 12, 17, 204n3
Qi Jinggong, 199n12
Qin Dynasty, 59, 194n7
Qing Dynasty, 8, 180n15
qiwu (equality), 68–69, 72–73, 169, 177
Qi Xuan Wang, 53
quality of life, 108, 130, 131, 203n12

recitals, 161–162
recordings, 144t, 145f, 146–147, 146f
reflection, 170
Reimer, Bennett, 158, 195n26, 198n29
relative perspective, 118–119
ren (benevolence), 38, 43–49, 46f, 53, 55, 155, 161, 169, 176, 187n7, 190n39, 204n5, 204n11; in classic Chinese philosophical works, 78; practice of, 47–48, 50f, 51–54; as way of living, 50f, 51–54
ren (human), 176, 190n39
ren dao (humanly *dao*), 79, 137, 155, 157, 164, 176, 189n35
ren lai (human music), 70–72, 148–149
roles: of music educators, 133–134; social, 40; teacher-learner roles, 34, 87, 87f, 128–129, 139, 170
root seeking *(xungen)*, 7
rou (flexibility), 69–70, 73, 169, 177

sage *(shengren)*, 49
scholarship, 15–18
schools of propositions, 181n26
secondary musical experiences, 143–147, 144t, 145f, 146f
self-cultivation, 141–142, 157, 165
self-improvement, 48–49, 165
self-reflection, 48–49, 170
senior citizens, 130, 133, 195n29, 201n42, 205n24
shan (kindness), 42–43, 44f, 169, 176, 188n28, 201n31; in music, 125; as way of *junzi* living, 50f, 51–52
Shang Dynasty, 199n11
Shangshu, 13, 194n17, 197n20
sharing music, 53
shehui (social culture and system), 5–6, 9, 13, 43, 45, 56, 79, 80, 97, 104, 108t, 135, 148, 153, 154, 161, 163, 171, 173, 204n3
shen (god), 157, 177
shengren (sage), 49, 157, 177
shi (situation), 112–114, 169
Shiji (Book of History) (Sima Qian), 13, 58–59, 191n2, 191n3
Shijing, 13, 41, 52, 124, 125
shu (numbers), 22–23, 196n10
Shun, 52
Sima Qian, 58–59, 185n13, 187n9, 191n2, 191n4
sincerity *(cheng)*, 41–42, 44f, 169, 176, 201n34; as way of *junzi* living, 50f, 51–52
social culture and system *(shehui)*, 5–6, 9, 13, 43, 45, 56, 79, 80, 97, 104, 108t, 135, 148, 153, 154, 161, 163, 171, 173, 204n3
social harmony, 11
social order, 54, 55
social roles, 40–41, 60, 79, 80, 112, 143
society, 5, 9, 11, 13, 19, 22, 39, 41, 44, 51, 53, 57, 79, 80, 99, 124–125, 134, 136, 141, 147, 176, 191n52
Song dynasty, 16
spiritual *(jingshen)* level, 5, 135
Spring and Autumn period, 9, 21, 37
students: teacher-learner roles, 34, 87, 87f, 128–129, 139, 170
Sun Zhenxing, 185n7
Su Shi, 181n17

synchronicity, 33–35, 114–115
synchronism, 114–115

Tai Chi, 206n2
Taiji, 26, 26f, 176, 196n9
tai yang (sun), 187n28
Tan, Charlene, 188n16
tang (soup), 199n13
Tang Junyi, 17
Tan, Leonard, 180n12, 181n20, 188n16, 192n19, 195n26
Taoism, 9, 175
teachers: lifelong teachers, 157–158; teacher-learner roles, 34, 87, 87f, 128–129, 139, 170
teaching, 157–158, 190n44, 205n22
telecommunications, 197n18
Thirteen Classics, 17
this-with-that approach, 195n26
tian, 192n15
tian dao (heavenly *dao*), 156, 164, 176
tian lai (heavenly music), 70–72, 148–149
tianxia, 81–82, 177
tiao, 83
tong (flowing through), 97, 169
traditional Chinese medicine, 206n2
translations, 15–17
Tu, Weiming, 14
Twenty-Two Masters, 17, 193n29, 202n2

unfamiliar musical experiences, 88–89, 90f, 128–129
urbanization, 198n1

virtue *(de)*, 59, 62–63, 176; complete cycle of, 63, 65f; *xuan de*, 63–64

Waley, Arthur, 16
Wang Bi, 22, 71, 193n29
wanwu (all things), 61, 63, 63f–65f
Warring States period, 5, 9, 21, 38, 188n15
water, 28, 28f, 70, 199n14, 200n15
way of life: habitual, 169–171; *junzi* (the exemplary person), 50f, 51–52; musical, 158–161; music education as, 161–166; practice, 167
wei, 177, 193n20, 201n30
Western civilization, 7, 12, 182nn34–35

Western Han period, 191n54
wuhua (materialization), 67
wuwei (non-egoistic action), 64–67, 66f, 169, 177, 192n19, 205n19
wuxing, 194n17
wuzhi (material culture), 5

xiang (phenomenon), 22–23, 98
xiao (filial piety), 204n5
xiaoren (villains), 123, 157, 177, 189n36, 205n13
Xie Jiaxing, 182n34
xing er shang (metaphysics), 5
xing er xia (physical matters), 5
xuan de, 63–64
Xueji (Record of Learning), 38–39, 195n28, 197n20
xungen (root seeking), 7
Xunzi, 18, 19, 180n11, 184n55, 184n57, 188n28
Xunzi, 13, 188n28

yang, 25–35, 26f, 37, 61, 62f–65f, 63, 176, 194n17, 197n22; in music education, 84–85; *yin-yang* relationships, 26, 26f, 90–92, 91f–93f, 119–120, 167
yang yao, 26–27, 26f
Yan Yuan, 180n15, 191n56
Yanzi, 122, 199n12, 200n15
yao, 26, 176
yi, 206n1
Yijing (The Book of Changes), 5, 9, 12–13, 18, 37, 40, 59–61, 77–79, 120–121, 153, 154, 165, 168, 175, 176, 180n13, 182–183n38, 185n2, 185n4, 192n5, 193n3, 206n1; complementarity with classic Confucianism and classic Daoism, 78–82; concept of change in, 95; contextual studies of, 16; *dao* in, 78–79; foundations, 21–35; interpretation of, 15–16; Jung on, 10, 114–115; *ren* in, 78; *yin* and *yang* in, 84, 90, 104, 206n2
yin, 25–35, 26f, 37, 61, 62f–65f, 63, 176, 194n17, 197n22, 199n5; in music education, 84–85; *yin-yang* relationships, 26, 26f, 90–92, 91f–93f, 119–120, 167
Yin Aiqing, 182n34

yin-yang relationships, 119–120, 167; as continuum, 90–92, 91*f*–93*f*; fish *taiji* diagram for, 26, 26*f*
yin yang wu xing, 194n17
yin yao, 26–27, 26*f*
Yin Yi, 122, 199n11, 200n15
Yizhuan (Ten Wings) (Confucius), 21–22, 24–25, 30, 37, 41, 78, 96, 97, 120–121, 141, 175, 176, 179n5, 182n38, 185n2, 185n7, 185n9, 185n13, 186n14, 186n15, 186n16, 187n25, 187n27, 187n4, 187n5, 188n24, 196n6, 201n34, 203n10
yong (courage), 47, 54
yue (music), 51, 123–126, 155, 176, 179n7, 200n18, 201n30, 203n11, 204n8, 204n10
Yueji (Record of Music), 20, 38–39, 148, 179n7, 187n11, 189n34, 190n47, 200n18–200n19, 201n33, 201n34
yue jiao (education of *yue*), 6, 54–55, 175, 179n7
Yuezhengke, 195n28, 197n20
Yuezhengzi, 43, 195n28
Yu Wenwu, 182n34

zhan gua (divination), 25
Zheng Junhui, 187n11

zhi (wisdom), 47, 54
Zhongyong, 38, 48, 78, 82, 83, 121, 188n23, 194n13, 199n8, 203n17
Zhou Dynasty, 36–37, 46, 199n9
Zhou Jiu, 124
Zhou Wen Wang, 22, 175, 180n13
Zhou Wu Wang, 52, 53, 125
Zhouyi, 175, 176, 185n2
Zhuangzi, 13, 59–60, 63, 67–69, 79, 83, 109, 113, 122, 136, 175, 183n38, 192n10
Zhuangzi (or *Nanhuajing*), 59–60, 62, 63, 67–69, 78, 113, 122, 136, 177, 193n22, 193n24, 193n28, 194n12, 203n21
Zhu Bokun, 185n3, 185n13
Zhu Xi, 16, 180n15, 183n39, 188n28
Zi Gong, 49
Zixia, 40, 195n27
zone of musical avoidance, 110–112, 111*f*, 130–132, 141–142, 158, 171
zone of musical passivity, 110–112, 111*f*, 118–119, 130–132, 141–143, 158, 171
zone of musical proactivity, 110–112, 111*f*, 118–119, 129–132, 141–142, 158–159, 162–164, 162*f*, 168–171
Zuo Qiuming, 199n12